THE THEATER

IN COLONIAL AMERICA

by

Hugh F. Rankin

THE UNIVERSITY OF NORTH CAROLINA PRESS
Chapel Hill

Copyright © 1960, 1965 by
The University of North Carolina Press
Manufactured in the United States of America
Library of Congress Catalog Card Number 65-16333
Van Rees Press • New York
2nd Printing
North Carolina State University Print Shop, Raleigh

FOR BETTY
My Leading Lady

PREFACE

Some years ago I spent a delightful interlude employed as a Research Associate for Colonial Williamsburg, Inc. Among other things, I was assigned a study of the colonial theater as it existed in Williamsburg. The weakness of such an approach soon became apparent; the theater in any era or any community has never existed in a vacuum, therefore the playhouse in Williamsburg could not be examined as an entity. The mobile existence of the actors alone precluded such a limited study, and to understand fully the nature and operations of the colonial theater it became necessary to range far afield.

During the eighteenth century the drama in England was undergoing a transition; in the American colonies it was gaining a foothold. At the time when David Garrick was introducing new dramatic techniques to the London stage, the company of comedians under Lewis Hallam and David Douglass were struggling to gain recognition in the New World. The wanderings of the players have not been easy to trace. In some communities an abundance of advertising in the local newspapers made the task easier and in some instances playbills were useful. Yet upon other occasions, there was literally a drought of sources, and only by scattered references and an occasional name in court records could the presence of the comedians be determined in any particular locale.

It seems that any study involving actors should take on a bit of a sparkle, for that group has always been an exciting segment of society which has captured the imagination of every social level. Yet I fear some of the tinsel and the gusto is lacking in the following pages. The greater part of the information was gleaned from colonial newspapers and even actors lack personalities when listed in a playbill. And had they not been indifferent to the payment of debts, it is likely that few of their first names would have been revealed to further distinguish them from the less boisterous element. Playbills, for the most part, list the players' last names prefixed by "Mr.," "Mrs.," or "Miss." Only when involved in litigation were they fully identified.

Tribute should be paid to some who did not aid directly, such historians as Carl Bridenbaugh, Edmund S. Morgan, and Louis B. Wright, whose studies of colonial life not only contain much that is useful in any study of the theater but also are valuable in helping to place the players in their proper perspectives. And there are those who have written on the American theater, George Freedley, Joseph Ireland, George C. D. Odell, Thomas Pollock, Robert Land, Eola Willis, Arthur Hornblow, and William Dunlap, to name but a few, whose earlier studies have not only afforded a point of departure but have filled in some of the thin areas as well.

Invaluable aid was cheerfully given by the library staffs of the College of William and Mary, the Institute of Early American History and Culture, The University of North Carolina at Chapel Hill, the Library of Congress, the University of Pennsylvania, Duke University, Harvard University, the New-York Historical Society, the Players Club of New York City, the City Museum of New York, the New York Public Library, the Library Company of Philadelphia, the Pennsylvania Historical Society, the Maryland Historical Society, the Library Company of Charleston, South Carolina, the Maryland Hall of Records, Tulane University, and the William L. Clements Library of the University of Michigan.

It would be impossible to list within these pages all those individuals who have aided. At The University of North Carolina at Chapel Hill valuable suggestions were made by Professors Hugh T. Lefler, Fletcher M. Green, and Robert M. Miller. Dr. Milton Smith, formerly of Columbia University, read the manuscript and offered comments that were most helpful. Dr. Paul Hostetler and Brooks McNamara of the Tulane Theatre Department helped with some of the rough spots, as did Dr. Joseph Roppolo of the English Department. Among my former colleagues at Colonial Williamsburg, Dr. E. P. Alexander offered constant encouragement. Dr. Edward M. Riley gave freely of his counsel and experience, as did Mrs. Mary Goodwin and Mr. James Short. Mr. Singleton P. Morehead and Miss Mary Stephenson were most generous in sharing with me their earlier researches on the Williamsburg theater. Mrs. Rose Belk did everything anyone could ask in tracking down needed materials. Dr. Thad Tate (now of William and Mary) and John Hemphill III (now of Southwestern College of Memphis), paused long enough in their own projects to make a note for me when they ran across something of a theatrical nature. Dr. Jane Carson devoted time to rescuing many a dangling phrase from the precipice of obscurity. Horace Sheely and Lauretta Ramirez did yeoman service when it became necessary to read countless rolls of microfilm. Susan Armstrong Low did a prodigious amount of work in compilation and research that left me free to concentrate on putting the study together. Mrs. Sue Sherman of Williamsburg was quick to give me important leads that she had discovered in her own theatrical researches. Mrs. Mary Black, whose enthusiasm for the theater is not only contagious but well-nigh overwhelming, worked her way through some of the duller research as though she really enjoyed it. And then there is my most patient wife, who has grown weary typing so many drafts.

So it is that the cast for this production has been large. They have done their parts well—I only hope the result justifies their efforts.

HUGH F. RANKIN

Tulane University
New Orleans, La.

CONTENTS

xi

ILLUSTRATIONS

The endpaper: Stevens' Lecture on Heads *as presented in
a London theater (courtesy of Harvard Theatre Collection)*

THE THEATER
IN COLONIAL AMERICA

So much for Us, the Pageants of an Hour
Who fret, and strut, and then are heard no more.
                              Prologue, Annapolis
                              September 1, 1772

· I ·

THE BEGINNINGS

———

Leisure time activities in England's American colonies, as in all colonial cultures, were quite naturally patterned after those of the mother country, although there was always the time lag occasioned by overseas expansion. Through the years, English dramatists had gradually modified the theater from an aristocratic to a middle-class institution, but the favor of the upper class was by no means alienated. As such, it was more readily acceptable to the American colonists, who were themselves modifying an English heritage into a culture that would one day be termed "American."

The theater, colonial or modern, did not and does not exist in a vacuum. The basic elements are play, actors, and audience, held together by a bond of interest. These elements were present in colonial America, but through the exigencies of the times had been diverted into other and more complex channels. The early settlers, moreover, were not concerned with a medium of entertainment. They were themselves actors in the more pressing true-life drama of carving homes out of the wilderness and the struggle for survival in hostile surroundings. There was no place for artificial comedy or tragedy.

1

Credit must be given to the Spanish and French for the earliest dramatic productions on the continent of North America, although such incidents were isolated in time and customarily assumed the form of extravaganzas and pageants, containing religious rather than secular connotations. As early as 1526, Spanish authorities were recommending the drama as a possible instrument for the conversion of the "idolatrous multitudes" of Indians, and within two years the priests were beginning to adopt the religious drama as a facet of their missionary activities. In a like manner, the Jesuits in Canada were utilizing the drama to convey their spiritual message to the savages as early as 1606, some six months before the founding of Jamestown.[1]

Few settlers in the English colonies held so liberal a view of the drama. In New England, Puritanism had crystallized, forging a solid bulwark against temptation and sin. Massachusetts Puritans migrated from England in an era when licentiousness and obscenity were considered to be desirable and necessary ingredients for successful drama, and their clergy had impeached the theater, from both the pulpit and the printed page. Playhouses, they charged, were responsible for emptying the churches, aiding the Pope, inducing the Lord to visit the plague upon London, corrupting maidens and chaste wives, and providing a market place for harlots and their customers. The theater was denounced as the "bastard of Babylon" and "the snare of concupiscence and filthy lusts of wickid whoredom." This "Chapel of Satan" was censured as a school that taught: "how to be false and deceive your husbands, or husbands their wives, how to play the harlot, to obtain one's love, how to ravish, how to beguile, how to betray, to flatter, lie, swear, forswear, how to allure whoredom, how to murder, how to poison, how to disobey and rebel against princes, to consume treasures prodigally, to move to lusts, to ransack and spoil cities and towns, to be idle, to blaspheme, to sing filthy songs of love, to speak filthily, to be proud, how to mock, scoff and deride any nation."

Any one of these charges could be documented in the plays of Shakespeare alone, yet these devout critics neglected to point out that each of these arraignments also could be found in the Bible. Neither did they consider the possibility that such biblical masterpieces as the Song of Solomon and The Book of Job were cast in dialogue form and might, in truth, be adjudged dramatic poems. Increasingly, the Puritans clung fast to their doctrine that those in charge of a community should be allowed to control its moral development. Protected by theological tenet, it seemed only natural to forbid entrance to those European factors that they had come to a New World to escape.

The acting of plays led to a flurry of Bostonian denunciations in 1685 when Samuel Sewall's temper blazed forth at a dancing master's twitting boast that "by one play he could teach more divinity than Mr. Willard or the Old Testament." And two years later, when tavern-keeper John Wing fitted up his establishment for a "stage-fight" and the gambits of a magician, a committee of four, including Sewall, persuaded Wing that not only was such a display unseemly, but " 'tis offensive." Sewall's punctilious apprehensions were stretched thin in 1714 with the whispers that a play was to be acted in the Council Chamber. Pointing out that not even the Romans, with all their lust and dissipation, had ever gone so far "as to turn their Senate House into a Playhouse," he angrily cautioned, "Let not Christian Boston, goe beyond Heathen Rome in the practice of Shamefull vanities." [2] No record indicates whether this outburst was sufficient to thwart the devil's delight, but no source reveals further attempts at play acting for the next thirty-six years. Theaters conveniently became identified with Catholicism, the great enemy of Puritanism, and the most minute stirrings of the drama in New England evoked an immediate cry of "Popery." It was a most effective weapon.

Further south, the early Dutch settlers had no particular theatrical heritage and, as a result, harbored no antagonism towards the drama. These thrifty folk, however, did object to the expense and waste of time involved, a point of view they retained long after becoming subjects of the English Crown. This principle is particularly reflected in the indentures for apprentices in the early eighteenth century: "He shall not absent himself Day or Night from his Master's service without his leave, to haunt Alehouses or Playhouses, but in all things as a faithful apprentice he shall behave himself toward his said Master, and all during the said term." [3]

New Englanders found sturdier allies among the Quakers and Presbyterians of Pennsylvania whose inherent convictions, as those of the Puritans, had long been nourished on a diet of abstract thought. Actors, in the minds of the Friends, were little more than "inlets of vice," and these usually tolerant Quakers "never confused liberty of conscience with license to behave as one might wish."

William Penn, despite his reputation for tolerance, was not one to agree with those playwrights who defended themselves against the attacks of Jeremy Collier and others by asserting that to exhibit vice was to establish a standard of virtue. In 1699, in his *No Cross, No Crown,* Penn had come forth with a powerful argument against the theater by posing the question, "How many plays did Jesus Christ and his apostles recreate themselves at? What poets, romances, comedies, and the like did the apostles and the saints make or use to pass their time withal?" This principle he had incorporated into the Great Law of Pennsylvania, a reflection of his efforts to establish a "Holy Community" within his colony: a provision that forbade "prizes, stage plays, masques, revels, bull-baitings, [and] cock-fighting." Despite the disallowance of the law by William and Mary in 1693, the ban against such frothy diversions quickly reappeared upon the statute books and just as promptly was disallowed once again. But William Penn was as persistent as he was religious, and from England he instructed James Logan to "prepare a nervous Proclamation against Vice," a basis for a Council-approved measure on November 27, 1700, prohibiting plays, bonfires, and "any rude or riotous sports." Even after this law met the inevitable fate of disallowance, similar endeavors in 1706 and 1713 were bolstered by added threats of fine and imprisonment but, like their predecessors, incurred the displeasure of the Crown. So it was that, from 1682 to 1713, Pennsylvania made strenuous efforts to gain permanent injunctions against fatuous entertainment, in each instance frustrated by the regal veto. Seemingly realizing the futility of their efforts, the Quakers refrained from further legal attempts to restrict the drama in Pennsylvania during the next forty-six years. Unsuccessful in limiting entertainment for the colony as a whole, the Society of Friends now could only try to dissuade their own sect from "the reading of plays, romances, novels, and other pernicious books." [4]

Yet, despite this vigorous opposition, and perhaps because of it, there may well have been a number of unrecorded plays produced in the early colonial period before the advent of a vigorous amateur or professional theater. In 1612, in his *Apology for Actors*, Thomas Heywood, expanding a theme developed by Shakespeare, wrote:

> The world's a theatre, the earth a stage,
> Which God and Nature do with actors fill.

Acting on the premise presented in Heywood's couplet, it is reasonable to suppose that the American colonial was similar in his thespian inclinations to his contemporaries in Europe.

Opposition, even when tempered with ecclesiastical reasoning, cannot always stamp out the inner whimsies of man, for it was in Puritan Massachusetts that one of the first recorded plays written by an American was produced. In 1690, at Cambridge, the students of Harvard College acted Benjamin Coleman's *Gustavus Vasa,* and because there is no notice of a subsequent performance, it must be assumed that the capricious students experienced the frown of Calvinistic authority. [5]

Sparse and vague sources record an attempt to initiate the dramatic arts in the city of New York. Some time between 1699 and 1702, one Richard Hunter petitioned Governor John Nanfan, begging leave to present plays and stating that the petitioner had "been at great charge and expense in providing persons and necessary's in order to the acting of Play's in the City." Although it has been established that his plea was favorably received, nothing implies that Hunter actually went as far as to produce plays. [6]

The first professional actor on record to perform in North America was a twenty-year-old vagabond by the name of Anthony Aston. His father, Richard Aston, was the compiler of a valuable work entitled *Placida Latina Rediviva,* and "tho' a lawyer, liv'd and dy'd an honest Man." Anthony had received a fair education and had plodded along as a law clerk until he became enamored of the stage in 1697. For three years, he barnstormed around England and then fell victim to reports of the fabulous fortunes acquired by the buccaneers of Jamaica. Instead of wealth, he accumulated only disappointment and was forced to turn to the law and soldiering as means of subsistence. Sailing to South Carolina, he arrived just in time to accompany Governor James Moore on the latter's abortive expedition against St. Augustine. In January, 1703, upon their return, the carefree Aston reported, "Well, we arriv'd in Charles-Town, full of Lice, Shame, Poverty, Nakedness, and Hunger:—I turn'd Player and Poet, and wrote a Play on the Subject of the Country." Aston, later to be styled "a vagrant ... perpetually setting the laws at defiance," next journeyed to New York where, falling in with old cronies, he spent the winter "acting, writing, courting, fighting." Spring found him in Virginia, from which he secured passage back to England. He made no mention of having acted in Virginia, although he boasted that "the noble Governor Nicholson treated me handsomely." [7]

Aston's visit possibly inspired other hopefuls to try their hand at the drama in New York, although their efforts were insignificant enough to remain in obscurity. Because of this or some similar reason, the Council, on May 6, 1709, forbade "play-acting and prize-fighting," an indication that the town may have been plagued by these evils.

This decree, however, did not prevent the succeeding governor, Robert Hunter, from writing the first play known to be printed in America, which appeared in 1714 under the lengthy title of *Androboros, a B[i]ographical Farce of Three Acts, viz: The Senate, the Consistory and the Apotheosis.* It was a clever, but rude, satire on the actions of the Assembly and Lieutenant Governor Francis Nicholson, the latter thinly veiled as Androboros or "Maneater." Dr. William Vesey, Rector of Trinity Church, came in for a share of criticism in the role of "Fizle." Vesey had journeyed to England, perhaps at the instigation of Nicholson, to protest Hunter's lukewarm attitude towards the interests of the Anglican church. This inelegant drama, coarsely written and filled with uncouth attempts at humor, bore the imprint "Moropolis" or "Fool's Town." [8] Never intended for public performance, the play was merely Hunter's robust method of ridiculing his critics.

Thus, despite early vigorous opposition waged against the theater in the American colonies, resistance was gradually worn down except in New England, where Puritan convictions remained as steadfast as the boulders of her rock-bound coast. There, hostility to the drama was so firmly entrenched that only the erosion of the passing years and changing times could wear it down. Even in the other colonies, laws restricting theatrical activities were sometimes passed as a sop to religious extremists but just as often were ignored. Only Virginia and Maryland never enacted legislation prohibiting the theater, and it was in Virginia that the theater was able to gain its first foothold in America.

THE FIRST THEATER
IN AMERICA

(Williamsburg, 1716-1745)

Virginia made an early entrance on the American stage. The colony was represented in the theater, although minutely, even before its first settlers landed at Jamestown. Shortly after the coronation of James I in 1603, Scapethrift and Spendall, two "Adventurers for Virginia," appear as characters in the play *Eastward Hoe*. And within the next decade, or so it has been claimed, the opening scene in Shakespeare's *The Tempest* was based on a Virginia letter describing the wreck of a part of the fleet taking Sir Thomas Gates to the colony in 1609.

Strangely enough, the first recorded opposition to the drama in the new colony had its origin in London theatrical circles. The failures of the first colonization attempts had provided a boon for the comedians of the Elizabethan stage. And it was probably their facetious conceit that led to the inclusion in the Daily Prayer prepared in 1602 for the use of the plantations this beseechment: "O Lord we pray thee fortifie us against this temptation: let Samballat & Tobias, Papists and Players and such other Amonits & Horonits, the scum & dregs of the earth, let them mocke such as helpe to build up the walls of Jerusalem, and they that be filthy, let them be filthy still."

A similar posture was assumed by the Reverend William Crashaw eight years later in a sermon delivered before Lord Delaware in February, 1610. In the judgment of this ecclesiastic, the enmity of the actors was a consequence of their thwarted ambition to emigrate to the new world. The colonization of Virginia, Crashaw warned, "hath three Great enemies ... euen the Divel, Papists and Players. . . . But why are the Players enemies to this Plantation, and doe abuse it? I will tell you the causes: First, for that they are so multiplied here, that one cannot live, by another, and they see that wee send of all trades to Virginiea, but will send no Players, which if wee would doe, they that remaine would gaine the more at home. Secondly ... because we resolve to suffer no idle persons in Virginiea, which course if it were taken in England, they know they might turne to new occupations." [1]

This was little more than an exercise in evangelical polemics. There were no places for players in early America; starvation was much more of a reality for the settlers in Jamestown than it was for the unemployed actors of London. The days of the colonists were too fully occupied with the struggle to survive, and the nights held too many dangers for even casual considerations of the relatively trivial entertainments offered by the drama. Tragedy was more than a representation on the stage—it was an ever-present fact.

Legal attempts to suppress or restrict the drama were practically unknown in early Virginia. It is an interesting fact, and perhaps a relevant one, that the royal governor who lived in the colony thirty-five years—Sir William Berkeley—was himself a playwright of some note and had been associated with the Cavalier drama at court and in London. His *The Lost Lady*, first acted in 1637, one year before its first printing, proved popular enough to be reprinted in 1639. With its revival in 1661, that inveterate playgoer, Samuel Pepys, had censured the performance because it did "not please me much." A second Berkeley play, *Cornelia*, seems to have been performed upon at least one occasion during the Restoration.[2]

Religious opposition to the theater was never a serious consideration in Virginia. The Anglicans, who had conceded tacit recognition to the theater in England, seemed inclined to pursue a similar course in the new world.

Virginia was not long contained within the limits of the little isthmus that was Jamestown. Land was cleared, and crops were planted, harvested, and shipped to the London market. Ambitious men acquired great tracts of land out of which they created great plantations, and the vanguard of European culture began to settle over what had been a frontier civilization. Accumulated wealth brought some leisure time, and with leisure came an inclination towards more pleasurable pursuits. Sizable libraries could be found on many plantations, and from the extant inventories it seems that more than one planter accepted the injunction of Henry Booth, second Baron Delamere and first Earl Warrington, whose *Works* were first published in 1694. With regard to the dramatic arts, Booth had suggested, "To read a play or romance now and then for diversion may do no hurt; but he that spends most of his time in such books will be able to give a very ill account of it." Perhaps the most enthusiastic devotee of the drama in Virginia was William Byrd II. In the late seventeenth century, he had been in residence at the Middle Temple in London, where he not only became an intimate of William Wycherly, one of the boldest of comedy writers, but also made the acquaintance of William Congreve and Nicholas Rowe. An enthusiastic patron of the London theater, Byrd was to maintain an active interest in the drama throughout his life, with plays accounting for one-sixth of his rather extensive library. And there were others. In 1740, the personal library of William Eustace of Northumberland County included "a parcel of play books." This literary interest in the drama, however, was not a sole prerogative of the gentry; Nathaniel Hill, a school master in Henrico County, was found at his death to have owned some sixteen playbooks.[3]

No colonist, however, was so bold as to flout the Roundhead Parliament by acting plays in defiance of its edict prohibiting such amusements. Yet, it may well have been the overseas re-action to the gay life that accompanied the Restoration of Charles II which prompted the first known play to be acted in the English colonies. It was a local talent production, acted in Accomac County, on the eastern shore of Virginia, August 27, 1665. The play, *The Bare and the Cubb,* was staged in Cowle's Tavern near Pungoteague, with a cast of Cornelius Watkinson, Philip Howard, and William Darby. To one Edward Martin, acting a play seemed akin to heresy, and scurrying to John Faw-sett, the king's attorney, he reported the play and demanded that the offenders be brought to trial. The defendants were haled before the county court by Fawsett, but the case was continued, the justices of peace ordering Wilkinson, Howard, and Darby to appear at the "next Court, in those habiliments that they then acted in, and give a draught of such verses, or other speeches and passages, which were then acted by them." At the following session of the court, the justices apparently were pleased with the performance of the accused, for the verdict was that the players were "not guilty of fault," and because of "the Charge and trouble of that suit did accrew," they further directed that Martin, the accusing witness, pay all costs of court.[4] This ruling might be considered the first favorable review of a play in America.

Judicial approbation gave license to amateur theatricals in Vir-ginia. Certainly, there was no recorded protest in 1702 when the students of William and Mary performed *A Pastoral Colloquy* without molestation or subsequent criticism. And it is not un-likely that they performed before other than their fellow schol-ars, for the college was no longer isolated at the defense outpost of Middle Plantation. Around it was rising the town of Wil-liamsburg, the new capital of Virginia.

William III, for whom the new town had been named, was the same monarch who had disallowed Pennsylvania's attempted ban of the theater, and his successor, Queen Anne, refused to sanction a similar measure for "it restrains her Matys. Subjects from Innocent Sports and Diversions." Williamsburg's people maintained the cult of their English heritage, for they "live in the same neat Manner, dress after the same Modes, and behave themselves exactly as the *Gentry in London*." [5] With a royal benediction proclaimed over the drama, and with the natives of Williamsburg striving to mimic their more cultured models across the sea, Virginia was ripe for the introduction of the professional theater.

William Levingston, a merchant of New Kent County, had migrated to Virginia sometime before 1715 and is said to have been the son of a Scottish merchant and member of Parliament from Aberdeen. In addition to his merchandising activities, he operated a "peripatetic dancing school" in New Kent and neighboring counties. Instruction was furnished by two indentured servants, Charles Stagg, listed as "Dancing Master," who was assisted by his wife Mary. They had been bound to Levingston in September, 1715.

In the spring of 1716, Levingston broadened his activities by establishing a dancing school in Williamsburg, boasting that a suitable building was under construction. To inaugurate his classes without undue delay, Levingston submitted a petition to the Board of Visitors of the College of William and Mary begging the use of the college building to conduct his classes. On March 16, 1716, he was granted the "use of the lower Room at the South end of the Colledge for teaching the Scholars and others to dance until his own dancing school in Williamsburg be finished."

In the interim, Levingston and Stagg decided to expand their operations in the entertainment field. Sometime between March and July, they concluded an agreement to erect a theater in Williamsburg. Just what stimulated this idea is not known, but it may well have been the solicitations of interested townspeople, the urgings of the Staggs, or Levingston himself may have seen the possibility of additional revenue from a hitherto untapped source. Whatever the motive, by November, Levingston had, "at his own proper Cost & Charge sent to *England* for Actors & Musicians for the better Performance of the sd. Plays."

The Staggs were a talented couple. In addition to their proficiency in the "Science of Dancing," it seems they possessed some knowledge of the stage. Recognizing this, Levingston had, on July 11, 1716, released them from their indentures but still retained their services under contract. Under the terms of this covenant, not only were the Staggs to operate the theater, but they were to train other actors to the "best of their Skill." In drafting this new agreement, both Levingston and the Staggs drove shrewd bargains. Stagg agreed to pay Levingston £60 each "Lady Day" (March 25) for a period of three years, but was allowed to deduct a sum of £5 monthly for the time that he was engaged in acting for their joint benefit. In turn, Stagg was permitted to retain all entrance fees and profits received from the dancing school since his arrival in Virginia. Within eighteen months, Stagg agreed to reimburse Levingston for money and merchandise advanced him, in addition to expenses incurred for "horses, ferriages, or Otherwayes" in the administering of the dancing classes. As for the playhouse, Levingston agreed to erect "at his own proper Costs & Charge ... One good Substantiall house commodious for Acting such Plays as shall be thought fitt to be Acted there." Although Levingston was to receive an equitable rent for the building, both parties were to share equally "in all Charges of Cloaths Musick & other Necessaries," while profits were to be divided after the deduction of expenses. After binding themselves as partners in the entertainment field, each agreed to "use their best Endeavours to Obtain a Patent or Lycence from the Governour of Virga. for the Sole Privileges of Acting Comedies, Drolls or Other kind of Stage Plays within any part of the sd. Colony" for the next three years, even longer if possible.[6] There is, however, no indication that Stagg and Levingston received this monopoly on theatrical productions in Virginia.

With actors and musicians supposedly on their way from England, it became essential that Levingston erect the theater building as early as possible. He moved to York County from New Kent, a measure calculated to allow him personal supervision of his new venture. On November 5, 1716, he secured deeds of lease and release for three lots from the Trustees of the City of Williamsburg for a consideration of forty-five shillings and an annual rental of "one grain of Indian Corn ... if it be demanded." These three lots, numbers 163, 164, and 169, faced on the Palace Green, and Levingston was bound, by the stipula-

tion in the 1705 Act of Assembly for building the Capitol and
the city of Williamsburg, to erect on each lot within a period
of two years "one good dwelling house or houses" of specified
dimensions.

July, 1718, was the termination date for Levingston's lease,
and it must be assumed that the playhouse and other dwellings
were completed by that time as required by statute, for he was
allowed to retain the property. In building the theater, Levingston may have turned to the Staggs for advice, relying upon
their recollections of English playhouses, or it may have been
that he relied upon his own imagination or printed descriptions
of such buildings. The structure, when completed, measured
eighty-six feet, six inches long, with a width of thirty feet, and
it rested on a narrow brick foundation. A plain weatherboard
building with a shingled roof, it contained at least five windows
for light and ventilation. Within, the building was floored and
plastered; possibly the exterior was painted red, a practice customarily followed in later years.[7]

The spring of 1718 saw the first notice of a play being staged
in the new theater. On May 28, Governor Alexander Spotswood
sponsored a "publick Entertainment," including the presentation of a play, in celebration of the birthday of His Majesty,
George I. Spotswood, however, was at this time engaged in a
controversy with the Assembly relative to the completion of the
new governor's residence and he, it was charged, "lavishes away
the Countrys Money contrary to the intent of the Law." An
angry Council ignored the governor's festivities, repaired to the
capitol, and planned a more spectacular celebration of their own.
They "invited all ye Mobb to a Bonfire," providing their guests
with free liquor; toasts to the good health of the governor were
conspicuously absent. On June 24 of that year, an angry and
bitter Governor Spotswood, in a pungent complaint to the
Board of Trade, insisted that the vote of the Council be abolished
"in the passing of Laws." [8]

It seems quite proper to assume that this play of the governor's, if it was acted, was presented in the new playhouse by the
Levingston-Stagg Company, conceivably by those actors for
whom Levingston had sent to England some two years before.

It is also likely that the thrifty Scot resorted to importing indentured servants who had acquired some acting experience. Only a meager effort would have been necessary to persuade destitute London actors to bind themselves to a period of servitude as an assurance of eating regularly. Mary Ansell and Mary Peel, two female servants indentured to Levingston, may well have been actresses with the troupe. Little Thomas Sellers, "one-eyed, flat-footed, and Battle-ham'd," who was indentured to the Staggs and who was endowed with a talent for the violin and a penchant for running away, may have furnished musical accompaniment for both dramatic productions and dancing classes. Other possibilities were Nicholas Hurlston, conceivably a professional, and Alice and Elizabeth Ives, who perhaps performed the duties of wardrobe mistresses.[9]

The earliest date of a specific mention of the theater is May 21, 1721. In the intervening five years since securing the original property, Levingston had enlarged his holdings by two additional lots (numbers 176 and 177). In addition to the playhouse, he had erected a dwelling, a detached kitchen, and other necessary outbuildings, including a stable. In the acre and a half adjacent to the theater, a bowling green had been laid out. Around 1722, the Reverend Hugh Jones, mathematics professor at William and Mary, made casual mention of the theater but applied the adjective "good" to the bowling green, an implication that the playhouse was less than imposing.

From all indications, Levingston had completely abandoned his merchandising activities by 1721 and had established himself as an entrepreneur in the field of entertainment. He secured a license to operate his house in Williamsburg as a tavern, but with the understanding that he would "constantly find & provide in his ordinary good wholesome & cleanly Lodgings & diet for Travellers & Stableage"; that there would be no "unlawful gaming"; and that on the Sabbath he would not allow his patrons to "Tipple or drink more than is necessary." [10]

Notwithstanding his many projects, or perhaps because of them, Levingston's financial status steadily worsened. There are suggestions that he set himself up as a surgeon to better his fortune. Repeatedly, he brought legal action against delinquent creditors. His servants, almost from the beginning, involved Levingston in one legal entanglement after another. One, by the name of William Jones, was indicted in 1720 for attempting to incite other servants of the community to rebel and murder their masters. Others frequently ran away when not otherwise contributing to their master's difficulties or litigations. To ward off impending financial crisis Levingston, on May 29, 1721, was forced to mortgage his property to Archibald Blair. Levingston defaulted, and on June 24, 1723, Blair leased the property for five years to a person named in the deed as Robert Faldo (a legal pseudonym). To see another enjoying the fruits of his labors so enraged Levingston that, on the same day the new lessee assumed possession, the former owner "by force of Arms... Ejected expeled & Amoned" the new tenant from the premises. In the resultant court action, a jury declared Blair to be the rightful owner and, at the same time, awarded damages of one shilling to Faldo, who was allowed to reoccupy the property. Levingston was adjudged to have been the aggressor and ordered to pay the costs of the court. Shortly thereafter, the indigent Levingston removed to Spotsylvania County, endeavoring to begin anew by leasing land in an area that was ultimately to become the site of the town of Fredericksburg. He died sometime before 1729.[11]

The paucity of information, coupled with the absence of a local newspaper before 1736, veils the early operations of the theater in an almost impenetrable fog. An indication that the theater had fallen on hard times is seen in a passing observation by William Hugh Grove in his diary in 1732: "There was a Playhouse managed by Bowes but having little to do is dropped." Insofar as the records are concerned, Bowes remains a nonentity, but he may have been an employee of Blair, if the owner of the property elected to continue theatrical entertainments. Perchance, the playhouse was used as a dance studio by the Staggs. There is ample evidence that Stagg continued his instruction in the dance, although there are implications that he may have, upon occasion, dabbled in activities of a more commercial nature. Sometimes before January 21, 1736, Charles Stagg died, by the standards of his day, a fairly well-to-do man.[12]

Stagg was in his grave when, in January, 1736, Mrs. Cent-livre's *The Busy Body* was staged in Williamsburg by a local group; from all appearances, this was an amateur effort or, at best, a hybrid combination of the remnants of the Levingston-Stagg troupe joined with the community's dilettantes. William Byrd II wrote a sly, facetious letter from Westover, inquiring as to the reception of one actor, Dr. Henry Potter, newly arrived from London and a "Writer of Plays," who had played the rôle of Squire Marplot: "... we should be glad of a little Domestick [news], which of your Actors shone most in the Play next [to] Isabinda, who I take it for granted is the Oldfield of the theatre? How came Squire Marplot off? With many a clap I suppose, tho I fancy he would have acted more to life in the comedy called the Sham Doctor. But not a word of this for fear in case of sickness he might poison or revenge your, etc." [13]

Perhaps it is only coincidence that Blair sold the property on which the theater was located shortly after the death of Charles Stagg. On February 20, 1736, he deeded the property to George Gilmer, the apothecary, for a sum of £155.

After the death of her husband, Mary Stagg continued to offer instruction in terpsichorean skills. For only a brief period did she retain a monopoly of the dance in Williamsburg. In 1737, Madame Barbara de Graffenried, daughter-in-law of the noted founder of New Bern, North Carolina, advertised her services in a similar capacity. Her husband Christopher, owner of a plantation on the James River, was experiencing financial difficulties, and just two years earlier his father had observed that "fortune doth not look upon you with favorable eyes." His wife aided by establishing a dancing school and sometime ballroom in their town house adjacent to the Governor's Palace. Among others, she received the endorsement of William Byrd II, who noted, "She really takes abundance of pains and teaches well." Byrd also asserted to Sir John Randolph (perhaps a little wistfully) that "were you to attacque her virtue in the furious month of May when the sap rises in women they say as well as vegetables, you will find her as chaste as Lucretia." For the next two years, Mrs. de Graffenried and Mrs. Stagg sponsored balls and assemblies in gay competition. On the nights when both offered similar entertainments, Mrs. Stagg embroidered her presentation by offering a simultaneous raffle for "Several valuable Goods" and, upon one occasion, "a likely young Negro Fellow." Her theatrical experience allowed her an advantage with the presentation of such additional attractions as "several Grotesque Dances, never yet perform'd in Virginia." The inhibitions of her social position would not countenance Madame de Graffenried to supplement her income by selling "Jellies, Mackaroons, and Savoy Biscakes," as did Mary Stagg. Yet, these rivals by no means had the field to themselves. In 1737, William Dering advertised that he taught dancing "to all Gentlemens Sons... according to the newest French Manner" at the College, and by 1739, an indentured servant, Stephen Tenoe, was giving dancing instruction in both Yorktown and Williamsburg.[14]

This light-hearted round of amusements fostered new, or continued, interest in the drama. There is, however, the possibility that what appears to be renewed interest is only additional information made available when William Parks began publishing his *Virginia Gazette* in 1736. The spring term of the General Court in that year found the capital thronged with visitors, many of whom were from the backwoods and who constituted a ready-made audience for almost any type of entertainment. And it was for them that the local novices performed *The Recruiting Officer* and *The Busy Body* to "much Applause." Included in a rather distinguished cast were the sister and son of Governor William Gooch, Mayor Abraham Nicholas, the "merry" Dr. Henry Potter, apothecary George Gilmer (who now owned the theater), supported by "a Painter, and several others." So well received were their efforts that contributions to the amount of £150 were subscribed to "encourage their Entertaining the Country with like Diversions at future Public Meetings of our General Court and Assembly."

Play production, likewise, had been given a semiofficial stamp of approval by the faculty of the College of William and Mary. Concluding that "dayly Dialogues" in the grammar school would facilitate the teaching of Latin and Greek, they suggested: "... if there are any sort of Plays or Diversions in Use among them, which are not to be found extant in any printed Books, let the Master compose and dictate to his Scholars Colloquies fit for such sorts of Plays, that they may learn at all Times to speak Latin in apt and proper Terms."

This expressed interest in classical drama by the pedagogues may have led "the young Gentlemen of the College" to band together in what might be termed the first college dramatic society (discounting the Harvard presentation of *Gustavus Vasa* in 1690). Although there is no record of any formal organization, the students demonstrated sufficient interest to present publicly two plays in the fall of 1736. On September 10, soon after the House of Burgesses assembled, they opened with a performance of Joseph Addison's *Cato*, admirably suited as a dramatic vehicle for college lads. *Cato* was "a most ponderous tragedy" with "a succession of declamatory scenes . . . elegantly written, perfectly moral, and correctly in nature." Although almost hopelessly turgid by modern dramatic criteria, it was a success in its day, not only because of its flexible political allusions, but because of its apostrophes of virtue, liberty, and patriotism.

This portrayal of the last of the Romans making a final stand for liberty was followed by plays of a more sophisticated nature performed by a more worldly-wise cast. The old favorite, *The Busy Body*, was acted by a company of "the Gentlemen and Ladies of this Country," presumably with most of the same actors who had appeared in the spring performance. Success prompted the scheduling of two additional plays, *The Recruiting Officer* and *The Beaux' Stratagem*. Disappointment was imminent when no suitable actress could be found to play the feminine lead, the "fine Lady" Dorinda in Farquhar's *The Beaux' Stratagem*. This obstacle was overcome with the arrival in town of a Miss Anderson, although it would seem that an effort was made to keep the identity of Dorinda a secret to create suspense and interest in the play. But, as in all whimsy, the secret leaked to at least some of the public. During the performance, the sophisticated licentiousness of the plot delightfully shocked many of the young and genteel ladies in the audience; "Arabella Sly" coyly confessed to the readers of the *Virginia Gazette* that she had received a "Hunch" from the elbow of her companion when she forgot to mask her giggles as a kiss was passed on the stage. Others of the younger generation, it was noted, spent more time casting love-sick glances at one another than devoting attention to the action on the stage.

On September 20, the last drama known to have been played on the stage of the first theater was produced. Again, it was the "young Gentlemen of the College" who this time made their appearance in Addison's *The Drummer, or The Haunted House.* A month later, Thomas Jones's stepdaughter was being consoled by her grandmother with, "I hear there will be no plays this court so my dear B[etty] Pratt will loose no diversion by being absent for heare is not nor is there likely to be anything to do." [15]

Entertainment once again was centered around the balls and assemblies of Barbara de Graffenried and Mary Stagg. And unless an occasional unreported play was presented, the theater remained dark and quiet. In the spring of 1738, an attraction that played Williamsburg may conceivably have rented the playhouse from Gilmer. This was a performance during the Williamsburg fair by a troupe composed of an unnamed man, his wife, and their two children, who boasted of their "Agility of Body, by various Sorts of Postures, Tumbling, and Sword Dancing, to greater Perfection than has ever been known in these Parts for many Years, if ever." [16]

That the theater was active during the next few years is nowhere indicated, and disuse is suggested by the need of extensive repairs in 1745. Possibly, the decline of the first theater in Williamsburg was hastened by that religious upheaval, the "Great Awakening," already on its sweep through the colonies by the late 1730's. In December, 1739, George Whitefield delivered his eloquent bombast from the pulpit of Bruton Parish Church, in words so powerful as to sober people and turn their thoughts from more frivolous concerns.

December 4, 1745, marked the beginning of the last epoch in the existence of the first playhouse. On that date, a deed was drawn, confirming an earlier sale, that conveyed the "House call'd the play House" and a surrounding area of six feet on all sides from George Gilmer to a group of thirty-one "Gentlemen Subscribers" for a sum of £250. The bowling green had disappeared by this date, although Gilmer retained title to Levingston's original dwelling that housed his apothecary shop. Included in the list of purchasers were the names of some of the most distinguished men of the colony; each had been required to pledge the relatively small sum of £1. 13s. A petition submitted to these subscribers, by the Corporation of the City of Williamsburg, stressed the town's need of a suitable building for use as a common hall and a hustings court. Heretofore, the courthouse of James City County had been used "on Curtesie," and despite a pressing need, municipal funds were inadequate to construct a new building for that purpose. Suggesting that the old playhouse was admirably suited and located as a center of community affairs, they petitioned the purchasers to "bestow Your present Useless House on this Corporation." On December 4, 1745, the same day that Gilmer's original deed to the subscribers was drawn, the property was transferred a second time to the ownership of the city.

Within three weeks, city officials were advertising for proposals to alter and restore the structure, now in an advanced state of disrepair. The land remained in the possession of the city until 1770, when it was sold to John Tazewell, but by then the playhouse had disappeared. After the Capitol burned in 1747, the General Court of Virginia sat in the building until more suitable quarters could be acquired.

One final moment in which the old building served as a house of entertainment came in 1766 when it harbored William Johnson's exhibition of experiments "in that curious and entertaining branch of Natural Philosophy called Electricity," accompanied by appropriate lectures.[17]

Such was the story of the first theater in America—conceived in ambition, born to a dancing class, nurtured in difficulty, and expiring in the midst of the human life drama of a hustings court.

· III ·

OTHER EARLY AMERICAN THEATERS

AND MURRAY-KEAN,

THE FIRST TOURING COMPANY

(*Charleston, Philadelphia, New York,
Williamsburg, and Annapolis, 1723-1752*)

Despite antipathy sometimes bordering on the violent, the theater gradually broadened its niche in colonial culture and entertainment. Even Quaker Philadelphia was subjected to an early invasion of the despised actors. As early as 1723, a troupe of entertainers, led by "a Player who had Strowled hither to act as a Comedian," arrived in the outskirts of the city and, after playbills were printed and distributed, went on "to act accordingly." James Logan, the newly elected mayor of Philadelphia, was distressed to the point of complaining, "How grievous this proves to the sober people of the place...." Had not Governor William Keith looked with favor and indulgence upon the activities of players, there is reason to suspect that

Logan may have endeavored to suppress the performances, notwithstanding their location outside municipal jurisdiction. In clarifying his own reticence, the mayor explained that, inasmuch as the Governor had previously "excused himself from prohibiting" stage attractions, Logan felt he could "by no means think it advisable to embroil myself with the governor to no purpose."

The following year, 1724, the disposition of this unhappy civic official was further ruffled as a newspaper advertisement called attention to a "New Booth on Society Hill," just outside the city limits, where the latest in "Roap Dancing" could be admired, with additional regalement furnished by "your old friend Pickle Herring." This new "Booth" was probably little more than the modern connotations of the word would indicate, but it did boast a stage, pit, and gallery, with choice seats located on the stage.

Conceivably, these entertainers of early Pennsylvania were the nucleus of a troupe said to have presented plays in and around Lancaster between 1730 and 1742, but their names, the plays they acted, along with all other pertinent information have been lost in time. Certainly, there appears to have been a hiatus in almost every type of amusement in Philadelphia, for in 1729 one virtuous citizen of that city publicly rejoiced that there were "no Masquerades, Plays, Balls, Midnight Revellings or Assemblies to debauch the Mind or promote Intrigue." [1]

In the spring of 1730, the drama suddenly reappeared in New York with the first known performance of Shakespeare on the American stage. The performers, like the Williamsburg actors of 1735, were an amateur group under the direction of the sprightly Dr. Joachimus Bertrand. On March 23, 1730, Dr. Bertrand advertised a performance of *Romeo and Juliet* by quoting several lines of dialogue and then adding: "But as this Tragedy will be the first to be acted at the Revenge Meeting House, which is fitting up for that purpose, I hereby invite the Ladies to be present the first Night, the part of the *Apothecary* to be performed by myself in propria Persona, which I hope will be kindly taken and look'd upon as a great condescention in a Physician." No one reported the success of this performance; nor is there mention of the subsequent use of the Revenge Meeting House, which appears to have been a local tavern, as a theater.

Not for two years was there further public mention of a dramatic effort in New York. Then a succinct notice in the local press announced a production of *The Recruiting Officer*, with Thomas Heady, barber and peruke maker to Governor William Cosby, cast in the role of "Worthy." The "new Theatre" referred to in this news item was located in one of the buildings owned by Rip Van Dam, President of the Council, who as such had served as governor of New York for nearly a year following the death of Governor John Montgomery. Located in the loft of one of Van Dam's warehouses, the claim has been made that this theater seated as many as four hundred spectators. The players, whether amateur or semiprofessional, proved themselves versatile and, within the next three weeks, performed at least four more plays: *Cato,* a repeat of *The Recruiting Officer, The Beaux' Stratagem,* and *The Busy Body,* before fading from public notice. But so well had they established themselves that a year later Rip Van Dam's building was still referred to as "the Play-House," and a 1735 map of Manhattan so identifies a building on the east side, near Beaver Street.[2]

For the next eighteen years, however, New Yorkers were forced to content themselves with entertainments other than formal drama. In 1734, a German artist displayed "the Wonders of the World by Dexterity of Hand"; his seating arrangements were intriguingly advertised as "best seats," "farther off," and "furthest off." Five years later, in the "long Room" of dancing master Henry Holt, a pantomime of the "Grotesque Characters" of Harlequin and Scaramouche was announced, and the advertising boasted of new scenes, costumes, and decorations. The fall of 1747 saw a Punch and Judy show arriving from Philadelphia, the puppets supported by "a most curious Posture-Master Boy ... and many other Curiosities too tedious to mention." Two years later, "Punch's Company of Comedians" played a return engagement, with the puppets intermittently acting plays from July to October "At a large Theatrical Room" commodious enough to accommodate a wax works and an automaton. Their season was brought to an end in true theatrical fashion, advertising a benefit "to relieve some of the poor Prisoners in the City Hall." [3]

While the theater in New York was suffering this irregularity the institution was gaining a firm foothold in South Carolina. Charleston, like Williamsburg, was shaping a neoclassic culture based on a plantation economy. Trade, nourished by a busy port whose rivers gave the city access to a vast hinterland, was increasing at a pleasing pace. Wealth and new-found leisure prompted an interest in the arts, first discernible through the medium of music. One of the first public notices of a musical presentation in Charleston appeared in April, 1732, when it was announced that a "Consort of Musick" would be presented in the Council Chamber for the benefit of a Mr. Salter. It proved to be a popular diversion, and similar affairs offering "Vocal and Instrumental Musick" eventually graduated to a pattern featuring a combination concert and ball.

In a like manner, the seed planted in 1703 by the carefree Anthony Aston had fallen in fertile soil, but it was not until the winter of 1735 that Charleston's first dramatic season was inaugurated. For lack of a proper playhouse, Thomas Otway's *The Orphan, or The Unhappy Marriage* was performed in the courtroom on Friday, January 24, 1735, and was so well received that it was repeated the following Tuesday. The better tickets for both these performances were priced at forty shillings, undoubtedly South Carolina paper currency. In the prologue spoken on the night of the first performance, the players pleaded their inexperience with:

> Faint our Endeavours, rude our Essays;
> We strive to please, but can't pretend at praise;
> Forgiving Smiles o'erpay the grateful Task;
> They're all we hope and all we humbly ask.

The Orphan proved popular. On February 8, the play was once again presented ("Encourag'd by your Smiles again we dare"), with the prologue stressing the strong moral overtones in a basically licentious and obscene play.

Seemingly convinced that their efforts constituted a solution to many sociological problems, the players boldly ridiculed the theatrical censorship of New England in the prologue when *The Orphan* was presented for the fourth straight time:

> The little Term that Heaven to Mortals spares,
> Is daily clouded with prolonging Cares;
> Nor *real* Virtue blames the pleasing Strife,
> To blend Amusement with the Shades of Life;
> Wise, innocent, serene, she smiles at Ease,
> Nor hanging Witches, nor adjoining Plays.

Not until February 18 was the bill changed, when Colley Cibber's ballad farce *Flora, or Hob in the Well* may well have been the first production of a musical play in the English colonies. Another innovation was the addition of an afterpiece, the old pantomime favorite of *Harlequin and Scaramouche*, played as usual "in Grotesque Characters."

The subsequent interval was possibly to allow the necessary time to rehearse a new play. The next performance, whatever the reason, was not until March 25, when John Dryden's *The Spanish Friar, or The Double Discovery*, a rather difficult and dull play involving two separate plots that are wholly independent of each other, was presented. Yet, it must have been well received; there was a repeat performance two days later.

With Dryden's play the theater closed for the season. The cast of this ambitious group was never published, but a reasonable supposition is that they were of the local gentry. The last performance of *The Spanish Friar* on March 27 had been announced as a benefit for the young lady who played the feminine leads, designated simply as "Monimia," suggesting the same girl who had played the heroine in *The Orphan*. It was still a man's world in which the roles of the female were chiefly domestic and biological. To have announced the lady's name in public advertisement would have overstepped the bounds of genteel Charleston society. Amateur or professional, the company more than fulfilled its announced purpose:

> From the old World in minature we shew
> Her choicest Pleasures to regale the new.[4]

So favorable had been the reception of the troupe's efforts that a subscription was undertaken to insure similar entertainment for the following winter. A list of pledges was solicited by Charles Shepheard, who had been responsible for ticket sales during the season and evidently acted as manager for the company.

Although the courtroom was still felt to be adequate for dancing, the attendance at the plays the past season had demonstrated that it was no longer suitable for the staging of the drama. Construction of a new theater was begun in Dock Street, and the public was assured of its completion by the following winter.

On Thursday, February 1, 1736, the "new Theatre in Dock Street" opened with George Farquhar's popular comedy, *The Recruiting Officer*. Such a large audience was anticipated that even the subscribers were cautioned to "bespeak places" before noon, "otherwise it will be too late." It was well that they did, for the popular "Monimia" of the year before, who this night was cast in the role of "Silvia," recited a prologue written especially for the occasion by Dr. Thomas Dale, Associate Justice of South Carolina. The fact that a prologue should have been written by so dignified an author was unusual, but even more uncommon (for the colonies, at least) was that the young lady appeared in male attire, in what was commonly called a "breeches part." Such disguises, common in Shakespeare's plays, became popular after the appearance of women upon the stage. Samuel Pepys, in 1661, recorded his pleasure at seeing an actress "on the stage in Men's clothes, and had the best legs that I ever saw, and I was very well pleased with it." In the prologue to this first American breeches part, "Silvia" boldly and unabashedly stated her purpose:

> To bid farewell to petticoats and stitching,
> and wearing breeches, try their force bewitching.

The so-called "Dock Street Theatre" bore that designation for only one performance. In the intervening week, the name of the street on which it was located was changed to Queen Street, and from this time on, the building was known as the "Theatre in

Queen Street." There were two additions to the usual repertoire of *The Orphan* and *The Recruiting Officer*, the more important being George Lillo's *The London Merchant, or The History of George Barnwell*. A new ballad opera, *The Devil to Pay, or The Wives Metamorphos'd*, was added, possibly to mitigate the stark tragedy of *The London Merchant*. One of the two performances of the martial comedy, *The Recruiting Officer*, was played at the special request of the officers of the local military garrison.

Charles Shepheard's was still the only name of a member of the company to appear in the newspapers, and apparently he was still either the manager or the agent of the company. There was always an interval of at least one week between plays, which, coupled with their limited repertoire, is in itself an indication that the actors were more amateur than professional. The spring season of 1736 closed with *The Orphan* on March 23, and six plays had been presented in as many weeks.[5]

In May, the ownership of the theater changed hands. The sale so frightened one devotee of the drama that he was quick to pen a lament to the *Gazette:*

> How cruel Fortune, and how fickle too,
> To crop the Method made for making you.

These premature fears proved groundless. On November 11, the following autumn, the theater opened with a presentation of Addison's *Cato* and added *Flora, or Hob in the Well* as an afterpiece when that play was repeated the following week. Sandwiched between a production of *The Recruiting Officer* on December 1 and *Cato* on December 17 was a ball held in the theater building, a practice that was destined to continue. The 1737 season came to an end on January 11 with still another performance of *The Recruiting Officer*.

This comedy, repeated in the spring, was the last play to be seen in Charleston for many years. This May 26 production was significant inasmuch as it inaugurated a relationship between the theater and the fraternal order of Masons that remained constant throughout the colonial period. The "antient and honourable Society of Free and Accepted Masons," active in Charleston since 1735, had presented a special request for this performance of *The Recruiting Officer*. It should be noted, however, that the "request" was more than likely initiated by Charles Shepheard, at whose house the Masons had their lodge. It was a gala performance. The evening began and ended with a prologue and epilogue written especially for the occasion, and it included a comic dance, "Harlequin and the Clown," a prancing innovation upon the Harlequin theme. A special vocal attraction, "The Song of Mad Tom," was done "in proper Habiliments, by a Person that never yet appear'd upon the Stage." When the Masons marched in a body to the theater and filed into the auditorium, they constituted the largest audience the house had yet known. As vocalists upon the stage sang the "entered Apprentice and Master's Songs," they were joined in chorus by the brethren in the pit, "to the Satisfaction and Entertainment of the whole Audience."

When the curtain fell upon this gay production, it marked the end of dramatic performances in Charleston for the next eighteen years. Concerts declined in a similar fashion, and the occasional dance assemblies of Henry Holt, Henry Campbell, and others were the only notable public entertainments offered in Charleston between 1740 and 1751. As in Williamsburg, this languishing interest in things theatrical may have resulted from an epidemical resurgence of religious interest. Just six weeks before the concluding performance in the Queen Street Theatre, John Wesley had preached so effectively in St. Philip's Church that one gentleman had exclaimed, "Why if this be Christianity, a Christian must have more Courage than Alexander the Great." And that most spirited of all evangelists, the Reverend George Whitefield, preached upon many occasions in Charleston during the next few years, always to a great concourse of admirers.[6]

Conversely, it was in the Quaker stronghold of Philadelphia, where religious opposition to the drama was to be expected as a matter of course, that the first traveling company of comedians made their original appearance. The city had seen little in the way of theatricals since Mayor James Logan's alarm in 1724. To be sure, there had been some exhibitions, but the nature of them had been so passive as not to excite emotions; freakish animals, a "Magick Lanthorn," and "Changeable Figures of Two Feet High," who produced comedies and tragedies on their miniature stage were the only professional entertainments even remotely resembling the theater.

There was, however, an undercurrent of interest in the drama. As early as 1744, some of the young ladies of the city had dazzled their swains with "Expressions, which swim on the Surface of Criticism" of current plays. And there were implications that the younger set had staged a play for their own amusement in the winter of 1749. In August of that year, Edward Shippen had written from London to young James Burd, "You acquaint me of your acting a play last Winter to the Satisfaction of all Spectators. . . . I am glad that *Spirit is kept up*, because it is an amusement the most useful to any young People, and I heartily wish it would spread to the Younger Sort, I mean School Boys." Shippen's enthusiasm, however, did not constitute an endorsement of the professional theater but was limited to the pedagogic values of play acting—it not only polished the student's articulation but "rids him of his natural Bashfulness." There had been no public announcement in the local press of the production of which he wrote.

On the other hand, this may have been the first stirrings of a company of players formally organized in 1749 under the dual management of Walter Murray and Thomas Kean. Their place of origin is unknown, but it was in Philadelphia that they made their first recorded appearance. Seeking a building in which to perform, they negotiated with William Plumstead for the use of his warehouse on Pine Street. There was not a more ideal person in all Philadelphia with whom they could have dealt; Plumstead had been read out of the Quaker meeting and had since embraced the Anglican faith. His prominence in local politics was to reward him with the mayoralty of the city within the year.

The struggling young company was too poor to advertise its performances, and as a result, information is at best sketchy. On August 22, Quaker John Smith, son-in-law of James Logan, dropped in on his friend Peacock Biggers for a cup of tea, and there discovered the daughter of his host thrilled by the prospect of seeing *Cato* acted that evening. Smith promptly "Expressed my sorrow that any thing of the kind was Encouraged &ca."

Cato is the only play known to have been acted in Philadelphia during the stay of the Murray-Kean Company, but there must have been others. It seems only reasonable to assume that the company played the dramatic creations of such popular playwrights as Dryden, Otway, Congreve, Farquhar, Rowe, and Gay, which they were to perform in New York the following year. And unless Murray or Kean drastically expurgated such plays as *The Beaux' Stratagem*, the words "whore," "cuckold," and "bastard" profaned the same pious air as that inhaled by the Quakers and Presbyterians of Penn's "Holy Community."

The audiences were remembered as "genteel"; they were shocked and "fell out" with a local girl, the stage-struck Nancy George, when she joined the thespians. Despite the growing strength of the Anglican church in Philadelphia, the Quakers and Presbyterians still wielded sufficient political power to, on January 8, 1750, force the Common Council of the City to take action to excise this canker, posing the argument that money would be drawn "from weak and inconsiderate People" who could scarce afford such luxuries. Notwithstanding their lack of jurisdiction, the Council unanimously condemned the performance of plays as an activity that "would be Attended with very Mischievous Effects," and the magistrates were ordered to bind the actors "to their good Behaviour."

In the face of such a display of open authoritative displeasure, it seemed wise that the Murray-Kean Company seek a more comfortable climate. In early February, 1750, the troupe departed from Philadelphia, leaving behind them sharpened literary appetites for things dramatic, a desire speedily gratified by the booksellers of the city.[7]

Arriving in New York this same month, the members of the company once again found themselves in a society in which the drama had long been dormant. That attempts were made to revive the local theater as early as 1739 is indicated by an old London manuscript by Archibald Home entitled "Poems on Several Occasions." One of his efforts bore the heading, "Prologue, Intended for the second opening of the Theatre at New

York, Anno 1739." It is also implied that plays were popular as a form of literature by one writer's bitter denunciation of the parents of his generation: "She is now ten years of age, her mind is ripe for plays. Here again is a noble field of vanity presented to Madam, her mind is wholly taken up with the pleasure it affords and an actress' part, repeated by heart, yields greater joy to her parents than if she knew the whole Catechism."

Soon after their arrival in New York, the Murray-Kean Company secured "a convenient Room for their Purpose in one of the buildings lately belonging to the Hon. Rip Van Dam Esqr., deceased, in Nassau Street, where they intend to perform as long as the season lasts, provided they meet with suitable encouragement." As in the Plumstead building in Philadelphia, the theater was probably housed in a warehouse and resembled a playhouse in few respects other than size. Originally there were no boxes, as only seats in the pit and gallery were advertised. Later, when a few box seats were added, the capacity of the house reached 161 in the pit, ten box seats, and 121 in what was a rather large balcony.

On March 5, the company opened with *Richard III*, "Wrote originally by Shakespeare," as altered by Colley Cibber in the accepted acting version throughout the eighteenth century. *Richard III* was repeated the following week, and proven favorites of more contemporary writers were produced later. *The Orphan*, "wrote by the ingenious Mr. Otway," was presented on April 27, "For the Benefit of The Charity School in this City," possibly to prevent opposition on moral grounds. Attendance at subsequent performances dwindled as the weather grew warmer, and on July 12, the extreme heat forced a four-day postponement until "it has the appearance of being Moderate Weather." But the drop in temperature did not materialize, and one week later it was advertised that *Love for Love* would be "The Last Night of playing this Season." [8]

Not until the cool nights of early September did the company reappear with *The Recruiting Officer*. On September 20, *Cato* was performed for the largest audience ever to attend a theatrical performance in New York, some of whom felt that "it was pretty well performed." The *Weekly Post-Boy* editorialized: "It may serve to prove that the taste of this place is not so much vitiated or lost to a sense of liberty but that they can prefer a representation of virtue to one of loose character." This scolding had some salutary results, for the plays presented during the next few weeks were in somewhat better taste.

In late November, with winter fast approaching, the managers made several alterations in the theater and proudly announced, "The house being newly floored is made warm and comfortable, besides which Gentlemen and Ladies may cause their stoves to be brought."

Benefits, the means by which an actor augmented his meager income, were frequent. Thomas Kean, as one of the managers, was first, and he wisely chose the ever-popular *Beggar's Opera*, announcing at the same time two notable variations. For the first time, box seats were to be available in the Nassau Street theater; possibly this was accomplished by the simple expedient of railing off a small portion of the pit. And a new member of the company was announced, Robert Upton, "a gentleman lately from London," who was skilled in the dance. On this first appearance, he performed a Harlequin dance, a Pierrot, and the popular "Drunken Peasant." Upton was not only talented but shrewd. He had been sent out from London as the advance agent for a company of comedians who were even then making preparations to sail to the colonies. Rather than make the necessary arrangements for their arrival, he had succumbed to the prospect of easy money, deserted his original employers, and sold his talents to Murray and Kean.

Kean's benefit proved so popular, perhaps because of the extra attractions, that the theater was unable to accommodate the audience. Announcements had stated that no tickets would be sold at the door, but this had proved impracticable because of the risk involved in offending regular patrons. Evidently some of the audience managed to evade payment altogether, for the house became so crowded that the price of admission was refunded to a number of those who had purchased tickets in advance. Criticism became so heated the following week that the *Weekly Post-Boy* carried an explanation by the publisher, James Parker, that no more than the usual number of tickets had been printed. In this same issue, Thomas Kean denied the rumor that there had been a "falling out" with his leading lady, Mrs. Taylor, and defended what must have been a rather sorry performance on her part, explaining that it was "owing to her not getting the part in time."

Benefit followed benefit, but few were as successful as Kean's. Mrs. Taylor received two benefits for this reason outlined in the playbill: "As there was not much company at 'Love for Love' (the play performed for her previous benefit) the Managers took the profit arising by that night to themselves, and gave Mrs. Taylor another benefit, who hopes the Ladies and Gentlemen will be so kind as to favour her with their company."

Heavy spring rains occasionally postponed scheduled performances, but on April 22, notice was given of an unusual benefit, the second for Thomas Kean. This one was to expedite his departure from the company, Kean "by the advice of several gentlemen in town who are his friends, having resolved to quit the stage and follow his employment of writing (wherein he hopes for encouragement)." His agreement with Walter Murray was that, in return for the entire receipts of this one night, he would relinquish any claim to the scenery, costumes, etc., belonging to the company, leaving his partner as sole owner. For his farewell performance, Kean originally selected *Richard III* and *Beau in the Suds,* but before the date of the benefit, a change was announced, substituting *The Busy Body* and *The Virgin Unmask'd,* the identical program of the previous week. An additional attraction was the singing of the celebrated ode, "Briton's Charter," by Charles Woodham. On the playbills, Kean made the customary plea that "all Gentlemen and Ladies, and others, who are his Well-Wishers," favor him with their attendance.

The company struggled along without Kean, possibly the best actor in the group. One benefit succeeded another, with even Master Dicky Murray, the son of the manager, receiving his night along with the rest. An effort was made to swell the repertoire through an advertisement requesting the loan of printed scripts of such farces as Henry Fielding's *The Intriguing Chambermaid.*

The summer of 1751 was comparatively mild, and the plays

continued throughout the warmer months. From the pathetic solicitations on the occasion of their benefits, a fair idea may be gained of the cast of this company which a later manager dismissed rather contemptuously as "some young men perpetrating murder of sundry plays in the skirts of town." On June 10, when Mr. Jago advertised his benefit, he prayed that the play would be patronized, "as he never had a Benefit before, and is just out of prison." This same issue of the newspaper carried the notice of Mrs. Davis' night, with her expressed hope that she would be favored, "as the play is granted to enable her to buy off her time," an indication of indentured servitude. The widow Osborn was the personification of the title of her play, *The Distrest Mother*, "As 'tis the first time this Poor Widow has had a benefit, and having met with divers late hardships and misfortunes, 'tis hoped all charitable, benevolent ladies, and others, will favour her with their company."

July 8, 1751, marked the end of the New York run for the Murray-Kean Company. Within a few weeks, one of the actors, John Tremain, inserted an advertisement in the *Weekly Post-Boy* declaring that, inasmuch as he had now "declined the stage," he proposed "to follow his business as a Cabinet Maker, at the house of Norwood near the Long Bridge" and that his wares were to be sold "at the cheapest rates." [9]

Despite their vicissitudes, the Murray-Kean Company enjoyed one of the longest runs in a single town in the history of the colonial theater—from March 5, 1750, to July 8, 1751, continuous performances, with the exception of the six weeks when they were forced to close because of summer heat. They were soon to reappear in Williamsburg, but they left a number of their troupe in New York, including Robert Upton, who once again deserted an employer.

Robert Upton was an ambitious and enterprising man. With the departure of the Murray-Kean Company, he began to form his own troupe; as a nucleus he collected the members of the Murray-Kean group who had elected not to make the journey to Virginia. Quite naturally, Upton and his wife claimed the starring roles for themselves. John Tremain was persuaded to lay aside his woodworking tools and return to the stage. The

"Poor Widow" Osborn, whose daughter had gone to Virginia, once again appeared on the boards.

After some time in rehearsals, Upton, on December 26, 1751, presented his first bill, combining *Othello* and Garrick's *Lethe, or Aesop in the Shades* and advertising lower admission prices than those of Murray-Kean. Notwithstanding such bargains, attendance was poor, and on February 13, Upton announced "his great disappointment not meeting with encouragement" and declared his intention of presenting only five or six more plays as benefits. With the first of these, which he claimed by his prerogative as manager, he apologized for his inability to follow theatrical custom and call personally upon each potential customer to solicit patronage, and "he humbly hopes they'll impute it to the want of information, not of respect."

With the announcement of Mrs. Upton's benefit on February 20, the declaration was made that this was "Absolutely the last time of performing here," coupled with the swaggering boast that "The Company assures the Publick that they are perfect, and hope to perform to Satisfaction." Despite the finality of this pronouncement, the company continued to play regularly until the week before Upton's ship sailed for England. On March 4, 1752, *The Fair Penitent* was Upton's last production. His last words on the American stage were contained in the farewell epilogue "adapted to the occasion." [10]

Meanwhile, the Murray-Kean Company had opened in Virginia. Williamsburg had seen few professional entertainers since late December, 1745, when William Johnson had demonstrated his electrical display. The arrival of a similar practitioner of the electrical art, who had come from Maryland by way of Norfolk, Suffolk, Hampton, and Yorktown, was announced for the October, 1749, term of the General Court. In addition to its amusement values, powerful curative powers were claimed for this voltaic element which were alleged to be an antidote for ailments ranging from toothache and deafness to "swelling of the spleen." Domestic entertainments included the usual balls and assemblies enjoyed by any eighteenth-century urban community, horse racing in season, and a periodic fair. The return of the theater was a welcome innovation.

In the *Virginia Gazette* of August 29, 1751, Alexander Finnie, proprietor of the Raleigh Tavern, announced his sponsorship of a new theatrical project. Undoubtedly, he had been in communication with Walter Murray, for he published the intention of the players to come to Williamsburg if a playhouse could be provided. Finnie proposed that the funds for the construction of a new theater be raised through subscription, and those "kind enough to favour this Undertaking" would, upon contribution of one pistole, be entitled to a box seat "for the first Night's Diversion." The building, he promised, would be completed in time to accommodate the large crowds expected in town for the October term of the General Court.

Time was short. Less than a week after Finnie's original announcement, he purchased two lots from Benjamin Waller at a cost of £40. These lots were located on the east side of Eastern Street (later Waller Street), and a customary provision in the deed required that Finnie build either "2 good dwellings" of sixteen by twenty feet or one large building of at least fifty by twenty feet.

Subscriptions were slow, but Finnie boldly pushed ahead with the building, in spite of the rumor that the actors were not coming after all. John Blair, President of the Governor's Council, noted briefly the prevailing gossip in his diary, "Hear ye Actrs. are dispersed Presid will *not* come." But the players did come and, as early as September 26, were announcing their first production for October 21, *Richard III* with an exotic added attraction of "a Grand Tragic Dance, compos'd by Monsieur Denoier, called the ROYAL CAPTIVE, after the Turkish Manner."

Although the theater was considered complete, it contained only the bare essentials of stage, pit, boxes, and gallery, and the Murray-Kean Company was still operating on the same shoestring it started with. The *Virginia Gazette* received little patronage from them, with the company relying upon the distribution of playbills on the day of the performance. Only three days after the presentation of *Richard III*, a card inserted in the *Gazette* revealed the financial difficulties of the troupe. Informing the public that the expenses incurred in the erection of the theater had been greater than anticipated, they solicited additional funds from "those Gentlemen who are Lovers of theatrical Performances," as a means "to procure proper Scenes and Dresses." Rather than choice seats, the subscribers were offered a share in the theater building itself. Finnie, to whom the property had been deeded originally, was not involved in this proposal, as the money was to be collected by Messrs. Mitchelson and Hyndman who, in turn, would issue theater deeds to the contributors. Two interesting administrative changes were revealed in this notice. Charles Somerset Woodham, who had sung "Briton's Charter" at the New York benefit of Thomas Kean, was now listed as a manager, his name appearing above that of Murray. It is quite possible that he had been persuaded to invest his savings in the company on the condition that he be made manager in charge. Certainly, it was Woodham who was billed by the creditors of the troupe. Thomas Kean, despite his ostentatious farewell performance and surrender of title to all properties of the company, was again listed as manager, and it must have been he who had essayed the difficult lead role in *Richard III*.

By the middle of November, with the adjournment of the General Court and the departure of the crowds, the company concluded its rather short engagement in Williamsburg. They moved on to Norfolk, opening there on November 17 in "Capt. Newton's Great Room," offering *The Recruiting Officer*, plus such extra "Entertainments as will be express'd in the Bills." With this brief notice, the company disappeared again, but it is likely that they played out the rest of the month in Norfolk, with a possible side trip to Suffolk, another town favored by strolling entertainers.

During their brief period in Williamsburg, the company revived some enthusiasm for the drama at the College. There was some talk of reviving the old collegiate favorite, *Cato*, as an acting vehicle for the students, and Mr. Preston, professor of moral philosophy, took it upon himself to demonstrate the evils of the drama. It would appear that he became carried away with his own histrionic efforts. John Blair penned a wry note in his diary on November 16: "This evening Mr. Pre[s]ton to prevent the young gentlemen at the college from playing at a rehearsal in the dormitory, how they could act Cato privately among themselves, did himself, they say, act the Drun[ke]n Peasant; but his tearing down the curtains is to me very surprising."

By December, the wandering players had returned to Williamsburg, but they left no records of any performance. On December 19, they announced their intention of playing in Petersburg no later than the middle of January. Either the actors were not properly clothed for the winter months ahead, or new costumes were needed, and there seems to be little doubt that their credit was poor, if not non-existent. "A Suit of Cloaths for the Players" was purchased through William Hunter of the *Virginia Gazette*.

Their success or failure in Petersburg, like so many of their performances, is unrecorded, leaving a gap in the chronicle of their peregrinations. They did not appear again in Williamsburg until the spring of 1752, and then it was with an announcement of the benefit for Mrs. Becceley, female singer and soubrette of the troupe. This, however, is in itself an indication that the company had been in Williamsburg for some time, as benefits were always played near the end of the season. Mrs. Becceley selected for her night the Farquhar comedy *A Constant Couple, or A Trip to the Jubilee*, with *The Lying Valet* as an afterpiece. Both Murray and Kean joined her in playing lead roles, and there were promises of songs between the acts, along with the dance of the "Drunken Peasant." That Mrs. Becceley selected the role of Angelica rather than Sir Harry Wildair (played by Kean), a role that English actresses occasionally played as a breeches part, suggests that her figure was not all that it should have been for a leading lady. Mrs. Becceley obviously had an agreement with the managers that guaranteed her a well-advertised benefit, for none of the other actors received such extravagant notices on their nights, not even the managers. In general, expenditures for advertising were so low as to be practically negligible.[11]

Two weeks later, the *Gazette*, on April 30, announced the intention of the company to leave Williamsburg for Hobb's-Hole (Tappahannock) for a two-week stay from May 10 to May 24, where the courthouse was the only building large enough to accommodate the players and their audience. From Hobb's-Hole they journeyed to Fredericksburg to take advantage of the large crowds attracted to that town by the June Fair. And it was in Fredericksburg, on June 2, that young George Washington saw (from the balcony) what was probably his first play on the American stage. There is the possibility that Fredericksburg had a theater building at this time, or a building that had been altered as such, for young Washington noted in his meticulously-kept ledger that he had made a loan to his brother Samuel "at the playhouse." [12]

With the closing of the fair, the actors hurried to Annapolis, arriving in time to announce their first production on June 18. Here they found themselves in a capital city similar to Williamsburg, with "the characters of the inhabitants . . . much the same as the Virginians." The people of Annapolis harbored few prejudices against the stage, although their prior professional entertainment had been limited to "Underlings of the Theatre, such as Rope-Dancers, Jack Puddings, and Tumblers," along with the inevitable lectures on electricity. Also, there was some literary interest in the theater as Jonas Green, publisher of the *Maryland Gazette*, frequently advertised plays and histories of the theater for sale.

The claim has been advanced that the theater in which the Murray-Kean Company opened was built of brick, especially constructed for their visit. This seems unlikely, even though the comedians did advertise their performances "At the New Theatre," which tradition locates on the Duke of Gloucester Street. It was also through their newspaper advertisements (which were much more frequent than in Williamsburg) that the troupe attempted to establish a local identity. Upon their first arrival in Annapolis, they billed themselves simply as the "Company of Comedians," but to titillate local vanity this was changed to the "Company of Comedians from Annapolis." [13]

The season began on June 22 with *The Beggar's Opera* and *The Lying Valet*, but no sooner had they opened than they announced their intention of "immediately" performing in Upper Marlborough, Piscataway, and Port Tobacco. The response in Annapolis was greater than anticipated, and it was not until two weeks later that a tag appended to an advertisement of *The Busy Body* explained: "As the Company have now got their

Hands, Cloaths &c compleat, they now confirm their resolution of going to Upper Marlborough, as soon as ever Encouragement fails here."

"Encouragement" did not fail until the middle of August, and though the General Assembly was to meet in the near future, the company took the road to Upper Marlborough, where they hoped to attract some of the fun-loving crowds drawn to that place by the races. They performed in what was termed the "New Theatre," possibly no more than a remodeled warehouse as only pit and gallery seats were sold. On August 20, they opened with the identical bill presented on their first night in Annapolis. Their visit to Upper Marlborough reached a climax on September 14 when, "at the Request of the Antient and Honourable Society of Free and Accepted Masons," a special performance of *The Beggar's Opera* and *The Lying Valet* was scheduled. Like the earlier, but similar, occasion in Charleston, this was a gala affair. Instrumental music to accompany the lyrics of the songs was furnished "by a Set of private Gentlemen." Other attractions offered on this special night were a solo on the French horn and "A Mason's Song by Mr. Woodham; with a Grand Chorus."

Despite this full house, and with the racing season not yet over, the Murray-Kean Company returned to Annapolis. They reopened at the capital with *The Constant Couple* and soon after began their benefits with *Cato* on the night of Mr. Eyanson, an actor who had joined the players since their departure from New York.

Desperation marked the struggles of the comedians in their efforts to survive. Poor attendance in Annapolis led them to momentarily desert that town for Chester, Maryland, where they opened on October 26. In Annapolis, they were succeeded by "Richard Brickell and Company," whose primary offering included three wax figurines of Hungarian royalty, a "Curious Brass Piece of Ordnance," and "Prospects" of European localities.

This exhibition fared little better than the actors, and it had departed by the first week in December when the comedians announced their return to Annapolis on December 11. Upon this occasion, there were two new faces in the lead roles of Richard and Richmond in *Richard III*, in the past played by Murray and Kean. These newcomers, Mr. Wynell and Mr. Herbert, were billed as "From the Theatre in Williamsburg." Actually, this casting was beyond their ability, for they had acted only in minor parts with the company then appearing in Williamsburg before they became disgruntled and joined the opposition to become stars, a rather sad commentary on the acting abilities of the Murray-Kean organization. While the company had been on the road, the Annapolis theater had undergone some refurbishing. A porch had been added to shelter patrons in inclement weather, while the interior had been finished throughout, insulating the auditorium so that it was now "fit for the Reception of Ladies and Gentlemen." [14]

After these presentations, the company disappeared as suddenly as it had appeared on the theatrical scene. They may have followed through with their announced intention of playing Piscataway and Port Tobacco, but it is just as plausible that their obvious insolvency crowded in upon them in Annapolis and there they disbanded, with the actors picking up their lives again as ordinary mortals.

For the most part, the Murray-Kean Company had been composed of stage-struck tradesmen and their wives; constantly in financial difficulty and often facing a hostile audience, they managed to survive three years and played in Philadelphia, New York, Williamsburg, Annapolis, and outlying towns. Their importance is reflected in the fact that they had unwittingly done the job that Robert Upton had been employed to achieve and had acted as an advance agent for those to follow, whetting the appetite of the colonials for the drama and upon occasion wearing down religious and moralistic opposition. Even now, as they were drifting back into obscurity, their most significant successor was producing plays in Williamsburg, initiating a fabulous career that had its beginning in London by way of Jamaica.

· IV ·

THE HALLAM COMPANY

(Williamsburg, 1752-1753)

Jamaica, strangely enough, could very well lay claim to fostering the professional theater in the American colonies. Economically, politically, and in many ways aesthetically, the island was not unlike the southern colonies on the mainland. It was on this West Indian island that one of the first planter aristocracies developed, and a healthy economy had its origins in the profits made from the buccaneers who disposed of their loot through its markets in the late seventeenth century. Out of this wealth, a gay social life had arisen, so frivolous that Edward Long was later to comment: "Considering the climate and its tendency to rouse the passions, we ought to regard chastity here as no mean effort of female fortitude."

In an environment of cheer and conviviality, the drama came as a natural and welcome development, and as early as 1682, a theater of sorts was reported in Jamaica, possibly to supply the roistering buccaneers with diversion. And in a 1740 history of the island, it was carefully noted that the planters of Jamaica "lately have got a Playhouse, where they retain a Set of Extraordinary good Actors."

A vigorous repertory theater in Jamaica actually began in 1745, when a young Irishman who called himself John Moody disembarked from a trading vessel. This eighteen-year-old youth, born in County Cork and the son of a hairdresser by the name of Cochran, had followed his father's profession in his early years. Bored with this dull and unexciting existence, he, like Anthony Aston, followed his star. Young Cochran journeyed first to London where he had endeavored to conceal his humble origin by changing his name to John Moody and claiming England as his native land, but a rich Irish brogue soon exposed his deception. Forsaking the city for the provinces, he became a strolling player, and "As he was naturally a comedian, of course his first efforts were directed to tragedy," even though a thick Celtic articulation did not prove particularly adaptable to the sonorous eloquence of the speeches in such plays as *Macbeth* and *Othello*. It was alleged that in 1745 he had participated in the second Jacobite Rebellion, perhaps an explanation for his flight to Jamaica.

Wandering through the island, Moody discovered an amateur company performing plays in a ballroom, and he offered his services to them. They allowed him "to revel in all the heroes of Shakespeare," which, despite his declamatory defects, so delighted the planters of the island that he became an immediate favorite. Moody was shrewd enough to recognize opportunity, and capitalizing on the enthusiasm of his new-found audience, he proposed to organize a regular theater in Jamaica after returning to England to recruit a company of professionals. Meeting with a warm response, Moody returned from London the following year with his actors to open the playhouse. His success bordered on the spectacular, and this former failure was soon on his way to accumulating a small fortune. The climate and fevers endemic to the island took their toll among the players, and once again he made the voyage to England seeking new actors. Among those who returned with him were several who, within a few years, were destined to play an important role in the development of the American drama: namely, David Douglass and the Owen Morrises. In all probability it was this company that entertained young George Washington in Barbados with his first play, Lillo's *The London Merchant, or The History of George Barnwell* on November 15, 1751, of which he observed, "The character of Barnwell and several others was said to be well perform'd. There was music adapted and regularly conducted. . . ." Soon after this, Moody returned to England, where he joined Garrick's company at Drury Lane. David Douglass and the other members of his company continued to tour, on shares, throughout the islands.[1]

Actors have never been noted for their ability to keep a secret, and word of Moody's extraordinary good fortune spread rapidly throughout the profession. Among those who were made aware of this new field for theatrical endeavor was a family long associated with the English stage—the Hallams. Adam and Anne Hallam had five sons, four of whom—William, Lewis, George, and Thomas—became actors, while the fifth chose a naval career. Adam Hallam never became a great favorite or an outstanding performer, but as early as 1731, he had been listed in the casts of the plays presented at the annual Bartholomew Fair. When the annual Canterbury races were run two years later, it was announced that comedians from both royal playhouses (then closed for vacation) would play in that town. Listed among the performers was the "Hallam Family," composed of Mr. and Mrs. Hallam, William Hallam, "Young" (Lewis) Hallam, a "Miss Hallam" and an Adam Hallam—the latter two undoubtedly related in some way to Adam and Anne, although the exact relationship is not known. Mrs. Hallam was starred as Lady Macbeth, with Miss Hallam in the role of the Duke of York, and it was the latter who spoke an epilogue of thanks to the town. Adam Hallam had also gained a measure of fame for his ingenuity in developing the stage armor used in *Richard III*. His peculiar mannerism "of pulling down his ruffles and rolling his stockings, joined to a good deal of diligence" so intrigued the manager of Covent Garden, John Rich, that Hallam was signed for an engagement of seven years at a considerable salary. At the expiration of this contract, however, he was dismissed and ended his days an itinerant actor. When Moody returned from Jamaica, Adam Hallam had just finished a creditable job of translating *The Beggar's Opera* into French.

The long engagement of Adam Hallam at Covent Garden may partly be attributed to the kinship of Anne, his second wife, with John Rich. Anne was an actress of "uncommon merit" and, despite her ample girth, was considered a beautiful woman. Because of her popularity with London audiences, she often appeared in roles that were not consistent with her figure. Her corpulence was so noteworthy that it was later said, "By her death, the boards of old Drury were relieved from a load of fourteen stone weight."

Thomas Hallam, who seems to have been the eldest of the sons, was the victim of one of the most bizarre and sensational accidents of the day. Charles Macklin, whose "skill in acting is acknowledged to be superior to that of any man," quarreled with Hallam over the possession of a theatrical wig. In a fit of passion, Macklin seized a cane from the hands of an onlooker and thrust it into the eye of Hallam, who died the following day. In the ensuing trial, although it was testified that Hallam "had no friends" and Macklin was "a Man of quiet and peaceable Disposition," the jury found him guilty of manslaughter. Macklin undoubtedly pleaded benefit of clergy, which carried no punishment other than branding on the brawn of the thumb, for he was, within a short time, playing his parts on the London stage with his usual aplomb.[2]

The next oldest brother, William Hallam, had begun his career in Covent Garden's Theatre Royal, but it appears that his primary source of income was his wife, who was termed "a top Actress at Covent Garden." After her death, William took to the fairs, where the "Diversions perform'd at his Booth facing the Hospital Gate met with the Success they merited from crowded applauding Audiences." An April 20, 1739, he announced the opening of a bowling green and the New Wells Theatre at "the bottom of Lemon-Street" in Goodman's Fields, but it was not until August, 1740, that this place of entertainment was formally opened. To avoid the consequences of violating the Licensing Act of 1737, which permitted the performance of legitimate drama only at the two patent houses of Covent

Garden and Drury Lane, Hallam's operations were in the nature of a replacement of a similar institution in Goodman's Fields, a "Theatre Tavern," that had been operated by one Philip Huddy for a number of years before 1738. Originally, Hallam's establishment was designated a "Wells," or "drinking Theatre," supposedly devoted to such legal amusements as "rope dancing, tumbling, singing and Pantomime entertainments" and patronized by an "abundance of genteel People." In reality, the New Wells in Goodman's Fields differed "little from a Playhouse," and "the Scenes and Machinery . . . [were] very good." However, it was not until November 26, 1744, that he produced his first full-length play, *The Recruiting Officer*.

William Hallam had gained some acting experience playing minor parts at Covent Garden in the 1730's, yet he never performed in his own theater. Among the plays he produced at the New Wells were *The Beggar's Opera, Love for Love, Hamlet, Jane Shore,* and *The Tempest*. Threatened with legal sanction because of the licensing law, he resorted to the usual evasion of inserting a play between the parts of a concert, with the play supposedly thrown in free. Increased pressure by the authorities led to the presentation of pantomimes and harlequinades only, but he returned to the production of plays when official surveillance lessened. Early in 1747, however, judicial proceedings were initiated against Hallam for illegally operating a theater, and he began to employ devious and ingenious subterfuges to circumvent the law. During the early months of 1751, patrons of the New Wells were admitted "for wine"—but Hallam sold the wine and the price was high. This practice was enjoined as a public nuisance, and in February, his case was brought before the lord chancellor, but Hallam still managed to keep his pseudo-playhouse operating until December 18, 1751, when it was closed for good.

Among the actors performing in the New Wells in Goodman's Fields had been William's brother and sister-in-law, the Lewis Hallams. Lewis Hallam had contented himself with playing supporting parts, while his more talented wife was acting the feminine leads in such plays as *Othello* and *Henry IV*. One of her last roles before the move to the New World was that of Portia in *The Merchant of Venice*.[3]

The news of Moody's success in the West Indies must have seemed a godsend to the indigent William Hallam, for he decided to tap this overseas source of possible solvency. Gathering a group of his former actors in his home, and perhaps joined by some of the unemployed players who haunted the inns in the vicinity of Covent Garden, Hallam led them in drawing up plans for the venture. As "backer," William Hallam was able to supply playscripts, scenery, and costumes from his now defunct theater. A theatrical company was organized that was to be operated on a sharing basis, with the number of shares limited to eighteen. The original number of adult performers was twelve, some of whom were entitled to a full share, while those married couples of lesser talents seem to have been expected to divide a share. Lewis Hallam was allowed an additional share as manager, with still another share assigned for the services of his three children: a fifteen-year-old girl whose name may have been Helen; and two sons, twelve-year old Lewis Hallam, Jr., and Adam, who had reached the age of ten. Four shares were to provide operating expenses and from them the profits, if any, were to be drawn. This sharing system was to become the principal method of reimbursing actors in colonial America, the same method by which members of small provincial touring companies of England received their pay. Division of the profits was to be made at the end of every performance after expenses had been deducted from the gross receipts. Lewis Hallam was to act as field manager of the company, while William was to remain in London as "viceroy over him."

It was early decided just what "cast" or roles each of the actors could claim as his own under the existing traditions of the theater. Although Mrs. Hallam was to play the feminine leads, her husband apparently realized his own shortcomings and assigned the male leads to William Rigby, perhaps the best actor in the entire troupe. Lewis Hallam reserved for himself the parts of principal comedian and serious old men. Next in importance was Patrick Malone, possibly a long-time friend of the family, for a person by that name was playing minor parts with the strolling players as early as 1732. He was to play many of the top supporting characters, both serious and comic, among them the roles of Shylock and Lear. Mrs. William Adcock was recognized as the second lady of the company, playing heavy tragedy, second comedy parts, and the more attractive old woman parts. Her husband, primarily a vocalist, was not only to furnish incidental songs but was also cast in singing roles. John Singleton was a light comedian and, possessing some literary talent, was to prove useful in the composition of original prologues and epilogues. The remaining members, Mr. and Mrs. Thomas Clarkson, Miss Palmer, Mrs. Rigby, Mr. Wynell, and Mr. Herbert "were of the class called useful." The Hallams left behind their eldest daughter, Isabella, who within five years was appearing on the stage at Covent Garden and later became famous as Mrs. Mattocks, for many years "the chief support of Covent Garden." [4]

As manager of the company, Lewis Hallam's duties were many and varied and, of necessity, were extended to include the entire range of dramatic operations: producer, director, stage manager, actor, accountant, public relations expert and, one would suspect, stagehand. Not only did he assign the parts in casting a new play but also found it necessary to mark the cues in the prompt books. Backstage employees had to be instructed in their duties and doorkeepers supervised. It was the manager's responsibility to acquire a wardrobe and to see that it received the necessary, though occasional, laundering. Itineraries and repertoires were subject to his constant revision. And the tact of a diplomat was required in his dealings with local authorities.

The repertoire of the company consisted of a careful selection of the most popular plays, including Shakespeare's, then appearing on the London stage. The company wardrobe was good by eighteenth-century standards, but the costumes were, for the most part, contemporary fashions. The scenery was better than average, although within nine years all the properties of the troupe were to be assessed at no more than the equivalent of $1,000. There was also the problem of theater buildings in the American colonies, but Lewis Hallam, through his own experience and his father's association with John Rich, should have been well versed in the construction and operation of a playhouse. Rich had gained a measure of fame for his mechanical developments at Covent Garden.

With considerable foresight, the Hallams, in October, sent Robert Upton to the colonies to solicit the necessary permissions to perform, erect suitable buildings, and to settle such petty details as might arise. To this first advance agent in American theatrical history, William Hallam "advanc'd no inconsiderable Sum," but Upton had cherished dramatic ambitions beyond his talents and joined "that Sett of Pretenders," the Murray-Kean Company. After his departure, his employers heard nothing from him and could only wait. Finally, in April, 1752, at the urging of "several Gentlemen in London" and ship captains from Virginia, they made preparations to embark. In early May, they sailed in the sloop of Captain William Lee, the *Charming Sally*.

The *Charming Sally* sailed to Virginia by way of Barbados, and, on calm days, the quarterdeck was taken over by actors rehearsing plays, to the delight of the off-duty sailors. Their acting was of the bombastic style with declamatory speeches, typified by James Quin, rather than the more modern and realistic natural acting introduced by David Garrick in 1741.[5]

On June 2, the *Charming Sally* dropped anchor at Yorktown, Virginia, and the players traveled overland to Williamsburg. Upon reaching the capital of the colony, Lewis Hallam very likely rented a house and lodged his troupe all under one roof, as he later did in New York. Hallam was a name not unknown in Virginia, for there had been people calling themselves that in the colony since 1636. There was a certain familiarity in the advertisement that appeared in the *Virginia Gazette* on June 12, 1752:

THIS IS TO INFORM THE PUBLIC

That Mr. Hallam, from the New Theatre in Goodmansfields, is daily expected here with a select Company of Comedians, the Scenes, Cloaths and Decorations are all entirely new, extremely rich, and finished in the highest Taste, the Scenes being painted by the best

Hands in London are excell'd by none in Beauty and
Elegance, so that the Ladies and Gentlemen may
depend on being entertain'd in as polite a Manner as at
the Theatres in London, the Company being perfected
in all the best Plays, Opera's, Farces, and Pantomimes,
that have been exhibited in any of the Theatres for
these ten years past.

Despite the phrase, "is daily expected," the company had
earlier arrived in town, and Hallam had submitted his application to Governor Robert Dinwiddie for permission to play in
Williamsburg. Actors, at the moment, were not popular, for the
Murray-Kean Company had not only been charged with "loose
behaviour" but with "the disturbance they had like to have
occasioned in private families." Hallam's arrival was unfortu-
nately timed, for resentment against the Murray-Kean group
was still smoldering, and no later than April, during the last
meeting of the General Assembly, there had been agitation for
an act "suppressing ordinaries and players." The Governor's
Council had gone so far as to initiate a bill "to prevent unlawful
playing of Interludes" within two miles of Williamsburg, but
this legislation had been rejected by the House of Burgesses.
On June 13, the day following Hallam's first announcement
in the *Gazette*, Governor Dinwiddie referred the manager's request for permission to perform to the consideration of the
Council. Still smarting from the defeat of their bill by the burgesses, the opinion of this body was that the governor "would
not permit or suffer them to act or exhibit any plays or theatrical
Entertainments in this Government." Dinwiddie, thereupon, refused his permission, an action which could have meant financial
disaster to the comedians, but Lewis Hallam was not easily dis-
couraged and boldly continued to run his notice in the two
succeeding issues of the newspaper.
This rejection of Hallam's petition by the governor very
nearly proved "the utter ruin of a set of idle wretches," and the
manager complained bitterly of the injustice of the action to
anyone who would lend an ear. George Gilmer learned that the
adventure thus far had cost the players at least £1,000. Perse-

verance was rewarded when, at last, "the voice of the Country, and proper application" broke down the resistance of Dinwiddie, who issued the necessary dispensation. In this period of anxiety, at least one of the players resorted to his own ingenuity to supplement his income. John Singleton advertised that he would give violin lessons to persons in Williamsburg, Yorktown, Hampton, and Norfolk.[6]

A playhouse was still necessary. Hallam thereupon purchased, for a consideration of £150. 10s. the theater building from Alexander Finnie, who had but recently announced his intention of selling his Raleigh Tavern and taking passage for England. The building, as constructed for Murray-Kean, was little more than an empty barn-like structure, and Hallam was forced to enlarge it, finish the interior walls, and otherwise alter "the Play-House ... to a regular Theatre, fit for the Reception of Ladies and Gentlemen, and the Execution of their own Performance."

The modifications considered necessary by Hallam to render Williamsburg's second playhouse into "a regular Theatre" are only problematical, but it would seem natural that he followed the basic precepts of eighteenth-century theater construction. Today, even the location is uncertain other than it was "behind the Capitol," but it was built so near the edge of town and so close to the forest that years later, Lewis Hallam, Jr., claimed that the actors were able to shoot game from the doors and windows of the playhouse.

It was a small building and, as in all eighteenth-century theaters, restricted in size by the limitations of sight and sound. From the scant figures available today, it would seem that the average outside dimensions of the typical theater in the American colonies measured eighty-one by thirty-seven feet. Within the dimly lighted structures, proximity to the stage was a necessity, and, even then, the "untoward Construction of the whole house" distorted both the speaking and singing voices of the comedians. Near the end of the eighteenth century, George Saunders was to admit, "In forming our first theatres, we certainly knew but little of favouring the voice, or if we did, we paid no attention to it, and were as careless with respect to vision."

A combination of dim flickering lights and bright paints, plus the fact that attention was focused on the action, successfully camouflaged the crude scenery and props on the gently sloping stage about five feet high that extended apron-like into the pit. Across its leading edge was a row of iron spikes, ostensibly to separate audience and actors. The claim has been made that above the stage of all colonial theaters was the Latin motto, *Totus Mundus agit Histrionem*, copied from the original at Drury Lane and translated by contemporaries as "The whole world acts the player."

In general, the auditoriums of the earlier colonial theaters followed no pattern other than the fancies of the builder—the basic principle usually applied was to crowd as many people as possible into the available space. Narrow benches were provided for those who had purchased pit tickets, and to create the illusion of comfort, they were sometimes covered with rush matting or green baize. The ease of the audience was seldom a consideration, and as late as 1790, in London's Covent Garden theater, each customer was allowed a maximum of twenty-one inches for "seat and void." Large square columns supporting the roof frequently obstructed the view of the stage.

In the more permanent structures, boxes usually lined the auditorium in a U-shape along both sides and across the rear. In the earlier theaters, there seems to have been only a lower level of boxes, while those built in the later years of the colonial era added an upper tier. In both instances, sharpened metal spikes were used to separate the boxes from the pit or, in the case of an upper row, the gallery, a very tangible class division.

Customarily, the gallery ran only across the back of the building, but in the larger houses, unless upper boxes had been installed, all three sides of the auditorium wall were utilized. These held the cheaper seats, and it was usually in this "upper-tier of pop-gun wit" that trouble materialized. In England, the footmen and the lackeys considered the gallery their special domain while, in the colonies, it became the province of the less genteel element of mechanics, artisans, laborers, and, eventually, a market place where women of easy virtue solicited their customers.

Lighting arrangements were no more elaborate than the rest of the furnishings. Above the stage several pendant chandeliers known as "hoops," containing a varying number of candles, furnished primary illumination. Sconces along the walls of the auditorium, left burning through the performance, lighted the audience area. Both tallow and spermaceti candles were used, with the cleaner and more expensive spermaceti candles in the hoops above the stage, a precaution against tallow-spotted costumes. Those of tallow, "a malodorous idea and a dripping fact," served the customers.[7]

Although somewhat vague, enough evidence survives in playbills and advertisements to suggest that Lewis Hallam followed many contemporary conventions of theater construction. On August 21, the remodeling was so nearly complete that he announced that the theater would be opened the first Friday in September, with a presentation of *The Merchant of Venice* and the farce *The Anatomist, or Sham Doctor*. Expecting a large crowd, and adhering to English practice, Hallam warned the ladies to bespeak their places early and, on the day of the performance, to dispatch their servants early in the afternoon to the playhouse to hold their seats "to prevent Trouble and Disappointment."

Some historians of the American theater have surmised that this first performance in Williamsburg was on September 5, rather than the true date of September 15, apparently assuming the *Virginia Gazette* guilty of a typographical error when the issue of August 28, 1752, stated that *The Merchant of Venice* would be acted "on Friday next, being the 15th of September." The explanation is much simpler: 1752 was the year in which England and her colonies adopted the Gregorian Calendar, and the days between September 2 and 14 were omitted.

Lewis Hallam chose well in selecting a play for his first production in America. *The Merchant of Venice* was not calculated to offend the most delicate of sensibilities, and Shakespeare was already a favorite in the colonies. The play, as presented, was Lord Lansdown's version, *The Jew of Venice*; nevertheless, the playbill carefully noted that it had been "Written by Shakespear." John Singleton, "a man of pleasing and gentlemanly manners" and a poet of no mean ability, composed the special prologue delivered by Mr. Rigby, "a general player of no ordinary merit." The lines of this rhythmic opening address suggested that the actors were missionaries of civilization and destined to bring culture to this outpost of the Empire:

> The Muse still labor'd to encrease her Fame:
> Summ'd her Agents quickly to appear,
> *Haste to* Virginia's *Plains, My Sons, repair,*
> The Goddess said *Go, confident to find*
> *An audience sensible, polite and kind.*
> We heard and strait obey'd; from Britain's shore
> These unknown climes advent'ring to explore:
> For us then, and our Muse, thus low I bend,
> Nor fear to find in each the warmest Friend;
> Each smiling aspect dissipates our Fear,
> We ne'er can fail to find Protection here;
> The Stage is ever Wisdom's fav'rite Care;
> Accept our Labours then, approve our Pains,
> Your smiles will please us as equal to our Gains;
> And as you all esteem the Darling Muse,
> The gen'rus Plaudit you will not refuse.

At the conclusion of the prologue, Rigby retired backstage, and the curtain rose on the first performance of a theatrical troupe destined to become one of the most significant in the annals of the American stage. The title role of Antonio was played by Mr. Clarkson, with Singleton as Gratiano, and Rigby as Bassanio. Patrick Malone, playing Shylock and, disregarding the latest interpretations of the role which made the Jew a sympathetic character, "made the part that Shakespeare drew a mere farce part." Hallam resigned himself to the part of Lancelot, while the beautiful and talented Mrs. Hallam was the only woman in the troupe capable of playing Portia. Hallam employed every trick in the profession, including the "Clap-trap," to gain the approval of the audience. Knowing the tendency of spectators to spontaneously applaud children upon the stage, regardless of their acting ability, he cast Helen in the part of Jessica and young Lewis, Jr., as a servant to Portia. Neither had ever before faced an audience, and despite the presence of his mother upon the stage and with only one line to speak, young Hallam found himself immersed in such acute stage fright that he burst into tears and fled the stage.

The "numerous and polite Audience" who witnessed *The Merchant of Venice* received the efforts of the comedians "with great applause." Little did they realize the significance of the play they received so favorably, for this production marked the inauguration of a more dignified drama in America and the beginning of the continuous history of the American theater.

As William Adcock, who played Lorenzo, sang his "Songs in Character," he was probably accompanied at the harpsichord by a man in a grey coat who peered at the music through his "Temple Spectacles" in the dim light, a man by the name of Cuthbert Ogle, the leading musician in Williamsburg at this time. It may also be assumed that he was joined by John Singleton and his violin when that talented individual's presence was not required on the stage.

The company was an instant success. Three nights a week they played to large crowds, and during those periods when the General Court was in session, receipts were sometimes as large as £300 per performance; yet "Notwithstanding they take so much money never were debts worse paid...." Forgetting his own dramatic efforts sixteen years earlier, apothecary George Gilmer continued to grumble, "The money kept burning till they opened and then it flew among this Association of indigent wretches with a lavishness you would be surprised at." [8]

An absence of playbills or advertisements in the local press of subsequent productions occasions a gap in the records of the plays presented. It is only reasonable to suppose that they played the same repertoire that they had acted at the New Wells and that they were to present in New York the following summer. If so, the season saw the acting of such favorites as *The Constant Couple, Love for Love, The London Merchant, or The History of George Barnwell, The Distrest Mother, Richard III, The Careless Husband, The Beaux' Stratagem, The Fair Penitent, The Twin Rivals, The Drummer, King Lear, Woman Is a Riddle, The Conscious Lovers, Jane Shore, The Gamester, The Earl of Essex, The Suspicious Husband, The Albion Queens,*

The Beggar's Opera, Romeo and Juliet, Henry IV, Othello, as well as a large selection of the more popular farces, or afterpieces, of the day.

Six or seven weeks after the opening of the theater, the Hallam Company was involved in one of the more spectacular social events of the season. Soon after November 1, the "Emperor" of the Cherokee Nation, accompanied by "his Empress and their Son the Young Prince attended by several of his Warriors and great Men and their Ladies," came "through many Briers, Thickets, and great Waters" to Williamsburg "to renew the Treaty of Friendship with this Government." Governor Dinwiddie, with rare diplomacy, treated the savages as visiting royalty. On Thursday, November 9, 1752, they were taken to the theater to see *Othello.* The pantomime afterpiece, possibly a variation on the Harlequin theme, "gave them great Surprize," although they must have been delighted with the gamboling of the mischievous Harlequin. When, however, during the course of the play, the actors fought with naked swords, the "Empress" turned to several of her warriors and bade them halt the action on the stage to prevent "their killing one another." The festivities of the following evening were not so violent but more spectacular. The entire town was illuminated with candles in every window, and there was a ball plus "a very elegant Entertainment at the Palace." Although there was no activity in the playhouse, Lewis Hallam was involved in the night's entertainment. He exhibited "several Beautiful Fireworks" in Palace Street before an assemblage that included not only the visitors but "a brilliant Appearance of Ladies and Gentlemen." [9]

Shortly after December 1, the theater was the scene of violence not set forth in any script. About eleven o'clock on the night of December 7, a white man accompanied by two Negroes forced his way into the darkened building, only to be discovered by Patrick Malone. Overpowering the actor, they "violently assaulted" him, flinging him upon the iron spikes that separated the pit from the stage. One spike penetrated his leg so deeply that he hung suspended until his cries were heard by some passing Negroes. A reward was offered for the capture of "The Villains that perpetrated this horrid Fact," but there is nothing to suggest that they were ever apprehended.

As the season wore on, the players began to outfit themselves for their travels through the colonies. Alexander Craig made saddles and harness for several, sometimes accepting play tickets as partial payment for his labors. Notwithstanding the large receipts reportedly taken in by the company, several of its members were suffering financial distress. After doing some work for Singleton, Craig noted in his account book, "I took his Bond of £3. 5. 1/2 & give it to Lewis Hallam to get the money at New York & remitt to me."

Two of the actors, Wynell and Herbert, had already left Hallam to join the Murray-Kean Company in Annapolis. Although they played lead roles with their new associates, a study of the parts in which they had been cast in the Hallam Company implies that their departure occasioned no great loss.

The season in Williamsburg lasted for eleven months. During this interval, Lewis Hallam had, upon the advice of "several Gentlemen," decided to go to New York, where, he was told "That we should not fail of a genteel and favourable Reception: that the Inhabitants were very generous and polite, naturally fond of Diversions rational, particularly those of the theatre: Nay, they even told us of a very fine Play-House Building, and that we were really expected. This was Encouragement sufficient for us. . . ."

Despite what had appeared to be a successful season in Virginia, the actors were heavily in debt to the merchants of both Norfolk and Williamsburg. Already, William Rigby had fled to escape his creditors. In the York County Court, judgments were handed down against Rigby, Charles Bell, John Singleton, and William Adcock. Rather than allow the dissolution of his company with his players languishing in debtors' prison, Hallam persuaded Edward Charlton, peruke-maker, and John Stretch, bookkeeper and deputy postmaster (to both of whom the actors owed money) to stand security for his distressed players. In all, the total debt and bail amounted to £59. 5s. 4½d. For the nominal fee of five shillings, Hallam deeded the Williamsburg theater to Stretch and Charlton, with a clause that, if Bell, Singleton,

Rigby, and Adcock paid their debts and redeemed their bail by October 10, 1753, the "present Indenture will cease, determine and become void." [10]

None of the actors named ever paid, and Lewis Hallam lost possession of the playhouse. It was just as well. Hallam himself would never again have use for a theater in Williamsburg.

· V ·

THE TOUR OF THE
HALLAM COMPANY

(*New York, Philadelphia, Charleston,
and Jamaica, 1753-1754*)

When Lewis Hallam left Williamsburg, he was experienced and wise enough in the ways of the theater to have secured a "character," or certificate of good behavior, from Governor Dinwiddie to display when applying for permission to play in the next town. This precaution availed him little in the apprehensions that semed to saturate New York in the summer of 1753. In that city, the players ran afoul of those prejudices kindled during the runs of the Murray-Kean and Upton Companies. A description, although not contemporary, implies that the conduct of the earlier companies could hardly be used as a character reference for those who followed. The New York *National Advocate*, in 1821, summarized the off-stage activities of a group that could only have been either the Murray-Kean or the Upton Company as a set of "roystering young men, full of tricks and mischief; who used to gambol in the fields where St.

Paul's church now stands, and who spent their nights in the boat house, and amused themselves with snap dragons and hot cockles, during the winter evenings."

A number of the more influential citizens, led by William Livingston, feeling that the theater should be considered among those luxuries injurious to morals, lodged a strong protest against granting these new comedians permission to play. The governor, reacting to this pressure, withheld his approbation, and Hallam once again pleaded his case before the people. On July 2, 1753, the New York *Mercury* reported "The CASE of the London Company of COMEDIANS, lately arrived from Virginia, humbly submitted to the Consideration of the Publick, whose Servants they are, and whose Protection they intreat." Within this supplication, Hallam listed all the trials and tribulations encountered by his troupe since their formation. The manager also disclaimed any relationship with the Murray-Kean Company, whom he contemptuously dismissed as "that Sett of Pretenders," before defending his own position: "If the worthy Magistrates would consider this in our Favour, that it must rather turn out a publick Advantage and Pleasure, than a private Injury; They would, we make no Doubt, grant Permission, and give us an Opportunity to convince them, that we were not cast in the same Mould with our Theatrical Predecessors; or that in private Life or publick Occupation, we have the least Affinity to them."

This appeal aroused the partisans of the drama, and their voices, joined to the "entreaties of the young beauties so urgent," wore down the opposition. The permission was eventually granted; it did not, however, meet with universal approval. Matthew Clarkson penned a sour lament: "We are to have the diversions of the Stage the Season. There are Severale actors from some part of Europe, who after much Solissitation have at last obtain'd leave of his Excellency to perform. They talk of Building a house for that purpose, and have offered themselves to Subscribe £100 for the Encouragement of it. This is a Melancholy Story among considerate persons that so small a place as this is should Encourage the toleration of such publick diversions. People are dayly murmuring at the badness of the times as tho' they were actually concern'd for their Interest, but their conduct proves a contradiction to it. For men in every profession are ever some of some party of pleasure or other, and as if they had not room enough to spend their money that way, they must for all put themselves under greater temptations in going to the play house. This I speak with regard to those who are scarcely above want; these sort of people are the most fond of it which makes the Toleration of Publick Diversion be greater Nusance to a Place Especially as it contains so few Inhabitants."

The inadequacies of the old theater on Nassau Street increased the popularity of the subscription scheme. Razing this building and utilizing the same site, Hallam "built a very, large and commodious New Theatre." It was announced that because the company intended "to tarry here but a short while, we hear they design to perform three times a week."

While the theater was under construction, another attraction arrived in town which may have diverted some money from the playhouse. In "a new House built for that Purpose," Anthony Joseph Dugee, who claimed Oriental affiliations, entertained his audiences with performances on the slack wire, and he was later joined by his muscular wife, billed as "The Female Sampson." [1]

In the face of this agile and brawny competition, Hallam opened his "New Theatre in Nassau-Street" on September 17 with the comedy *The Conscious Lovers*, coupled with the ballad opera *Damon and Phillida*. As in Williamsburg, he chose his opening play with care. Because of the favorable reputation of Sir Richard Steele, *The Conscious Lovers* was considered, as its author asserts in the preface and the original prologue, a play "to moralize the stage." Mrs. Becceley, the singing soubrette of the Murray-Kean Company, also began to make appearances with the "Company of Comedians from London"—additional evidence that the old troupe had disbanded. Her dramatic capacities were confirmed when she was assigned the major female supporting parts. Master Lewis Hallam, Jr., was now sufficiently recovered from his initial stage fright at Williamsburg to reappear in the first of a long series of regular roles. Helen, the oldest of the Hallam children, was cast in a minor part, while her father, Lewis, Sr., buried himself as a not-too-important character in the afterpiece. Rigby and Mrs. Hallam were the starring performers on this New York opening night; Rigby greeted the audience with a new occasional prologue, and Mrs. Hallam bade them farewell with an epilogue "address'd to the Ladies."

Sitting in the boxes was young Philip Schuyler who had sailed down the Hudson for a holiday in the city. Even before his departure from home, he had determined to attend the theater if the actors were in town as rumored, "for a player is a new thing under the sun in our good province." Paying their respects to the governor shortly after their arrival in town, Schuyler and his friends then "bought our play tickets for eight shillings apiece at Parker and Weyman's printing-office, in Beamer Street, on our return. We had tea at five o'clock, and before sundown we were in the theatre, for the players commenced at six. The room was quite full already.... A large green curtain hung before the players until they were ready to begin, when, on the blast of a whistle, it was raised, and some of them appeared and commenced acting. The play was called The Conscious Lovers, written, you know, by Sir Richard Steele, Addison's help in writing the Spectator. Hallam, and his wife and sister, all performed, and a sprightly young man named Hulett played the violin and danced merrily. But I said I could not tell you about the play, so I will forbear, only adding that I was no better pleased than I should have been at the club, where, last year, I went with cousin Stephen, and heard many wise sayings which I hope profited me something."

The "sprightly young man named Hulett" did not appear in the playbill for he had but recently joined the company as a dancer. His theatrical heritage was English, and his family and the Hallams had been acquainted in England where a Charles Hulett, possibly his father, had appeared at the fairs with the elder Hallam and had later played at Goodman's Fields. In the summer of 1752, William Hulett had appeared in Annapolis, Maryland, with a Mrs. Love as a dancing partner. Their subsequent arrival in New York was noted when Mrs. Love's husband, Charles, advertised the opening of a music school, offering instruction in the violin, viola, hautboy (oboe), bassoon, French horn, and flute. Love had "run away" with Mrs. Love and had attempted to support her as a portrait painter before taking to the English stage. All three of these new arrivals may well have been sent from England by William Hallam as reinforcements for the troupe. Mrs. Love was to gain some recognition as a ballad singer, while Charles, though experienced as an actor, was engaged to play the harpsichord in the theater. After Hulett's rather obvious success on opening night, his appearances were duly noted in succeeding playbills.[2]

As the season progressed, Hallam alternated Singleton, Rigby, and Malone in the lead roles as their talent warranted, but these three could not claim leading parts as absolute personal prerogatives. Adcock, Bell, and a newcomer named Miller played an occasional lead. Mrs. Hallam apparently was given her choice of roles. The children, with the exception of Adam, appeared regularly. Adam, now twelve years old and the youngest of the trio, appeared in only those productions calling for a large cast, with his most important part as the Duke of York in *Richard III.*

Although Lewis Hallam limited himself to comparatively minor appearances on the stage, he worked hard as manager. Advertisements sometimes displayed a crude, though popular, sense of humor. When he realized how pleasing the singing and dancing were to American audiences, more diversions of that nature were included in the programs. Although Hulett began to appear in some minor roles, his dancing was nearly always the featured entertainment between the acts. He was even allowed to add a tag in newspaper advertisements announcing that he also taught "Dancing in general." The entire cast would sometimes perform "a Country Dance" between acts.

Eighteenth-century audiences manifested certain characteristics that are similar to those of later generations: late-comers not only interrupted the performance, they sometimes delayed the first-act curtain. This practice became so prevalent that a warning was inserted in the bills that the curtain would go up precisely at the advertised time, with the explanation that "it would be a great Inconvenience for them [the audience] to be kept out late, and a Means to prevent Disappointments." A particularly brilliant audience attended in late December. The Masons, celebrating the Festival of St. John at Trinity Church, requested that *The Conscious Lovers* be played that night at the theater.

When added to the regular patrons, the members of the order, dressed in full regalia, filled the house to its capacity. Hallam devised a program suitable to the occasion: "Several pieces of vocal Music, in Praise of the Fraternity, were performed, between the Acts. An Epilogue, suitable to the Occasion, was presented by Mrs. Hallam, with all the Graces of Gesture, and the Propriety of Elocution; and met with universal and loud Applause."

By February 4, the benefits had begun, and the more aristocratic segment of the audience had increased to such a point that the boxes had to be enlarged "For the better Accommodation of the Ladies." The indulgence of the patrons was such that when William Rigby announced his benefit, he was bold enough to defy custom (because of his "Pleuretic Disorder,") and suggest that his benefactors send for their tickets rather than his calling upon them to solicit attendance on his night. When the Hallam children had their benefit in early March, both Lewis, Jr., and Helen appeared in minor roles, but young Lewis displayed heretofore unrevealed talent by singing "As Chloe Came into the Room" and "The Reasonable Lover." An excuse for Adam's appearance on the stage was called "A Punch's Dance." On March 18, the New York season ended with *The Beggar's Opera*, the benefit for Mr. and Mrs. Charles Love, marking Mr. Love's only advertised performance—a solo on the "Hautboy." One week later a succinct notice gave evidence that the season had been successful: "Lewis Hallam, Comedian, intending for Philadelphia, begs the favour of those that had any demands upon him, to bring in their accounts, and receive their money." The company was now, at least, solvent enough to pay its debts.[3]

Some time before the end of the New York season, Lewis Hallam had been approached by several gentlemen from Philadelphia, who invited him to bring his London Company of Comedians to their city—if the proper permission could be obtained. Several of the group pledged themselves to forestall almost certain religious opposition, and it was suggested that the manager apply to Governor James Hamilton for the necessary dispensation. Antagonism towards actors was no longer so

Sketch Said to be of Mrs. Douglass
Courtesy of Harvard Theatre Collection

strongly evident within the executive branch of the government of Pennsylvania since the death of William Penn, whose sons and heirs did not accept the basic precepts of their religion so rigidly as did their father. And to Philadelphia, the largest city in the colonies, had come wealth with sophistication.

As envoy to the governor, Hallam selected Patrick Malone, a man of engaging personality and possessed of "a tongue that could wheedle with the devil." Malone was also no dullard; he seized this opportunity to better his future through subtle blackmail. The price demanded for a successful mission was that he was to be guaranteed the parts of Falstaff in *Henry IV* and *The Merry Wives of Windsor*, as well as that of Don Luis in *Love Makes the Man, or The Fop's Fortune.*

Malone tried, but his diplomacy was no match for the tempers of the religious groups. News that the players were coming split the city into two hostile camps. An angry "A. B." in the *Pennsylvania Gazette* deplored "the infamous Characters of the Actors and Actresses" and their "inhumanely impudent Dances and Song." The minds of the audience, he railed, were "polluted and debauched," even if there were no objections to the play itself, because "the ingenious Contrivance of the Managers entirely prevents the Good Effect of any worthy Sentiment expressed in the Play, but introducing a painted Strumpet at the End of every Act, to cut Capers in such an impudent and unwomanly Manner, as must make the most shocking Impressions on every Mind. . . ."

Hallam went to the rescue of his emissary. Already, the Quakers of the city had presented a petition to the governor demanding the prohibition of plays, followed in turn with counter-petitions signed by friends of the theater. The persuasiveness of Hallam and his friends was more effective than the anguished cries and remonstrances of the religious element. Governor Hamilton issued the necessary sanction but, as a compromise, imposed rather stringent restrictions upon the players. The London Company was permitted to stage its plays with the understanding that they "offered nothing indecent or immoral"; violations would result in immediate rescinding of the permission. A total of twenty-four plays might be presented by the company, but the receipts of one night were to be appropriated for the use of the poor. To protect those who extended credit to the actors, Hallam was required to give bond to cover the payment of all debts contracted by his players. Despite these rigid injunctions, Hallam prepared to move the company to Philadelphia, first selling the Nassau Street theater to a society of German Calvinists for the equivalent of $1,250.

Opposition quickened with the arrival of the thespians. The actors were subjected not only to verbal condemnations from the pulpit but also to the literary efforts of churchmen whose rage bordered on fanaticism. Shortly before opening night, Hallam countered by publishing in the *Pennsylvania Journal* extracts of the more vitriolic attacks that he facetiously "Recommended to the Perusal and Serious Consideration of the Professor of Christianity in the City of Philadelphia." This only succeeded in stimulating a flood of publications denouncing the evils inherent in the playhouse. Protest meetings formulated strategy to destroy this serpent. The Quakers, who now composed only about one-fourth of the population, found allies among the city's strongest denomination, the Presbyterians, who, notwithstanding their vigorous denunciation of the theater, could find no wrong in sponsoring a lottery to pay for the new steeple of their church. The Presbyterians argued that lotteries could be controlled as an instrument for the work of the Lord, but the theater was too prone to stray from the path of righteousness even when masquerading as virtuous pedagogy.[4]

Plumstead's warehouse was still the most convenient building, and after Hallam's remodeling, it was to be termed "The New Theatre in Water-Street." Improvements to the auditorium were such that seats in the pit, boxes, and gallery could be advertised. On April 15, the season opened with a socially and morally innocuous play and afterpiece, Rowe's *The Fair Penitent* and Garrick's *Miss in Her Teens*. The new prologue and epilogue recited upon this occasion were motivated by a posture of self-righteousness and self-defense on the part of the players. William Rigby's prologue played upon the old theme, "The World's a Stage, where Mankind acts their parts." Conceding the stage had "sometimes stray'd from what was pure and just," the actor reminded his listeners that also:

> Has she not oft, with awful virtuous Rage,
> Struck home at Vice—and nobly trod the Stage?
> Made Tyrants weep, the conscious Murd'rer stand
> And drop the Dagger from his trembling Hand?

Rather than risk fanning the passions of the dissidents, Mrs. Hallam, in the epilogue, attributed the responsibility for censure of the stage to an old enemy of Protestant Pennsylvania—the Catholic church—as she spoke the lines:

> Much has been said in this reforming Age,
> To damn in gross the Business of the Stage,
> Some, for this End, in Terms not quite so civil,
> Have given both Plays and Players to the Devil.
> With red-hot Zeal, in dreadful Pomp they come;
> And bring their flaming Tenets warm from Rome.

The puffings of the more devout element did not prevent the first night's performance being received "with Universal Applause" by "a numerous and polite Audience." Newspaper accounts did not, however, mention the uproar that occurred out front in the midst of the play. The action on the stage was interrupted when one of the devout petitioners was discovered sitting in the pit. Order was restored and the play allowed to continue only after this "spy" had been ejected, "head and shoulders," from the playhouse.

This abuse of one of its constituents only served to solidify the opposition. There was a continuous disputation in the press relative to the virtues and vices of the stage, as "A. B." and "Y. Z." moralized upon a basic theme of the "dreadful View of the ruinous Effects of Passion let loose," an argument that had been put forth before the arrival of the Hallam Company. So potent was this campaign that an observer of a later date was to comment, "Through the whole season the venom of these ascetics spouted broadcast over the community."

Lewis Hallam spun a delicate web of subtlety in his defense. For his benefit, on May 27, he selected George Baker's 1703 play, *Tunbridge Walks, or The Yeoman of Kent*, with all objectional lines deleted and as a farce, Colley Cibber's old favorite, *Flora*, now re-titled *The Country Wake, or Hob in the Well*. As was the custom, the three Hallam children were allowed a benefit night, and their father seized this opportunity to stress the role of the drama in the advancement of integrity and morality. Carefully, he selected Edward Moore's new tragedy, *The Gamester* and Garrick's farce, *Miss in Her Teens*, both suitable vehicles for child actors, although the inept Adam was omitted from the cast. Both the playbills distributed in the streets and newspaper advertisements concluded with a paragraph proclaiming the righteous mission of the theater as represented in *The Gamester:* "As the principal Business of the Stage is, or should be to satyrize *Vice*, and represent her in her true Colours, that Youth, and the Unexperienced, may receive Instructions, and be the better able to guard against, and avoid her enchanting Deceptions... And indeed, in this Age of the World, a Play representing the ruinous Consequence of the bewitching Practice, is perfectly seasonable, and the Author, from his Performance, merits at least the Thanks of Mankind. This Tragedy is written in Prose, after the manner of *George Barnwell*, and as it has not long been published, there may not, perhaps, be many Copies of it in this Place; but some Account of the Dramatick Characters may be seen in the *Gentleman's Magazine* for February, 1753; After this it may then suffice to say, That, considering the moral Tendency of this excellent Piece, to see it acted on the Stage, is not, nor cannot be unworthy of any Rank of People; for it must be allowed by all that know the World, that this Custom is so prevalent now-a-days, that Men have less to fear, even from constitutional Passions, than from this many headed Monster, GAMING." [5]

Two weeks later, the "last Night of performing," was Mr. Adcock's benefit, and *Tamerlane* and *A Wife Well Managed* were presented "By Desire." This note of finality, however, did not signify the end of the season. There was still the commitment of the charity performance. Fulfillment of the obligation was realized on June 17 with the presentation of *The Careless Husband* and *Harlequin Collector* for the benefit of the Charity School of Philadelphia. Upon this occasion, the pit and the boxes were laid together, and a special plea requested the members of the audience to refrain from venturing backstage during the progress of the play, "it being impossible to perform the Entertainment, if there is the least Obstruction behind." The "Obstructions" apparently remained in their seats where they belonged, for it was reported that the benefit was "acted before a very crowded and polite Audience" for the purpose of "pleasing soft-eyed CHARITY." Not only did this performance swell the coffers of the school, but it likewise resulted in the players acquiring an ecclesiastical champion in the person of the Reverend William Smith, who, in addition to his sanctioning the benefit for the academy, lent the theater an air of respectability by his presence.

Hallam policed the behavior of his players well, and this, coupled with their willingness to perform for charitable purposes, was a factor leading to the granting of permission for an additional six performances. The season finally ended on Thursday, June 27, with *The Provok'd Husband* and *Miss in Her Teens.* In her farewell epilogue, Mrs. Hallam reiterated the ageless theme of the stage in the lines:

> That here the World in Miniature you see,
> And all Mankind are Play'rs as well as we.

One event occurred in Philadelphia that was by far the most significant of the season of 1754—a visit from William Hallam. After the "Company of Comedians from London" had more or less successfully established themselves in Virginia, William had reopened, in November, 1752, the "New Wells" in Goodman's Fields. All five plays that he produced, and in which he acted, were for the benefit of himself. This experiment obviously had not been profitable for, while in Philadelphia, he consented to Lewis Hallam's purchase of his shares in the troupe. After William's return to London, the only record of the remaining years of his life was a benefit given for him at Sadler Wells in 1756 because "of being turned out of his house."

Lewis Hallam was perhaps more fortunate than he realized in that the number of performances in Philadelphia had been limited. Soon after his departure, the Reverend George Whitfield arrived in the city to preach "to large and crouded Auditories." Had the pattern of the past repeated itself, the theater would have fallen on hard times.[6]

Earlier historians of the American stage have assumed that Hallam sailed from Philadelphia directly to Jamaica in 1754. However, they sailed more south than southeast, and on October 3, the "Company of Comedians from London" announced a performance of *The Fair Penitent* at Charleston, South Carolina. The interval since leaving Pennsylvania and this performance afforded ample time for the voyage and the construction of the "New Theatre" in which they performed. Charleston, at the time, was struggling to rebuild the damage of the great hurricane of September 15, 1752, when over five hundred buildings had been leveled, one of which was probably the old Queen Street Theatre.

From the first production, received "much to the satisfaction of the Audience," to the final performance of the season, the pattern established by the Hallam Company in other localities prevailed, but in no instance were the actors identified in the local advertising. *The Fair Penitent* was followed by *A Bold Stroke for a Wife, The Orphan, Cato, The Recruiting Officer,* and possibly the remainder of their repertoire, but these were not advertised in the local *South Carolina Gazette.* Perhaps, the unusually large crowds in Charleston for the meeting of the General Assembly made extensive advertising unnecessary. As usual, there was a special request performance for the Masons, replete with the customary special Masonic songs, prologue, and epilogue, which was played to a full house on December 27, 1754.[7]

Shortly after this, George Whitefield arrived in Charleston, and Hallam discreetly sailed with his company for Jamaica with a view to taking advantage of the bonanza there as reported by John Moody. There, he discovered the heirs to the Moody organization still playing in the islands under the management of David Douglass. At the time, Douglass was preparing to embark for England to recruit actors for his company whose ranks had been thinned by disease and inertia. Hallam's appearance removed the necessity for the long voyage. The two troupes combined.

The climate of Jamaica, where "death stalks forth in almost every breeze," proved fatal to Lewis Hallam. Weak and ailing from his exertions on the continent, he fell victim to yellow fever on one of the periodic sweeps of that disease through the islands. Despite this loss, the company refused to disband. After a respectable period of mourning, Mrs. Hallam married David Douglass, and her new husband assumed sole responsibility for the management of the company. There was nothing to restrain their operations. The fun-loving Governor Sir Henry Moore had appointed Teresa Constantia Phillips, noted courtesan and woman of lenient virtue, to the post of Mistress of Revels. Her duties included the supervision of entertainment, and it is to be suspected that she held a loose rein on the activities of David Douglass and his actors.

Not only did the troupe perform in the British West Indies, but it also acted before audiences in those islands under the control of Denmark.[8] It was late in the summer of 1758 before they decided to return to the mainland colonies.

· VI ·

THE DOUGLASS COMPANY'S
FIRST AMERICAN TOUR

(New York, Philadelphia, Annapolis, Upper Marlborough, and Williamsburg, 1758-1761)

T he theatrical troupe that David Douglass brought to the American colonies in 1758 still clung to the attractive name "a Company of Comedians from London"—suggesting that the best in dramatic entertainment was to be expected.

Drastic changes had occurred in the personnel of the company. Only Mrs. Douglass, her two sons, Lewis and Adam Hallam, and Mrs. Charles Love remained as links with the group that had sailed for the West Indies some three and a half years earlier. Little is known as to the fate of the other members of the old Hallam Company. It is fairly certain that John Singleton remained in the islands; in 1767, in Barbados, he was to publish a long poem in blank verse, *A General Description of the West Indian Islands,* which was well enough received to insure its republication in London in 1777. It seems quite possible that the remaining members of both the Hallam and Douglass companies elected to remain in Jamaica to form a company of their own, but the records are few in that area.

David Douglass, the new manager, was "by descent and education, a gentleman." Originally trained as a printer, he had practiced that trade until he was seduced by the stage and joined Moody's company in Jamaica. Mediocre in talent, his actions upon the stage have been described as "rather a decent than shining actor, a man of sense and discretion." As a manager, he drove himself almost as if he feared a turn of fortune would pull him back into that respectable, but drab, existence among type, rollers, and printer's ink.

Mrs. Douglass, still a woman of exceptional beauty and poise, maintained her right to continue playing those youthful roles that she had claimed as her prerogative under her former husband's management. Although she had reached an age when her physical proportions were those attributed to matrons, her experience and dramatic ability enabled her to act "stately or querulous as occasions required."

Three adolescents, two of whom were destined to become favorites of the colonial stage, appeared as members of the Company of Comedians. One of these was Mrs. Douglass' niece, one Nancy Hallam, perhaps the daughter of the indigent William Hallam, who may have died by this date.

The other was Lewis Hallam, Jr., now a youth of nineteen, whose ability as an actor had grown far more than had been promised when he fled in terror from the Williamsburg stage as a lad of twelve. He had matured during the sojourn in Jamaica, and it has been said that he had been tutored in the intricacies of his profession by William Rigby of the old company. Some of his time had been spent studying the dialects and manners of the Jamaican Negroes, lessons that he was able to put to good use in later years. A thin body of only medium height was made more impressive by an erect posture. A slight cast in one eye, the result of a fencing accident, gave an almost imperceptbile, yet odd expression to a face dominated by a sensuous mouth and a sharp nose. Light on his feet, young Hallam was adept in both fencing and dancing, two requisites of his profession. Never exposed to the more realistic and natural acting introduced by David Garrick in 1741, he had been trained by players of the old school of dramatic rant, and there was the trace of the podium in his declamations. On stage, his actions were "stiff and prim," while his delivery irked some spectators who complained he was always "either mouthing or ranting." He was at his best while reciting prologues and epilogues, which he did with such finesse as "constituted the grace before and thanks after the dramatic banquet." Even with his admittedly rapid development, Lewis Hallam's ability was not, at this stage of his career, great enough to allow him to play the majority of the male leads in the repertoire. Yet he did, possibly because he and his mother owned most of the stock in the company.

The troupe included two other persons who bore the name of Hallam. One was the young Sarah Hallam whom Lewis had married in the islands, and who had neither talent nor inclination for the stage. The other was the younger brother, Adam, who had improved little in his dramatic capacities since last he was in the mainland colonies; even had he owned the company outright, the public would not have tolerated his appearance in important roles. The eldest of the three children the Hallams had brought with them to America, Helen, no longer traveled with the actors.

From Douglass' old troupe in the islands came three of the more durable members of the new company. Owen Morris and his wife had been among the original members of the Moody Company. He was especially good in "the tremulous drawle of old men, in low jest and buffoonery," although in later years his efforts were to be characterized as "despicable." His wife, apparently some years younger than her husband, was a beautiful and accomplished actress and was to be cast in many important supporting roles. Catherine Maria Harman, at this time second in importance to Mrs. Douglass among the actresses, "bore away the palm as duenna" and was possessed of a rich, though tragic, theatrical heritage. Her mother had been Charlotte Cibber, daughter of the poet laureate and wife of one Richard Charke who was a violinist and "knave with a sweet voice." They had traveled to Jamaica with a group of musicians who had been brought out to indulge Governor Sir Henry

Moore's passion for music. Abandoned by her husband, Charlotte was to die in 1759. The child of this unhappy union, Catherine Maria, had become the wife of one Harman, a mediocre actor at best, and the two of them had eventually become members of the Douglass Company.[1] Actors and actresses of lesser importance were Mr. and Mrs. Tomlinson, Mr. Horne, and Mr. Reed.

Near the middle of October, 1758, the company had disembarked at New York. They had arrived armed with impressive "characters," or certificates of qualification and good behavior, signed by such notables as Governor Hamilton of Pennsylvania and Baron Von Brock, Governor of the Danish West Indies. As Hallam had sold the Nassau Street playhouse in 1753, Douglass almost immediately began the construction of the first of many theaters he was to erect in the American colonies. For a location, he selected a "Sail-Loft" on Cruger's Wharf, an area surrounded on three sides by water. Presumably, this building was a regular theater with boxes, pit, and gallery, but the fact that it was soon to disappear lends credence to the supposition that the theater on Cruger's Wharf was little more than a temporary expedient and again was used as a sail loft once the players had departed.

Douglass had been lulled into carelessness by the easy and tolerant operations in the islands. He should have been better versed in the ways of the theater than to undertake a dramatic performance without first securing the necessary permission of the magistrates. Times were not good in New York. In 1758, exports had sunk to their lowest point since the beginning of the French and Indian War, and there were complaints that money should be expended for the poor rather than fribbling entertainment. Douglass' ultimate application, "to his great mortification," was blocked by the "positive and absolute Denial" of ruffled authority. Pleading an embarrassment of finances, the manager petitioned, "in the humblest Manner," that his players be allowed to perform until his economic situation improved enough to permit further travel. The magistrates, however, turned a deaf ear to his elegant appeal and "peremptorily refused it." To many, this would have spelled disaster, but Douglass was a man of ingenuity. After airing his troubles in the New York *Mercury*, he announced that within a few days he would open "an HISTRIONIC ACADEMY."

Judging by his actions in later years, there is little doubt that Douglass contrived to circumvent the will of authority by producing plays under the guise of pedagogy. He had not, moreover, reckoned with the intelligence of the administration. So great was the pressure following his initial announcement that, within a few days, the manager accepted the inevitable and published a rather abject and apologetic retraction. Assuming an air of shocked virtue, Douglass disavowed all unwarranted intentions and vigorously protested any notion that he would ever "aim at an Affront on Gentlemen, on whom I am dependent for the only Means that can save us from utter Ruin." With all the wide-eyed innocence of a child he insisted that "so vain, so insolent a Project, never once entered my Head" and explained that he had only proposed to deliver "Dissertations on Subjects, *Moral, Instructive* and *Entertaining*," essentially instruction in the art of public speaking. He reiterated the desperate financial straits of his players and denied any "supposed Presumption" by "A Very Humble, and Very Devoted Servant." [2]

Atonement had its reward. The magistrates relented and granted permission, but only for a brief season. On New Year's Day, 1759, "the Theatre on Mr. Cruger's Wharff" opened with *Jane Shore,* in which "a most crowded Audience" was entertained with the "LUXURY of grief." Rather than follow the usual custom of presenting a new occasional prologue and epilogue on opening night, Douglass revived an old epilogue defending the stage against its critics. Actually this piece originally had been used by the old Hallam Company in Philadelphia in 1754; it had been revised and sent to the new manager by Adam Thompson of that city. In the epilogue, after Mrs. Douglass had stated her case,

> Much has been said at this unlucky Time,
> To prove the treading of the Stage a Crime,

she listed the many useful and moral lessons that could be taught by the theater.

Douglass lost no time in publishing the prologue in the *Mercury* in answer to his critics. This was purely a defense mechanism, for from opening night on, the actors played to crowded houses. Although curtain time was not until six o'clock, the gallery was opened by four o'clock to allow the cheaper seats to fill before the gentry arrived to take their places in the boxes and pit. Tickets were sold at various designated places in town; there was no need for a box-office, as "positively no money will be taken at the Door."

The repertoire of the Douglass company was essentially the same as it had been under Hallam. Three nights a week they acted such proven favorites as *The Recruiting Officer, Othello, The Beaux' Stratagem,* and *The Drummer.* A new tragedy was performed on Wednesday, January 24, when John Home's *Douglas* had its American premiere. This tragedy with its moralistic overtones was to prove one of the most successful plays presented by David Douglass in the colonies and was to remain a popular attraction on the American stage for the next one hundred years.

Colley Cibber's alteration of Shakespeare's *Richard III*, always popular for its accent on action and blood-letting, was announced on February 7 as "Positively the last Time of acting in this City." This abbreviated season could have accomplished little more than reduce the insolvency of the players, but they were able to take to the road until the resentment of the magistrates abated.

From February until late spring, the actors disappeared. Quite possibly, they played the smaller towns between New York and Philadelphia, and this may well have been the year they visited Perth Amboy. This port at the mouth of the Raritan had all of the requisites of a good theater town—it alternated with Burlington as the capital of New Jersey, it was the home of the governor, a garrison of soldiers was stationed there, it was predominantly Anglican, and it boasted a society of aristocratic tendencies "far superior to that of New York or Philadelphia." William Dunlap, who was born in 1766 and spent his youth in that town, remembered that he had often "heard old ladies speak, almost in raptures, of the beauty and grace of Mrs. Douglass, and the pathos of her personation of Jane Shore." [3]

Douglass had learned his lesson well in New York. Long before his planned arrival in Philadelphia, he had secretly contacted Governor William Denny of Pennsylvania, and on April 5, permission to perform had been granted on condition that the receipts of one night be donated to the hospital. At the same time, the manager contracted for a new theater, to be constructed under the supervision of two double-named local craftsmen: Alexander Alexander undertook the erection of the playhouse; while William Williams, tutor of Benjamin West, was employed to paint new scenes. Possibly relying on information furnished by his wife, Douglass very wisely located his playhouse on Society Hill, at the south-west corner of South and Vernon Streets, outside the city limits and the jurisdiction of municipal officials.

From outward appearances, antagonism towards the stage in Philadephia seems to have waned. Eighteen months earlier, the students at the college had performed *The Masque of Alfred* (with the addition of suitable hymns) as "an Oratorical Exercise ... before large Audiences, with great Applause." No objections had been directed towards this dramatic exercise of the younger generation, as all female parts had been eliminated, and "every Thing that could injure their Morals" had been "carefully avoided." Only a year later, the Reverend William Smith had gone so far as to predict in his *American Magazine*: "... who can tell but the coming generation may have theatres by law established, and grow as fond of actors and actresses, *men and women singers*, as the polite, well-bred ladies and gentlemen of the beau monde in Britain: of whose follies, as well as fashions, we are the most humble, zealous mimics."

But the outspoken Smith was not one calculated to win support for the theater among the Friends or Presbyterians. In the first place, he was an Anglican rector, and his intemperance and slovenly habits were not pleasing to those of more pious leanings. In fact, the Quakers and Presbyterians, having now been joined by the Lutherans and Baptists, presented a more formidable and resolute stand against the drama than ever before. The

Lewis Hallam, Jr.

Courtesy of the Walter Hampden Memorial
Library of the Players Club, New York

*Nancy Hallam as Imogen, Painted by
Charles Willson Peale, 1771*

Courtesy of Colonial Williamsburg, Inc.

secret of the new construction on Society Hill was soon rumored; the design of a building large enough to house a theater —even a colonial theater—was difficult to conceal. Once this was determined, the religious factions closed ranks and rose up against this evil in their midst. Their first move was to appear before Judge William Allen, requesting an injunction against the players. In rejecting their suit, the judge observed "that plays brought him more moral virtue than sermons." Yet, on the night the theater opened, Judge Allen was unable to attend; he was mourning the death of his wife. No doubt many of those subjects of his rebuke secretly rejoiced in this manifestation of the wrath of a jealous God.

On May 22, the Quakers petitioned the governor directly. On the same day, their allies, the Presbyterians, submitted a similar document, declaring the stage to be "a most powerfull Engine of Debauching the Minds and corrupting the Manners of youth" and suggesting that such extravagances should not be tolerated during the current war with France.

When no immediate reply seemed to be forthcoming from the governor, the religious phalanx applied increasing pressure to the General Assembly, and that body, on May 31, 1759, passed "An Act for the More Effectual Suppressing of Lotteries and Plays," providing a fine of £500 for those "several companies of idle persons and strollers [who] have come into this Province from foreign parts" and attempted to perform or sell tickets to plays in Pennsylvania.

This unforeseen development left William Williams and Alexander Alexander with the unpleasant prospect of losing a considerable sum already expended for materials for the playhouse. They, too, petitioned the governor to consider their plight. Governor Denny himself was in something of a dilemma, for the revocation of the permission to play could be interpreted as a reflection upon his integrity. Then too, as he told his Council, the "Prohibition of plays was a most unreasonable restraint . . . from taking innocent diversions." The Council, on the other hand, although they did not necessarily condone the theater, saw in the suppression of lotteries the loss of the chief means of support for the academy, the charity school, and the college.

Backed by his Council, the governor neatly side-stepped the issue by supporting amendments to the act delaying the effective date of execution until January 1, 1760. So it was that Douglass gained a five-month season unhampered by legal restrictions. Even after the act became law, it was to remain in force only eight months before being disallowed by the king in Council, September 2, 1760.

Douglass rushed the final phases of construction. During this interval and while the issue was being debated, the players made their living as best they could. Mr. Horne, who advertised himself as "one of the young Gentlemen belonging to the Company," offered instruction in the French language to all who wished to take advantage of his services.[4]

On June 15, 1759, the Society Hill playhouse opened with a program of *Tamerlane* and Fielding's ballad opera, *The Virgin Unmask'd*. An occasional prologue and epilogue were rendered by the son-mother combination of Lewis Hallam and Mrs. Douglass, which, although not recorded, must have centered on the old theme of the theater as a school for morals. Mrs. Love was featured in songs between the acts. The opening play was followed by relatively inoffensive selections, including *Richard III* and *The Provok'd Husband*, the latter gay comedy inserted to liven up the more somber and gory productions. On Friday, July 13, Douglass, in a move that appears to have been an offering to conciliate the Presbyterians, staged *Douglas*. In the announcement, he inserted four lines from the original London prologue as a suggestion of the moral virtues of the play:

> This Night a Douglass, your protection claims:
> A Wife! a Mother! Pity's softest Names:
> The Story of her Woes indulgent bear,
> And grant your Suppliant all she begs, A TEAR.

As an appeal to the Calvinistic conscience, he emphasized that the tragedy had been "written by the Rev. Mr. Hume [*sic*], a Minister of the Kirk of Scotland." He did not, however, feel it incumbent to explain that the Reverend John Home had lost his pulpit for having written "a profane stage play."

A Mr. Allyn, an average actor who was destined to play minor roles with the Douglass Company for the next nine years, appeared in the cast for the first time when *Hamlet* was played on July 26. On August 10, scenes which must have been painted by William Williams were featured in the production of the old tragedy, *Theodosius, or The Force of Love.* Attention was focused on "the transparent Alterpiece, shewing the Vision of Constantine the Great, before his Battle against the Christians, the bloody Cross in the Air Inscrib'd about it [in] Golden Characters *In hoc signo Vinces.*" There was also the proud boast that "The Decorations are entirely New and Proper." Another new member with a familiar name was added to the cast of *The Beggar's Opera* on August 24. This was a Mr. Scott, quite possibly the actor of the same name who had originally appeared with the old Murray-Kean Company.

Governor Denny's political machinations had rendered ineffective the efforts of the anti-theater groups, but they still sniped at the actors and the playhouse in the newspapers. Terming the theater "the House of the Devil," they called upon all sensible men to: "Consider, therefore, the Play-House, and the Master of Entertainment there, as it consists of Love Intrigues, blasphemous Passions, profane Discourses, lewd Descriptions, filthy Jests, and all the most extravagant Rant of wanton, vile profligate Persons, of both Sexes, heating and inflaming one another with all the Wantoness of Address, the Immodesty of Motions, and Lewdness of Thought that Wit can invent."

Because of the flood of criticism, Douglass rearranged his repertoire to feature the plays of Shakespeare and the less offensive efforts of contemporary playwrights. Shakespeare, of course, was presented in the altered or expurgated versions then current on the London stage. Longer, sometimes the most significant, passages of dialogue were deleted, and as a concession to the new fondness for things comic and musical, the spectacular was added to the dramatic whenever possible. On October 25, for instance, *Macbeth* was performed in Davenant's operatic version, with the "original Musick as set by [Henry] Purcell; Witches Dance, and all the Decorations proper to the Play." The singing witches were played by Messrs. Allyn, Harman, and Tomlinson in the

English tradition of males portraying recognized "dame" parts.

Illustrating this proclivity for the ostentatious was the performance at which the local Masons honored Douglass on his benefit the night of November 2. The play was *Romeo and Juliet*, surrounded by all the dramatic froth customary upon such occasions. Douglass, a member of the fraternity, spoke the prologue "in the Character of a Master Mason," while his wife recited the epilogue as a "Mason's Wife." In the play itself, the spectacular assumed a morbid hue "With the Funeral Procession of Juliet to the Monument of the Capulets, and a solemn Dirge, as it is performed at the Theatre Royal in Covent-Garden." Such was the pattern for the presentation of this play throughout the remaining years of the colonial stage.

The relatively small number of players with the company often forced the more gifted to play two parts, especially in such musical productions as *The Beggar's Opera*, for singing talent was not abundant. In this fall of 1759, Lewis Hallam received his first challenge to his claim to the more attractive leading roles. On December 1, an actor by the name of John Palmer was cast in the title role of *Macbeth*. Palmer was a man of striking features and figure who had but recently joined the troupe. Unsuccessful in his early career as a strolling player in England, he was eventually to become one of the brighter luminaries of the London stage after his return from the colonies. In the six months he played with the Douglass Company, he was to act the leads in many plays, a rather cogent commentary on the ability of the company, as well as that of young Lewis Hallam. Among those roles in which Palmer supplanted Hallam was the comedy lead in *The Suspicious Husband* and he played Romeo to the Juliet of Mrs. Douglass, who, though far from fourteen, steadfastly insisted on her right to the part.

Another newcomer to the personnel of the company during the Philadelphia run was a dancer, George Abbington, who first appeared in entertainments between the acts of *Romeo and Juliet* on December 21. Trained in London as a theatrical dancer, Abbington had for the past year conducted a dancing school in Philadelphia.

With the conclusion of all benefits, two charity performances were given instead of the one required in their original permission. *The London Merchant, or the History of George Barnwell* was advertised on December 28, 1759, for the purpose of "purchasing an Organ for the College-Hall in this City, and instructing the Charity Children in Psalmody." In keeping with the sacrosanct purposes for which the benefit had been announced, music was added, played "by some Gentlemen of this City ... for which purpose a neat Harpsichord will be provided." Even Hallam's prologue was in praise of music rather than his usual extolling of the moral virtues of the stage.

The following night, when the weather was so bitter that the Delaware River was frozen solid, *Hamlet* was presented as a benefit for the hospital. The fact that this house of mercy should have to stoop so low to secure funds led to rumblings of discontent among the devout. So strong were these dissident criticisms that the hospital officials felt it necessary to publish a statement to the effect that they had "no Authority given them to refuse any Sums of Money, which may be lawfully contributed thereto." They further disclaimed any responsibility for the benefit, for it had been "done without the consent of the said Managers, in Consequence of the Injunction of the late Governor Denny at the time he granted Liberty to the Stage Players to erect a Theatre near this City."

Douglass' allotted time had expired, and he began his preparations for closing the houses by January 1, 1760. Not only had his company provided entertainment for the less pious citizens of Philadelphia, but they had been able to awaken dormant literary interests. It was Alexander Graydon's observation that: "Although the theatre must be admitted to be a stimulus to those vices, which something inherent in our nature renders essential to the favoured hero of the comic drama and novel, it was yet useful in one respect. It induced me to open books which hitherto lain neglected on the shelf. . . . I became a reader of plays, and particularly those of Shakespeare, of which I was an ardent and unaffected admirer." [5]

From Philadelphia, the company traveled to Annapolis, "the most cultivated and dissipated city in the American plantations." A claim has been made that they first played in Upper Marlborough, but there is no evidence to support this assertion. The winter of 1759-60 was one of the worst in years, and because of extreme temperatures the comedians did not open in the Maryland capital until March 3. In Annapolis, the players basked in a congenial atmosphere after their trials in New York and Philadelphia. Not only did the governor grant the necessary permission, but he lent dignity to the playhouse by attending the opening performance of *The Orphan* and *Lethe*. A "Gentleman of this Province" composed a special prologue for the occasion, and Mrs. Douglass welcomed the audience with:

> Lo! to new Worlds th' adven'rous Muse conveys
> The moral Wisdom of dramatic lays!
> To warm the Breast, and humanize the Soul!
> By magic Sounds to vary Hopes and Fears;
> Or make each Eye dissolve in virtuous Tears!
> 'Til sympathizing Youths in Anguish melt,
> And Virgins sigh for Woes, before unfelt!
> Here, as we speak, each heart-struck Patriot glows
> With real Rage to crush Britannia's Foes!

These patriotic sentiments and the plays that followed "were perform'd with great Justice, and the Applause which attended the whole Representation, did less Honour to the Abilities of the Actors than to the Taste of their Auditors."

The company had experienced, as usual, some changes in personnel. Nancy Hallam no longer was listed in the published casts of the plays, and Mr. Harman had completely disappeared. Mrs. Harman still appeared in her accustomed roles, but whether her husband had died or deserted her cannot be determined. A Mr. Sturt appeared in the first of the minor roles he was to play for the next two years. A new family unit had joined the players in the persons of the mother-daughter team of Mrs. and Miss Dowthaitt, who were relegated to minor parts along with a Miss Crane, also a new member of the troupe. Apparently Douglass had earlier persuaded them to come from Jamaica to join the players at Annapolis, for they were not local amateurs. An old familiar face appeared in *The Beaux' Stratagem* on

March 20. Walter Murray, the manager of the old Murray-Kean Company, joined the actors on that date and continued playing with them as long as they remained in Maryland.

An enthusiastic reception was tendered the players in Annapolis, but a series of unforeseen incidents limited attendance. During March, the most severe snowstorm of the year kept many theatergoers at home. According to custom, the theater was also closed during "Passion Week" and did not reopen until April 7, when Romeo was played "by a young Gentleman for his Diversion." Near the end of April, the governor adjourned the Assembly until July, thereby eliminating any prospects of increased attendance from the legislators. A rumor that smallpox was prevalent in Annapolis spread throughout the colony; though the *Maryland Gazette* repeatedly assured its readers that the town was free of the disease, nevertheless many people would not risk coming to the capital for fear there was some basis for the report. The townspeople, however, made no effort to quarantine themselves, for when *The Provok'd Husband* was played for the benefit of Mrs. Douglass, the Masons honored her by announcing, "The Fraternity will do her the Honor to walk in Procession, and appear in the House in their proper Cloathing."

Shakespearean plays reigned as favorites in Annapolis. One of the few lead roles that Douglass claimed as his own was that of Othello, played opposite his wife's Desdemona. Adam Hallam still played regularly in minor parts, which did little more than require his presence on the stage, and he was also able to perform some of the simpler dances that were offered as added attractions. Despite the repeated injunction, "No Persons to be admitted behind the Scenes," customers frequently wandered backstage during the progress of the play. Walter Murray's new velvet-collared great coat was taken "as supposed by Mistake" the very night the farce was entitled *The Wonder, or an Honest Yorkshireman.*

The benefits continued to work their way towards the end of the season. Mrs. Morris chose for her night Lord Lansdown's altered version of *The Merchant of Venice*, now called by its original title *The Jew of Venice, or The Female Lawyer*. Adam Hallam played Gratiano upon this occasion, the pinnacle of his success as an actor. Mrs. Douglass was still Portia, albeit a middle-aged one, while her son portrayed a comic Shylock.

Mr. Scott's benefit of *The Gamester* on Monday, April 8, marked the end of the 1760 season in Annapolis. In the special prologue "addressed to the Ladies," Mrs. Douglass expressed appreciation for their support:

> Ye gen'rous FAIR, ere finally we part,
> Accept the Tribute of a grateful Heart.

Continuing, she suggested that less tolerant Pennsylvania follow the example of Maryland:

> Oh! may your Influence still propitious prove,
> To cheer our distant Labours, as we rove!
> Till Sister-Colonies assert our Cause;
> And Their's resound fair Maryland's Applause! [6]

From Annapolis, the comedians made their way to Upper Marlborough. Despite its small size, this was a good theater town on those frequent occasions when races were held. There was no theater building in town, and Douglass played in "a neat convenient tobacco-house, well fitted up for that purpose." There were no box seats, but the building had been fitted up with a gallery. Seven shillings, sixpence, the regular price for box seats, was charged for admission to the pit, while the usual pit price of five shillings was collected for gallery tickets.

On May 22, the tragedy of *Douglas* and the farce *Lethe* were presented as the opening program. For the convenience of the many persons from outlying communities who were in town for the races, and "who chuse to go home after the Play," the hour of performance was moved forward from six to four o'clock. Another innovation appeared in the designation of a ticket agent. In Annapolis and in other cities, it had been customary to purchase tickets at the local printing office or at the bar of a favorite tavern, but in Upper Marlborough this chore was handled by

Benjamin Brooke, the local sheriff. One would suspect this to be a method of collecting debts owed by the actors.

The season in Upper Marlborough lasted six weeks, with the last advertised play, *Romeo and Juliet*, announced for July 1, 1760. By this time, John Palmer had taken leave of the company and was on his way back to England. With this more accomplished actor out of his way, young Hallam reclaimed his major roles, in this instance playing Romeo to his mother's Juliet.[7]

The Douglass Company later appeared in Williamsburg, having played short engagements in the villages between that place and Upper Marlborough. They had arrived in the Virginia capital sometime before October 2, when a local merchant, William Allason, noted that he had "paid for 2 Play Tickets." Strangely enough, for so extraordinary an occasion, no mention was made in the *Virginia Gazette* of the presence of the actors. Only two explanations suggest themselves: newspaper advertising was not considered necessary in a town crowded with visitors for the fall term of the General Court; or the company was experiencing financial difficulties. It is quite possible that Douglass resorted to the old English custom of "giving out the play," a practice dating back at least to 1667 when Pepys noted "little Mis. Davis did dance a jig after the end of the play, and then telling the next day's play." In the London theater, it was not unknown that the audience be allowed to vote by "Ayes and Noes" on the next attraction.

Certainly, the Virginians were in a receptive mood for theatrical performances. Only five years before, the Reverend Samuel Davies had arraigned his congregation on the moral indictment that "Plays and Romances" were "more read than the history of the blessed Jesus." Yet, the theater had remained dark unless there were local amateur undertakings; that is, it remained dark except for casual visits of such oddities as "that elaborate and celebrated Piece of Mechanism, called the MICROCOSM or THE WORLD IN MINIATURE." The Virginians welcomed any new diversion; just a little over a year earlier a traveler had commented: "They are immoderately fond of dancing, and indeed it is almost the only amusement they partake of."

From October, 1760, until May, 1761, the London Company

remained in Virginia. It is unlikely that they restricted their activities to Williamsburg during this period but played other towns of the neighborhood: perhaps Norfolk, Suffolk, Petersburg, and Fredericksburg. When he was in Williamsburg, one of the most ardent patrons of the playhouse was a rising young planter by the name of George Washington. In 1760, he noted in his ledger that he had spent £7. 10s. 3d. for "Play Tickets at Sundry Times," and in March, 1761, his expenses for this type of entertainment amounted to £2. 7s. 6d.

It is reasonable to assume that the same plays were presented, performed by the same cast, as in the earlier attractions of this first American tour by the Douglass Company. As late as May 8, they were still in town, for on this date Alexander Craig sold Lewis Hallam a pair of shoes, and it was also in Williamsburg that two of the actresses left the company after a year's trouping. Mrs. and Miss Dowthaitt did not reappear on the American stage for two years, until the company played next in Philadelphia.

Douglass himself, once again struggling with financial problems, did not depart Williamsburg until the first of June. His purpose for delaying his departure was to institute a chancery suit in the General Court in behalf of Lewis Hallam, in an effort to regain possession and title to the theater property for the late manager's heirs. The suit was unsuccessful, although it was still cluttering the docket as late as 1769.[8]

Douglass, through experience sometimes bitter, was still learning the trials of an eighteenth-century theatrical manager. Upon his leaving Williamsburg, he carelessly neglected to arm himself with that most necessary certificate of respectability, a "character," and was forced to delay all operations until he obtained that document. A recommendation, eventually signed by the "Governor, Council, and near one hundred of the principal gentlemen of Virginia," stated:

> Williamsburg, June 11, 1761
> The company of comedians under the direction of David Douglass has performed in this colony for near twelve-month; during which time they have made it

their constant practice to behave with prudence and discretion in their private character, and to use their utmost endeavours to give general satisfaction in their public capacity. We have therefore thought proper to recommend them as a company whose behavior merits the favor of the public and who are capable of entertaining a sensible and polite audience.[9]

Douglass was not without need of the best possible recommendation, for at this period he essayed to play the most difficult area of his career—New England.

· VII ·

PLAYING THE EASTERN COAST

(*Rhode Island, New York, Virginia,*
and Charleston, 1761-1766)

Although Massachusetts was the most populous colony in New England, it was useless for Douglass to attempt an
assault upon that citadel of Puritanism. Strict moral prohibition
of theatrical performances had become a legal reality in the
winter of 1749-50. It had all started innocently enough, when
two young Englishmen, assisted by some of the gallants of Boston, performed *The Orphan* in a coffee house on State Street.
Unhappily, this coincided with an unexplained riot in the street
outside the makeshift playhouse (some said it was caused by
those demanding entrance), which only served to accentuate
the evil influence of the drama. In consequence, a statute passed
by the General Court in April, 1750, stated as its purpose the
prevention of the "great mischiefs which arise from public stage
plays"; it provided for fines of £20 for those who staged a play,

with lesser penalties of £5 for each actor and spectator. This threat to the pocketbook was more likely to discourage play acting than moral sanctions.

Ten years later, when a local group planned to act *Cato* for their own amusement, they were suspected of "Vice, Impiety, Immorality" and were forced to cancel their project. Some plays, however, were clandestinely performed; *The Orphan* was acted before some 210 persons on March 13, 1765, although one spectator grumbled that it was "miserably performed." Such presentations were the exception rather than the rule, and, ordinarily, those enamored of things theatrical pampered their fancies by assembling in groups to hear the reading of plays. In fact, in the early days of the Revolution, young Lieutenant Williams of His Majesty's 23rd Regiment, complained that Boston had "no such thing as a play house, they were too puritanical a set to admit of such lewd Diversions, tho' ther's perhaps no town of its size cou'd turn out more whores than this cou'd. They have left us an ample sample of them." It was not until 1792 that Boston was to legally support a professional theater.[1]

No statutes restricted theatrical performances in Rhode Island, although there were strong sentiments against revelry. Douglass arrived in Newport in the late spring of 1761. On the surface, a theatrical venture into Rhode Island would seem a bold venture, but there was logic behind such a move. Even at this early date, Newport had taken on the air of a summer resort for those wealthier southern planters who fled northward to escape the heat and endemic fevers of their own environments. Still, Douglass found a strong wave of opposition, further complicated by his negligence in not securing a "character" from Governor Francis Fauquier before he left Virginia. A representative rushed southward to rectify this oversight, and the document, as eventually presented, bore the date June 11, 1761.

In the interval, the versatile manager schemed to circumvent the necessity of formal permission to play by an ingenious innovation. Handbills distributed through the streets of Newport announced:

Kings Arms Tavern—Newport
Rhode Island

On Monday, June 10th, at the Public Room of the
Above Inn will be delivered a series of

MORAL DIALOGUES

IN FIVE PARTS

Depicting the Evil Effects of Jealousy and other Bad
Passions, and Proving that Happiness can only Spring
from the Pursuit of Virtue.

MR. DOUGLASS will represent a noble and magnani-
mous Moor named Othello, who loves a young lady
named Desdemona, and after he has married her, har-
bors (as in too many cases) the dreadful passion of
jealousy.

Of jealousy our being's bane,
Mark the small cause and the most dreadful pain.

MR. ALLYN will depict the character of a specious
villain, in the regiment of Othello, who is so base as to
hate his commander on mere suspicion, and to impose
on his best friend. Of such characters, it is to be feared,
there are thousands in the world, and the one in question may present to us a salutary warning.

The man that wrongs his master and his friend,
What can he come to but a shameful end?

MR. HALLAM will delineate a young and thoughtless
officer, who is traduced by MR. ALLYN, and getting
drunk, loses his situation, and his general's esteem. All
young men, whatsoever, take example from Cassio.

The ill effects of drinking would you see,
Be warned and keep from evil company.

MR. MORRIS will represent an old gentleman, the father of Desdemona, who is not cruel or covetous, but
is foolish enough to dislike the noble Moor, his son-in-
law, because his face is not white, forgetting that we all
spring from one root. Such prejudices are very numerous and very wrong.

Fathers beware what sense and love ye lack.
'Tis crime, not color, makes the being black.

MR. QUELCH will depict the fool, who wishes to become a knave, and trusting one gets killed by him. Such is the friendship of rogues—take heed.

When fools would knaves become, how often you'll
Perceive the knave not wiser than the fool.

MRS. MORRIS will represent a young and virtuous wife, who, being wrongfully suspected, gets smothered (in an adjoining room) by her husband.

Reader, attend: and ere thou goest hence
Let fall a tear to hapless innocence.

MRS. DOUGLASS will be her faithful attendant, who will hold out a good example to all servants, male and female, and to all people in subjection.

Obediance and gratitude
Are things as rare as they are good.

Various other dialogues, too numerous to mention here, will be delivered at night, well adapted to the minds and manners. The whole will be repeated on Wednesday and Saturday. Tickets, six shillings each; to be had within. Commencement at 7. Conclusion at half past 10, in order that every spectator may go home at a sober hour, and reflect upon what he has seen, before he retires to rest.

These "Dialogues" were so well received that, despite an adverse vote at a special town meeting, Douglass hastily constructed a playhouse on Easton's Point as soon as his "character" arrived from Virginia. There is little evidence suggesting the plays that were presented in Newport, although on September 7, *The Provok'd Wife* was announced as a benefit for the poor. The manager was able to thwart the petitions of the anti-theater group by the presentation of passes to members of the Assembly. To add to their difficulties, a sudden hurricane flattened several buildings in the area and "came near to spoiling the entertainment" at the theater. The last play of this season in Newport, *Douglas*, was performed as a second benefit for the poor and "meant as an expression of gratitude for the countenance and favour of the town." Perhaps it was the £1,030 collected in the two benefits that led some to comment, "the behaviour of the company here has been irreproachable," and "the character they brought from the governor and gentlemen of Virginia has been fully verified." The fact that the comedians were to return to Newport the following year is in itself a suggestion that the season had been financially rewarding.[2]

From Rhode Island, Douglass took his players to New York. At some time in the past, he had contacted a builder in that city and completed the necessary arrangements for the construction of a new theater. The work had gone well and the playhouse was ready for occupancy just two weeks after their last performance in Rhode Island. The new theater was located on the southwest corner of Nassau and Chapel (now Beekman) streets. The costs of constructing this ninety by forty foot building totalled £650, and it could accommodate an audience of, at least, 325 spectators.

There was some concern expressed at the return of the players, and this possibly may be the reason that Governor Cadwallader Colden restricted them to the equivalent of two months of playing. New York was sinking deeper into an economic depression as a result of the British decision to draw off its military and naval forces to concentrate their war efforts on the French islands of the Caribbean. Merchants joined with religious groups in protesting that the comedians drained too much money from the town, money that might well be spent on necessities. Contrary to his usual custom of playing three nights a week, Douglass limited performances to only two per week, with the obvious intention of stretching the season through the colder months before another move became necessary.

Nicholas Rowe's moralizing domestic tragedy, *The Fair Penitent*, was the first offering on November 18, 1761, followed a week later with *Hamlet*. As usual, Lewis Hallam played the melancholy Dane, while his stepfather advanced from the role of the ghost to that of the king, a part he was to play throughout the remaining years of his career. Two names appeared for the first time in a cast of the London Company of Comedians. One was John Tremaine, of the old Murray-Kean Company, who once again laid aside his cabinetmaker's tools to gratify his passion for the boards. The other was Sarah Hallam, Lewis's wife, who made a rare, perhaps her only, appearance before an audience.

No sooner had the players established themselves than an amusing, yet vehement, war of words appeared in the local press between two writers using the pseudonyms of "Philodemus" and "Armanda." Philodemus began the exchange by stating that all ladies who went to the theater were lacking in modesty. An angry Armanda not only vigorously defended the actors but retaliated by styling Philodemus "a superannuated animal that has past his grand climacteric, and whose early times of life had been employed in luxury and debauchery, and now being satiated, concludes that all is vanity and every pleasure criminal." In retort, after posing the question as to whether the playhouse or the Bible were the better teacher, Philodemus countered with what he obviously considered the worst possible slur, intimating that his tormentor was herself nothing but a strolling player. Armanda, however, after a vigorous denial of the accusation the following week, seemed content to call off the feud and the woman, once again, had the last word.

While verbal blasts and counterblasts were amusing readers of the newspapers, Douglass entertained his fraternity, the Grand Master and the Masons, with a special performance of *The Gamester* on December 28, with the manager, as usual, reciting the prologue in appropriate costume. Although every advertisement and every playbill continued to carry the postscript "No Persons can be admitted behind the SCENES," they were but so many ineffective words to many of the patrons of the theater. The stage was frequently cluttered with those "Gentlemen" who not only imposed their presence behind the scenes, seeking out the actresses, but frequently, in mimic of the fops of London, wandered onstage during the performance in order to better display their fine clothing.

In New York, this practice became so general that Douglass was forced to issue the plea: "Complaints having been several Times made, that a Number of Gentlemen crowd the Stage, and very much interrupt the Performance: and as it is impossible for Actors when thus obstructed, should do that Justice to their

Parts they other wise could; it will be taken as a particular Favour if no Gentleman will be offended that he is absolutely refus'd Admittance at the Stage Door, unless he has previously secured himself a Place in either the Stage or upper Boxes." When *Romeo and Juliet* was acted one week later, the customary elaborate funeral procession was employed as an excuse "to give us the entire use of the Stage." These repeated requests were but whistling into the winds of tradition, and Douglass finally capitulated with the weary statement, "We presume it wou'd be unnecessary to inform the Town that we must be indulg'd with a clear Stage on this Occasion."

The two months allotted to the players expired, but an extension was granted, perhaps because of Douglass' willingness to give a performance of *Othello* for the benefit of the poor. When he called in all tickets that had been previously purchased but had not been used, he explained that the proceeds of the benefit were "to be impartially apply'd" to those destitute families not provided for by the city and that the names of those in charge of distribution of funds were to be published. Upon this and similar occasions, the pseudo-democratic practice of merging the boxes into the pit was followed, with prices reduced in both the expanded pit and gallery. Only the barest expenses for lighting materials and wages of non-acting personnel were deducted from the total receipts of £133. 6d. Net proceeds amounting to £114. 10s. were turned over to George Harrison and John Vander Speigle for distribution to the needy.

In addition to his struggle to keep the young bucks of the town off stage during the performance, Douglass endeavored to stop another precedent long respected in the theater. Traditionally, actors or actresses for whom a benefit was scheduled personally called upon known devotees of the drama to solicit their patronage. Douglass periodically inserted a tag to both his advertisements and playbills: "The Ceremony of waiting on Ladies and Gentlemen at their Houses with Bills, has been for some Time left off in this Company; the frequent Solicitations on these Occasions having been found rather an inconvenience to the Persons so waited on, than a Compliment."

An occasional alteration was made in the physical appearance of the theater. As a sop to the vanity of holders of box seats, partitions were added "to render them more commodious for select Companies."

David Douglass seems to have exercised strict supervision over his players both inside and outside the theater, for there was a gradual lessening of complaints against actors in general. Also, the city was acquiring a more cosmopolitan air as immigration swelled its population to around eighteen thousand. When, on Monday, April 26, 1762, *The Committee, or The Faithful Irishman*, was staged as the second charity performance, this time for the New York Charity School, their good behavior, plus the willingness of the company to aid the unfortunate, led Hugh Gaines to editorialize in his New York *Mercury:* "This is the second Play the Company has given this Season to public Uses; which with their unblamable Conduct during their Residence here, and the Entertainment the Town has receiv'd from their Performances, has greatly Obviated many Objections hitherto made against Theatrical Representations in this City."

Not all objections were so definitely "Obviated" as Gaines implied, especially with one who gratified his critical judgment with action. In the same issue with Gaines's paean of praise, an angry Douglass placed a card: "A Pistole Reward will be given to whoever can discover the person who was so very rude as to throw Eggs from the Gallery upon the Stage last Monday, by which the Cloaths of some Ladies and Gentlemen were spoiled and the Performance in some measure interrupted." [3] The egg, as an expression of dramatic criticism, had come into its own!

Soon after this experience, in the early summer, the Company of Comedians appeared once again in Newport. After a few performances, they moved on to Providence, where again they encountered the spreading thorns of bigotry and intolerance. Rather than further irritate the sensitive morals of the community, Douglass termed the crude barn of a theater he had hastily erected a "Histrionic Academy." Once again he stretched his subtlety to the extreme, advertising that the primary objective of the actors was to "deliver dissertations on subjects instructive and entertaining" and to instruct their audience "to speak in public with propriety."

This subterfuge, however, failed to deceive those zealots who were experienced in stripping the devil of his camouflage, for they set up the cry that the players be driven from the shadow of the hills of Providence. Some champions of the actors did come forth, one in the person of Benjamin Mason, who, writing to John and Nicholas Brown, said: "I think it will be a hard thing upon them [the actors] if your people have suffered them to go on with their Building & not Allow them to Act, at Least as Long as would pay their expenses." This was too little and too late. On the exact date of Mason's plea for equity, a town meeting was called "by warrant," in which it was proposed and passed "that no stage-plays be acted in said town." Douglass paid no attention to a resolution that contained no teeth, and he continued acting as before. His demonstrated scorn for the will of local moralists only strengthened their determination to drive the actors from Providence. A march on the theater, supposedly of spontaneous origin, with a view to pulling down the building was blocked when merchant John Brown planted a cannon in their path and threatened to fire if they persisted. With the failure of mob action, the opponents of the theater adopted legal methods to gain their end. They now struck with a petition to the General Assembly, requesting that body to "make some effectual law to prevent any stage-plays, comedies, or theatrical performances being acted in this Colony for the future." The 405 names affixed to the document were enough to demand political action, and in August, 1762, the legislature approved "an Act to Prevent Stage Plays and other Theatrical Entertainments in this Colony" which carried stringent penalties for noncompliance. To prevent the actors from claiming innocence of the law, as well as to give early notice of the statute, the act was ordered proclaimed through the streets of Providence to the beat of the drum.

It may have been that the manager entertained some notion of slipping over into New Hampshire, for it was this same year that the House of Representatives of that province refused an unidentified troupe of comedians permission to act on the grounds that plays had a "peculiar influence on the minds of young people and greatly endanger their morals by giving them a taste for intriguing, amusement and pleasure." With the prospect of advancing cold weather, and an even colder reception in New England, Douglass turned to the more hospitable South.[4]

The assertion has been made that Douglass and his comedians played in the West Indies for the next four years. Such is not the case. Actually, most of this period was spent in the southern colonies. They played in Virginia for approximately a year, although there is but fragmentary evidence to offer in substantiation. The following November, 1763, upon their arrival in South Carolina, the *South Carolina Gazette* reported the actors as coming from Virginia. In November, 1762, they were certainly in Williamsburg, for during that month George Washington was in town and purchased "Play Tickets," and in April and May of 1763, he recorded similar expenditures on five different occasions. The company also seems to have played in Petersburg, for on January 20, 1763, Thomas Jefferson wrote John Page that "I have some thoughts of going to Petersburg if the actors go there in May"—an indication that he may have seen them earlier in their tour. Petersburg would have been a logical choice for Douglass, as it seems likely that the town boasted a theater by this date. Such is the sum of information implying a full year of acting in Virginia.[5]

Near November 1, 1763, Douglass and his troupe disembarked at Charleston. Formerly, his troupe had been advertised as the "London Company of Comedians" or simply a "Company of Comedians," but now, seeking to suggest a local identification, he shrewdly renamed his actors "The American Company of Comedians." His credentials were impressive; public announcements stated, "They are recommended in a particular manner by many gentlemen of eminence in the northern colonies, both as to their abilities in their profession and their private conduct [which] for several years past has been truly exceptional." Douglass had no sooner rid himself of his sea legs than he was contracting for a new theater building and located it once again on Queen Street "upon the very Spot where an established Church formerly stood." Measuring seventy-five by thirty-five feet, the building was completed within six weeks of the initial ground-breaking.

On December 14, 1763, the theater, "completed in a very elegant manner," was opened with *The Suspicious Husband* and *Lethe*, to be followed by such old favorites as *The Gamester, The Provok'd Husband, The Mourning Bride, Douglas,* and *The London Merchant, or The History of George Barnwell,* which was now being advertised simply as *George Barnwell.* Possibilities of capacity houses multiplied with the sitting of the General Assembly in Charleston on January 4, 1764. From this time on, receipts averaged between £90 and £140 for each of the three performances every week. Considered in the light of population of the area, this income represents a most successful season in a city whose people numbered between nine and ten thousand, near one-half of whom were Negro slaves. But a sophisticated atmosphere had pervaded the town as its people, imitating London society, "worked hard to cultivate Culture."

Several new actors joined the company, although some were obviously no more than local amateurs, filling in until Douglass could make a projected voyage to England in search of new players, especially those who had the talent to satisfy the craving for musical interludes and "English comic opera." The acute shortage of actors was accentuated when Adam Hallam began to appear in roles that were inconsistent with his ability. The most significant and gifted of the new members was the beautiful and vivacious Margaret Cheer, whose lovely voice compared favorably with her talents as an actress. Three months after her arrival from England, Alexander Garden's letter to David Golden still contained a note of suppressed effervescence: "Mr. Douglass has made a valuable acquisition in Miss Cheer who arrived from London much about the same time Mr. Douglass arrived with his company. Soon after that, she agreed to go on the stage where she has since appeared in some Chief Characters with great applause particularly in Moninia in the Orphan & Juliet of Shakespear & Hermione of the Distrest Mother. Her fine person, her youth, her Voice, & Appearance &c conspire to make her appear with propriety—Such a one they much wanted as *Mrs* Douglass was their chief actress before & who on that account had always too many Characters to appear in."

On March 26, 1764, David Douglass appeared in *The Orphan*

of China and *The Anatomist*. As neither he nor Mrs. Douglass was listed in subsequent casts, it must have been about this time that they took passage for England. The company continued to play through the first part of April, with the last benefit, for Miss Crane and Mr. Barry, a performance of Mrs. Centlivre's comedy, *A Wonder! A Woman Keeps a Secret!* Under ordinary circumstances, the last benefit would have marked the end of the season, but on May 10, *King Lear* was acted. This could have been either a charity benefit, although it was not so advertised, or an expedient to supplement the income of the actors who were awaiting the sailing of their ship. Soon after, the company sailed for Barbados, where, even without the guiding hand of their manager, they continued to entertain the pleasure-loving islanders.

Although no actors strutted across its stage, the Charleston theater was not entirely unused during this interval. A Mr. Pike found it a suitable hall to hold his "annual Ball for the young ladies and gentlemen under his tuition." The same issue of the newspaper carrying this announcement, October 31, 1765, also reported the triumphant return of David Douglass from England after an absence of over a year: "On Friday last, Mr. Douglass, director of the Theatre in this town, arrived from London with a reinforcement to his company. We hear he has engaged some very capital singers from the theatres in London, with a view of entertaining the town this winter with English operas. It is imagined, when he is joined by the company from Barbados, that our theatrical performance will be executed in a manner not inferiour to the most applauded in England. The scenes and decorations, we are informed, are of a superiour kind to any that have been seen in America, being designed by the most eminent maker in London." No false claims had been advanced as to the excellence of the new scenery. It had been made by the best craftsman in London—Nicholas Thomas Doll of Covent Garden.

No descriptions exist of this "superiour kind" of scenery, although it would seem that it was no more elaborate than that of the average eighteenth-century theater. Splashed in bold colors on material of a burlap-like quality, detail was sacrificed for bold outline to take advantage of the dim light cast by the flickering candles. Consisting of a backdrop and side scenes, the average width was twenty-four to twenty-nine feet, the height around sixteen feet, although there is evidence that Douglass sometimes used flats as high as twenty feet. Designed to part in the middle, the scenes slid to the sides of the stage in top and bottom grooves, while the backdrops were fastened to rollers rather than frames because of greater facility in transportation. Scenes were by no means designed to fit the action of any particular play; usually there were stock representations of a "street," a "forest," a "parlor," or the like. Nor was it unusual to see chairs or tables painted on the fabric, although these properties were on stage if required.

Scenery was shifted in plain view of the audience, playscripts containing such directions as a scene "opens and discloses." In some instances, the actor would walk towards the apron with the wings closing behind him, while, at other times, he would make his exit to the rear of the stage, the scenes shifting behind him.[6]

Douglass had persuaded six actors and actresses to leave London for America, his choices guided by the penchant of the Americans for the gay and musical. Among them was a Miss Hallam, whose age at this time would make her the Nancy Hallam who had been playing minor roles and children's parts six years earlier. Her excellence "in the singing way" suggests that she may have been sent back to London for voice training. No longer was she to play children's parts, for during her absence she had acquired that pert vivaciousness that sparkles either on or off the stage. Miss Wainwright, a lovely young lady, was also to be noted for her vocal talents; she had been tutored by the famous Doctor Thomas Arne, London's renowned voice teacher and composer. The temperamental Henrietta Osborne was also to make singing performances, but she was more accomplished as an actress and dancer and possessed of a figure that made her a favorite among the males in the audience. Stephen Woolls, another student of Doctor Arne, was more singer than actor. The dandy, Thomas Wall, although musically inclined, was more an actor-lecturer. William Verling, restless and even more temperamental than Henrietta Osborne, was consumed with overwhelming ambition and became restive when forced to share the center of the stage with anyone. To display this new talent, Douglass had acquired four new playscripts, two comedies, *The Way to Keep Him* and *The School for Lovers*, and two musical pieces, *Love in a Village* and *The Oracle*, in addition to one very entertaining and amusing lecture. Sustained by his new scenery, new plays, and new players, David Douglass was now in a position to offer the best theatrical fare yet seen in the American colonies.

While the theater was being readied for occupancy, some of the actors applied their artistry to related areas. Thomas Wall offered to teach the "Guittar" at bargain rates, while the Misses Hallam and Wainwright appeared in a concert with Peter Valton, the organist of St. Philip's Church.

The other members of the company did not return to Charleston, perhaps because of commitments made in the islands, or perhaps they preferred the safety of a less turbulent atmosphere until the eruptions resulting from the passage of the Stamp Act had run their course. Bolstering his little group with Mr. Emmett, a fill-in from the year before, Douglass opened the theater on a cold January 17, 1766, with *The Distrest Mother*, followed by *Douglas* and *Love in a Village*. Mrs. Osborne had the first benefit, on February 27, selecting for her night *The Constant Couple* and *The Mock Doctor*. The juvenile lead of Sir Harry Wildair in *The Constant Couple* was well suited for a breeches part, and Mrs. Osborne took this occasion to display her contours in male clothing, a practice that was to bring her popularity in the colonies. In addition, Miss Wainwright was Henrietta Osborne's partner in a minuet and also sang "Hapless Lovers Who Sigh in Vain." The gay evening was brought to a close with Mrs. Osborne's recitation of the humorous epilogue, "The Picture of a Playhouse, or, Bucks Have at Ye All," the first recorded instance of this popular monologue having been delivered in the colonies.

On March 4, "A Subscriber" praised Mrs. Douglass's selection of the tragedy, *The Gamester*, for her benefit, and incidentally noted, in rambling syntax, the growing popularity of Nancy

Hallam: "If Miss Hallam in *Cinthia*, which I presume is the character she will perform, does not discover a Greater force of Genius, that the Audience hitherto, notwithstanding the applause she has received, have imagined her to possess." Fortunately, this letter was submitted in time to be inserted above the advertisement announcing the play. It may well have been composed by the clever Douglass.

The makeshift company with the abbreviated cast continued in Charleston throughout the spring, heavy rains sometimes forcing postponement of a scheduled play. The productions were liberally sprinkled with additional entertainments, possibly an expedient designed to shift the attention of the audience from the abridged casts. There was singing by Stephen Woolls, Miss Wainwright, and Miss Hallam, while Henrietta Osborne appeared in hornpipes, "The Statue's Dance" and the simpler dances, made sensuous by her appearance in male or equally revealing clothing. William Verling played almost all of the male leads, with Douglass in the chief supporting roles.

Arthur Murphy's comedy, *The Way to Keep Him*, was presented for the first time in America as William Verling's benefit on March 20. He let it be known that he was a Mason, and the brethren rallied to his support. The Grand Master ordered all the lodges in town, together with all transient members of the fraternity, to march to the theater in procession. Douglass, who customarily recited the special prologue on such occasions, retired in favor of Verling, who appeared "in the Character of a Master Mason."

In a like manner, Miss Hallam's benefit on April 3 saw the first American performance of William Whitehead's *The School for Lovers*, advertised as "Positively the Last Night this Season." Local talent was featured in the added attraction upon this occasion; one extra entertainment was billed as "an Ode set to Musick, called 'Gratitude and Love' Written by a Gentleman in the Province. The Musick composed by Mr. Valton." Despite the finality in the announcement of Miss Hallam's benefit, *Cato* was played on April 16, 1766, as a benefit for the poor, the first advertised charity performance given in Charleston.

For some reason, there was discontent among Douglass' recruits. Thomas Wall announced his intention of remaining in Charleston to teach the guitar, and Henrietta Osborne published a notice calling upon her creditors to present their bills for payment, as she was to "immediately depart this Province for Europe." William Verling disappeared from the stage at this time but made occasional, though significant, reappearances in early American theatrical history.

Although the unhappy state among his key personnel brought a cessation of play acting, Douglass still entertained in the theater by giving George Alexander Stevens' *Lecture on Heads*. It would seem that this was a pirated version of this rather popular lecture, for it was not published in London until the following year. Quite possibly, he had secured a script from some unscrupulous actor in London or had heard the lecture and memorized the words, a practice not uncommon at the time.

On May 6, the manager of the American Company advertised for those "who have Demands on him to come and receive their Payment," but it was sometime after June 1 that he finally left Charleston.[7] Before he sailed for the northern colonies, Douglass was able to persuade Thomas Wall to renounce his intention of remaining in Charleston. After their departure, the theater was silent except for such occasions as Mr. Pike's annual ball.

· VIII ·

QUAKERS, PLAYS, AND PLAYERS

(New York and Philadelphia, 1766-1767)

As Douglass played through the South, the theater in New York had for the most part remained closed. In April, 1764, the Chapel Street playhouse had been advertised for rent, the building described as "very convenient for a Store." Whether it was ever put to such use is not known, but it was not until early 1765 that it was again employed for the purpose for which it had been erected.

Upon this occasion, the actors appearing upon the stage of the Chapel Street Theatre were members of a make-shift organization under the direction of Mr. Tomlinson, who advertised his troupe as "a Company of young Gentlemen." Tomlinson, who had played with Douglass until recently, may have been sent from Charleston by the manager to await the return of the remainder of the company from the islands. Rather than mark time, Tomlinson and his wife Anna gathered a group of young theatrical aspirants and opened the playhouse. In late February and early March of 1765, the group had acted a program of

The Fair Penitent and *The Lying Valet* twice—each occasion advertised as the "Benefit of Mr. Tomlinson." *The London Merchant, or The History of George Barnwell* was played as a benefit for "the Prisoners in the New Gaol." After this brief appearance, these ambitious thespians disappeared for a year, possibly to avoid the threat of violence that hung in the air.

This was a period of flaring tempers and angry words, of a people who insisted that their liberties had been trifled with in that obnoxious bit of legislation termed the Stamp Act. Out of wrathful words came stubborn action. Non-importation agreements tied up ships in the harbor, and idle sailors thickened the mobs roving the streets of New York. Those who dared express approval of the act were forced to make public apologies and were toasted in the taverns with the hope that they might be exposed to "a perpetual Itching without Benefit of Scratching." The very loose and semi-patriotic organization calling themselves "the Sons of Liberty" went as far as to place the theater under their surveillance in the spring of 1766. A contemporary observer reported, "A grand meeting of the Sons of Liberty [was held] to Settle matters of the moment, amongst the many whether they shall admit the strollers, arrived here to act, tho the General [Gage] has given them Permission." Subsequent events imply the group arrived at a negative decision.

These "strollers" were the Tomlinson troupe, perhaps returning from a tour of the rural areas to escape the violence of the city. They followed the same pattern of production as on their previous visit. If they were aware of the disapproval of the Sons of Liberty, they showed no indication of it, even though that group had publicly burned a number of playbills at the same time they fired a stack of stamps, " 'tis said found in the Streets ... all to prevent their Spirits to flag." Five days later, on April 9, 1766, Tomlinson's group acted Farquhar's *Twin Rivals* and offered to repeat the comedy on May 5. It seemed that all antagonisms towards the players were on the wane, "As the Packet is arrived, and has been the Messenger of good News relative to Repeal, it is hoped that the Public has no Objection to the above Performance." It was also considered politic to feature "a Song in Praise of Liberty."

Passions fundamentally grounded in anger are not easily slaked. Mobs still roamed the streets of New York, now venting their restlessness in premature celebration rather than denunciations. Still, there were complaints that the playhouse should not be allowed to reopen at a time when money was so badly needed for the payment of debts. Even more important was the information in letters from London that repeal was not yet a fact, that the repealing act had passed only two readings in the House of Commons, possibly delayed because of General Gage's letter detailing the unwillingness of the New York Assembly to billet troops in compliance with the Quartering Act. Agitation immediately burst forth again as the "Bells were immediately silenced and a great discontent ensued owing to their having been so premature in their rejoicings &c. &c."

Nevertheless, Tomlinson felt secure enough to carry through his announced intention of presenting *The Twin Rivals* on May 5. That day, a rumor spread that those who attended the playhouse that evening "would meet with some Disturbance from the Multitude." This whisper intimidated some, and a spring rain kept others of the would-be audience at home. More adventurous souls disregarded the warning as small talk and went to the theater as planned. Midway through the first act, the flame of a single candle flickered as a tiny signal in the darkness outside the playhouse. There was a loud "Huzza" from the mob as they burst through the doors into the pit, and they "began picking of pockets, stealing watches, throwing Brick Bats, sticks and Bottles and Glasses." A screaming and thoroughly frightened audience pushed its way into the street while others, their clothes almost stripped from their bodies, leaped from open windows. Miraculously, there was only "One boy Killed and many people hurt in this licentious affair." Once the spectators had cleared the building, the mob methodically began to pull down the theater, carrying away the lumber to the Common, shouting "Liberty! Liberty!" all the while. That night, between ten and eleven o'clock, a great bonfire blazed—the funeral pyre of the Chapel Street Theatre.[1]

This incident, plus the reports of similar sentiments in other colonies, was enough to convince Douglass that his company should remain in the West Indies until the fall, which would also allow him time to construct a new theater in Philadelphia. He held no hope of returning to New York until tempers in that city had subsided.

Philadelphia, with all its religious factions, was, indeed, a city of paradoxes. There were cries to outlaw the drama, yet no voices were raised in objection to the masthead of William Bradford's *Pennsylvania Journal* which featured a bare-breasted female to distract the eye of the reader from the printed word. There had been no protests in 1763 when a benefit had been performed in London's Drury Lane to raise funds for the colleges in Philadelphia and New York. In the latter instance, however, there had been an ocean between, and the selection had been *The Cure of Saul*, "A Sacred Ode." Publisher Andrew Steuart had received no criticism when he reprinted current favorites of the London stage, for which he found a steady sale.

But when it was learned that Douglass' "dangerous School of Vice" was returning to the city, many were the cries raised in obloquy. "The Censor" led off the attack with a condemnation of the drama in general. Tragedy, he flayed as the vehicle by which "Vices are brought into Credit," and as for comedies: "I can scarcely speak of them with any Temper. Under the plausible Pretense of making a Man acquainted with the World, Cursing, Swearing, Duelling, Whoring, Drinking, &c. are introduced, and seldom in such a Manner as to excite Horror in the Mind, but are passed off with a Laugh." [2] Thus it was that the righteous prepared to do battle with the pagan disciples of Thespis, a crusade that was continued even after their customary petitions to the governor had failed. Verily, the devout of Philadelphia were made of stern and obstinate clay.

The new theater serving as the target for these literary outbursts was located just south of the city on Cedar Street in Southwark, a swelling suburb "inhabited by people of circumstances." Not only was this reputed to be the best theater yet constructed in the American colonies, it was the first designed with an eye to permanence. The exterior of the theater was built of a first floor of crude brick construction, supporting a frame structure that was painted the dull red so favored by eighteenth-century theater managers. The roof line was broken by a bell-shaped cupola, added as an aid to ventilation. Construction costs of this building of ninety-five by fifty feet had totalled approximately £360. That the building was more functional than decorative is borne out in a description of the interior of the Southwark Theatre in 1786: "The building, compared with new houses, was an ugly ill-conceived affair outside and inside. The stage was lighted by plain oil lamps without glasses. The view from the boxes was intercepted by large square wooden pillars supporting the upper tier and roof. It was contended by many, at the time, that the front bench in the gallery was the best seat for a fair view of the stage." [3]

The "new Theatre in Southwark" opened on November 12, 1766, with *The Provok'd Husband* and *Thomas and Sally*, with the playbills emphasizing that the players were now the "American Company of Comedians." Because of the large crowd expected on opening night, "Ladies and gentlemen will please to send their servants to keep their places in the Boxes, at 4 o'Clock." Such precautions, however, were not unique, for box seats were never reserved for any particular performance, and purchasers of theater tickets were free to use them for any play that struck their fancy. The *dramatis personae* in the playbills now listed the Douglasses, the Owen Morrisses, the Allyns, Lewis Hallam, Thomas Wall, Stephen Woolls, Margaret Cheer, Miss Wainwright, Nancy Hallam, and once again, the Dowthaitts. The Tomlinsons of the ill-fated New York venture had now joined Douglass, as had a Mr. Mathews who specialized in the dance. Mrs. Douglass was beginning to relinquish more of her feminine leads to Margaret Cheer and had wisely begun to assume the more matronly roles that a middle-aged figure demanded.

There were no other appreciable changes in the cast until after the New Year. On January 2, 1767, "a young Gentleman" played Moneses in *Tamerlane* and, a week later, reappeared as Horatio in *Hamlet*. This was, in effect, the tryout of a young actor who was shortly to be listed in the casts as Mr. Graville and whose real name was Samuel Greville. This same presentation of *Hamlet* also marked the first appearances of Mrs.

Eighteenth-Century "Rope Dancing" as Performed in London's
Theatre Royal in Covent Garden
Courtesy of Harvard Theatre Collection

Of the Worſhipful the MAYOR of WILLIAMSBURG

(For the BENEFIT of Mrs. PARKER)

At the old THEATRE, near the CAPITOL,

By the VIRGINIA COMPANY of COMEDIANS, on FRIDAY the 3d of JUNE,
will be preſented

The Beggar's Opera.

Captain *Macheath*, by Mr. VERLING.

(Being his firſt Appearance in that Character)

Mr. PEACHUM,		Mr. CHARLTON.
LOCKIT,		Mr. FARRELL.
MAT of the MINT,		Mr. PARKER.
NIMMING NED,	by	Mr. WALKER.
Crook Fingered JACK,		Mr. BROMADGE.
BEN BUDGE,		Mr. MALLORY.
FILCH,		Mr. GODWIN.

Mrs. PEACHUM, and LUCY LOCKIT, by Mrs. OSBORNE.

JENNY DIVER,		Miſs DOWTHAITT.
Mrs. COAXER,	by	Miſs YAPP.
Mrs. SLAMMEKIN,		Mrs. DOWTHAITT.
MOLL BRAZEN,		Mr. WALKER.

Mrs. DIANA TRAPES, by Mr. PARKER.

Miſs *Polly Peachum*, by Mrs. PARKER.

After the Opera Mr. GODWIN *will perform the DANCE called*
The DRUNKEN PEASANT.

PEASANT,	by	Mr. GODWIN.
CLOWN,		Mr. PARKER.

To which will be added a FARCE, called

The ANATOMIST,

O R

Sham Doctor.

Le MEDICIN (the French Doctor) by Mr. GODWIN.

Old GERALD,		Mr. PARKER.
Young GERALD,		Mr. CHARLTON.
CRISPIN,	by	Mr. VERLING.
MARTIN,		Mr. FARRELL.
SIMON BURLEY,		Mr. WALKER.
ANGELICA,		Miſs YAPP,
DOCTOR's WIFE,	by	Mrs. DOWTHAITT.
WAITING WOMAN,		Miſs DOWTHAITT.

BEATRICE, by Mrs. PARKER.

The MUSICK of the OPERA will be conducted by Mr. PELHAM,
and others.

Playbill of the New American Company, June 3, 1768
Courtesy of Colonial Williamsburg, Inc.

Thomas Wall and a Mr. Platt, both of whom were destined to play minor roles. There was a new dancer to aid Mr. Mathews, a young lad by the name of James Verling Godwin. Godwin had received instruction in theatrical dancing from John Baptist Tioli, late of London, who had been operating a dancing school in Philadelphia for over a year.

A young and wide-eyed college student, "Neddie" Burd, described the play and actors for his sister with an air of incredulity: "Uncle J. C. made me a present of a Ticket to see the Play. Mr. Hallam is the best Actor according to the common Opinion, but I am fonder of Mr. Allyn. Miss Cheer & Miss Wainwright are the best Actresses; the latter is the best Woman Singer & Mr. Woolls is their excellent Man Singer. James Godwin who used to be Mr. Tioli's dancing Boy dances & acts upon the Stage. They say he gets £4 per Week. A young gentleman by Name Mr. Gravel has commenced an Actor on Account of his Debts, for He is accounted an extravagant Young Fellow. He was of a good Family in South Carolina. And was sent to Prince Town College with a view of qualifying him for the Gown—But disliking the strict Rules of that Seminary He came to our College, & shortly after he left it too & commenced a Student of the Law under Mr. Galloway, but his Mother having married again, She refused to supply his Extravagance upon which he is now taken to the Stage for his Support, notwithstanding the kind Offers of Mrs. Galloway to maintain him till he is settled in the World, if he will quit his Designs. He is a very handsome young Fellow & has a clear Voice—He has acted twice but has no action which is the very Soul of good Playing. The People in general here rather pity than condemn him: this is the Consequence of loose Morals & may serve him as a Lesson to others."

Such was the debut of Samuel Greville who, assuming that Godwin had come to the colonies as an apprentice to Tioli, was the first known native American to become a professional actor, unless, of course, one wishes to dignify the efforts of the members of the Murray-Kean Company.

In early January, Douglass made one mistake for which he was forced to make restitution. Because of a small house, he allowed a less popular play to be substituted for the one advertised, for which he was so roundly criticized that he hastened to publish a public apology in the local press to appease the lust for authority inherent in every audience.

The players could ill afford to antagonize any friend of the theater in Philadelphia, and no apology would ever be able to placate the religious faction, whose frowns were directed not only towards his "Synagogue of Satan" but any other form of entertainment. To his brother-in-law the fun-loving Alexander Mackrabie complained, "I am quite tired of plodding for ever in this confounded Quaker Town. Plague take it!" He then went on to explain the extremes to which he was forced to go to savor the pleasures of youth: "Seven Sleighs with two Ladies and two men in each, preceded by Fidlers on horseback set out together upon a snow of about a foot deep on the Roads, to the Public-House a few Miles from Town, where we danced, sung, and romped and eat and drunk and kicked away care from Morning till Night, and finished our Frolic in two or three Side-boxes at the Play."

Not all who went to the Philadelphia theater found complete satisfaction. Drama was beginning to carve its niche in American culture and becoming subject to thoughtful criticism by those who considered themselves competent judges of things dramatic. One such, signing himself "Critic," acknowledged Lewis Hallam to be "genteel in his Person and Action" but censured his delivery: "There is much Fault to be found with Mr. Hallam's Method of articulating. He has begun, and continues, in a bad Habit of speaking; he seems to suck in, or at least not to utter the first Letters of the Words he speaks. . . . There is no necessity of destroying the least articulate Beauty of Language, thro' Fury, Eagerness or Passion." Such strictures neither disturbed nor dampened the ambition of Hallam. At twenty-five years of age he was the top actor in America, playing everything from the romantic Romeo to the "Crouchback," Richard III. Fortunately, for the young actor, eighteenth-century dramatic practices demanded no adherence to type. In Tate's altered version of *King Lear and His Three Daughters*, the beardless Hallam played the white-haired Lear, while Douglass, who was well past forty, portrayed the youthful Edgar.[4]

Criticism in Philadelphia, however, was never limited to acting techniques. Although the season of 1767-68 might possibly be termed the most brilliant of the entire colonial period, Douglass and his actors were constantly harassed by the carpings of religious zealots possessed of a literary flair. Many evenings of reflection were spent by the fireside during the colder months, and the conclusions reached and the vehement protests, written with pens dipped in gall, appeared in all three Philadelphia newspapers during the winter. The theater was compared with "Tippling Houses" and referred to as "that School of Debauchery among us." "A Friend to All Mankind" cried despairingly, "Good God! to what depth of insensibility are these unhappy people fallen!" "Philadelphus" reprinted a series of anti-theatrical essays by the English divine, William Jay, in the *Chronicle* which likened the playhouse to image worship and damned it as ribald and profane. "Eugenio" insisted that not even the sublime poetry of Shakespeare could atone for low buffoonery, while the "still voice of Religion is drowned amid the transport of passion." Even the stately *Cato* felt his sting because of its supposed countenance of suicide. "Altera Pars" not only ridiculed the players but accused patrons of the theater of attending this temple of sin only to witness their own wickedness reflected upon the stage in "wild rant, immodest passions, and profane language." His conclusion bore the stamp of dogma in the declaration "The Stage never had one innocent play."

For the first time, proponents of the theater marshaled their erudition in opposition to the more unworldly element. "Z" composed a ringing denial of any and all accusations leveled at the players and defended the character of the actresses with the assertion, "Miss Cheer has never honoured me with a dish of tea, nor have I received from Miss Wainwright *any more important favour.*" "A Free Thinker" accused "Philadelphus" of being "one of the hypochondriac gloomy crew" and, with tongue in cheek, cited as one of the advantages to be gained from the drama: "The art of seducing a maid is perhaps no other way to be gained than by the theatre." "A. B." loosed his barbs in a camouflage of compassion with "O you poor, blind, hard-hearted people, to condemn others because they do not see as you do. There are many stumbling blocks in the road of life, consider the consequences, especially if you say the Lord's Prayer." Bulwarked with this public support, Douglass, for the first time, did not offer apologetic pleadings, nor did he attempt to placate the religious faction. He entered into the dispute by publishing his own pungent comments. Dusting off an essay written in New York some five years earlier, he assured his readers that he had "with all the composure imaginable over-looked the torrent of incomprehensible abuse which has been of late, so plentifully bestowed upon the theatre." He was convinced that his persecutors had no knowledge of the "nature and tendency" of the drama and summed up his basic argument in persuasive disputation: "Has the stage been abused? So has the Pulpit.... But ought a good Clergyman to suffer on this account? By no means." A mild endorsement from an Anglican ecclesiastic was received when the Reverend William Smith published his *True Pleasure, Cheerfulness, and Happiness... With Some Remarks on the Theatre, Addressed to a Young Lady in Philadelphia*. No doubt, there was some favorable comment when Mr. Woolls and the Misses Wainwright and Hallam appeared in a concert held in the Second Street Academy for the benefit of the poor. At least, it was a bid for respectability.

Despite strong support, Douglass made some concessions to the mores and sentiments of the Quakers and Presbyterians. When Congreve's *Love for Love, With the Humours of Ben, the Sailor*, was played on February 20, the manager was careful to announce: "Mr. Congreve's Comedies are allowed to abound with genuine wit & a true Humour; but, in compliance with the licentious Taste of the Times in which they were written, the Author has in some places given the Rein to the wanton Muse, and deviated from those Rules a more refined Age, and chaste Stage require; *The Reviver* of this Play, has taken the Freedom to crop such Luxuriances, and expunge every Passage that might be offensive either to Decency or good Manners." [5]

Other concessions were made by Douglass to his audiences to satisfy the continuing demand for the light and the lyrical. *Romeo and Juliet* was no longer just a romantic tragedy of young love. In addition to the now familiar "funeral Procession of Juliet, to the Monument of the Capulets; and a solemn Dirge," the play was now sprinkled with songs and incidental dances. The sprightly Margaret Cheer also made a more believable Juliet than the queenly Mrs. Douglass.

With the expansion of his repertoire, and despite the additional players in his company, Douglass was sometimes forced to call upon non-acting personnel to take a turn upon the stage. Mr. Broadbelt, who seems to have been happiest when engaged in administrative duties, was occasionally called in to supplement the regular cast. A Mr. Appleby also appears to have been a non-acting employee of the company who was sometimes pressed into temporary service as a player.

Douglass constantly strove for new effects and new techniques. Both Godwin and Mathews continued to specialize in dancing roles, both sometimes appearing on the same bill. Godwin also was cast in several supporting roles. Creative ingenuity was employed in the development of new visual impressions. On April 2, when *The Gamester* was played, the advertisements carried the boast that, in addition to the new scenery that Douglass had brought from London, "The Machinery, Deceptions, Decorations," for the accompanying Harlequin were entirely new.

On April 13, 1767, there was the announcement that "a new Comic Opera, called, The DISAPPOINTMENT: OR, THE FORCE OF CREDULITY," would be acted on April 20. This marked the first occasion that a play written by a native American had been advertised as a production of a professional theatrical company. The same issue of the *Chronicle* also carried a notice that the play had been published and could be purchased locally. The author was listed as Andrew Barton, a pseudonym adopted by twenty-year-old Thomas Forrest of Germantown. Written as a comic satire, *The Disappointment* was a vigorous and good-natured, but coarse, two act critique of contemporary manners. Its slender plot revolved around a hunt for Blackbeard's treasure, presumably buried near Cooper's Point on the Delaware River. With the character "Raccoon," Forrest introduced the first Negro character in American drama and his was the first attempt to adapt Negro dialect to the stage. The libretto contained eighteen songs, or "Airs," but no music was furnished. The words were to be accompanied by popular tunes of the day: for instance, it was directed that "Air IV" be sung to the music of the rollicking "Yankee Doodle." Richard Swan, Philadelphia's foremost hatter, and printer Anthony Armbruster, the primary butts of the satire, were apparently persons of considerable influence, for they were able to block the presentation of the play. Although John McPherson observed that the printed version had been generally well received and that its readers "found no fault in it," the play was cancelled when Swan "swore that it might begin in a Comedy, but that he would make it end in a Tragedy." Three days after the original announcement, the newspapers carried a notice of the substitution of *The Mourning Bride* with the terse explanation: "The DISAPPOINTMENT, that was advertised for Monday, as it contains personal reflections, is unfit for the Stage."

Douglass, having whetted the appetites of local playgoers for a native drama, was quick to oblige, advertising *The Prince of Parthia*, "written by the late ingenious Mr. Thomas Godfrey of this city," to be played on the night of April 24. Godfrey, son of the original inventor of the navigational instrument that was to become known as Hadley's quadrant, had been praised by one of his contemporaries as "one of the first Sons of the Muses on this Side of the Atlantic." The youthful playwright had died in Wilmington, North Carolina, August 1, 1763, leaving as his literary legacy several poems and the manuscript of *The Prince of Parthia*, which had been published in 1765. The scene was laid in Parthia sometime around the beginning of the Christian era, and the plot concerned itself with events supposedly drawn from history, dealing only in grand passions and noble sentiments expressed in dialogue of soaring turgidity. Certainly, there was nothing in this classical script to offend either morals or virtue. The unpopularity of the play is attested by the fact that it was never again acted by the American Company.

Not only did Douglass exercise his versatility in coping with problems that involved public relations, but upon occasion he was forced to resort to adroitness in dealing with the minor crises constantly arising within the ranks of the troupe. When the cast for *Cymbeline* called for more male actors than were available, he dressed the aging Mrs. Harman in breeches to play the part of Pissanio. When Thomas Wall lost his chest containing a thousand personal benefit tickets, Douglass had new ones printed featuring the masonic emblem as a familiar symbol easily recognized by the doorkeepers. To temper the hot June nights, the theater was "properly aired," and, shortly afterwards, it was announced there had been "some Alterations made in the House, in order to render it Cool." Spermaceti candles, usually reserved for the stage, were substituted for those of tallow in the auditorium, thereby reducing the irritants to the audience of smoke and hot, dripping wax. As always, spring rains occasionally forced postponement of scheduled plays, especially on benefit nights when it was to the advantage of the actor to play to full houses.

Indecision marked the closing of the Southwark playhouse. On June 29, *Cymbeline* was advertised as "Positively" the last play of the season. On July 2, the same emphatic adjective was used to announce a benefit for Mr. Broadbelt, who had earlier renounced a benefit because of the heat and expenses but now had "altered his Resolution." The season finally dragged to an end on July 6 when *The Constant Couple* was played as a benefit for Mrs. Wall, who "by the Advice of her Friends, and as the Weather is more favourable than usual at this Season of the Year, has ventured to take a Benefit, which she had before declined." [6]

The players were idle during the remaining summer months. Douglass traveled to New York to make the necessary arrangements for the erection of a new theater, as well as to sound out the opposition against the players. There was still a strong religious current running through the city, and the best-selling book in New York (now in its sixth edition) was *A Sure Guide to Hell, by Beelzebub.* On the other hand, there ware favorable indications. A Mr. Bayly and a Mr. Tea had, throughout the spring, entertained the town with plays performed by their puppets or "artificial comedians." Their theater had been at "the sign of the Orange-Tree, on Golden Hill," and they had mimicked theater practices to the extent of giving a performance for the benefit of the prisoners in the city jail. The two promoters had contributed their personal talents by appearing in dances and harlequinades. On May 18, they had presented a "live" performance of *The Orphan* with a cast composed of "Gentlemen, and Ladies, for their Amusement." Adequate scenery, decorations, and "A good Band of Musick" were featured in the notice.

This hybrid company had discontinued operations when Douglass arrived in New York. Wisely, he issued no public statements relative to the theater. Not only was the dismantling of the Chapel Street Theatre still green in his memory, but parliamentary reaction to the refusal of the New York Assembly to quarter British troops had so incited the Liberty Boys that scarce a night passed that they were not burning effigies or marching through the streets crying "Pitt and Liberty." Although much of the open defiance had died with the arrival of troops, there was still a seething undercurrent that Douglass did not wish to disturb. To defray expenses, Douglass rented "Mr. Burn's Assembly Room" as early as July 17 and initiated a lecture series featuring Stevens' *Lecture on Heads* each Tuesday and Thursday "for the short Time he has to stay in Town." Stephen Woolls supported these programs with popular vocal selections. On July 31, Douglass felt compelled to lower the price of admission by one half, possibly because of the recent American publication of Stevens' celebrated dissertation. On August 6, he gave his last lecture in New York, and he and Woolls returned to Philadelphia.[7]

Sometime in the past, the services of a bearded young Irish giant had been contracted for. Twenty-one-year-old John Henry, after making a rather pathetic debut in London's Drury Lane, had fled to Jamaica, where audiences were not so demanding. In the West Indies, he had made the acquaintance of a former singer who had been billed as Miss Clark of Covent Garden but was now using her married name, Mrs. Storer. She was still a handsome woman, although the mother of four daughters—Helen, Ann, Fanny, and Maria. John Henry seems to have considered that these girls had been brought into the world for his special benefit. Of the four, only Fanny managed to elude the

clutches of the young actor, who "easily wins the laurels as the
first incautious amorist of the American stage, although be it
said to his credit, he restricted his activities (so far as we know
and that was far enough) to the Storer girls."

In Jamaica, Henry had married the eldest of the girls, Helen,
who had borne him two children. The entire family, including
Mrs. Storer and the other three daughters, had sailed for America in the brig *Dolphin*. The voyage was uneventful until, within
sight of the American mainland, the vessel burst into flames as
a result of an accident in the hold. With her babies trapped in
the cabin, Helen Henry threw herself into the holocaust in a
futile effort to save them and perished in the flames. Henry and
the rest of the family managed to reach shore safely. Leaving his
mother-in-law and two daughters to mourn their loss, Henry,
accompanied by Ann Storer, continued his journey to Philadelphia to join Douglass.[8]

Douglass had already opened the Southwark Theatre, but only
to deliver the *Lecture on Heads*, and had been joined by Lewis
Hallam who recited "the Dissertation of the Hearts of a British
Sailor, and his Agent for Prize-Money." An orchestra accompanied Stephen Woolls, Miss Wainwright, and Miss Hallam in
musical interludes during intermissions.

The company opened in Philadelphia for a short fall season,
allowing time for the construction of the new theater in New
York and taking advantage of the large crowds in Philadelphia
at this time. The first play was *The Roman Father* on October 9.
The prospect of even an abridged season delighted Alexander
Mackrabie, who happily reported, "We have Races here next
week, and a Review, and Plays. This is the busiest Season in
Philadelphia."

Both John Henry and Ann Storer made their debuts in the
colonies in *The Roman Father*, with each billed as "from the
Theatre in Jamaica." A Mr. Roberts also began the first of many
appearances in minor roles, but except for these three new members, the cast was essentially the same as in the spring. Douglass
continued to emphasize the spectacular; the bills and advertisements stressed "a Procession of Roman Youths and Virgins,
with an Ovation."

Early in November, Douglass began issuing periodic warnings that the theater would soon be closed for some time, and those in possession of tickets were urged to use them as quickly as possible. On November 19, 1767, the first performance of George Colman's and David Garrick's new play (1766) *The Clandestine Marriage* was staged, with a Mr. Malone—no doubt the Patrick Malone of the old Hallam Company—in the part of Traverse. This play was repeated one week later as the concluding performance of the Philadelphia season, with Mrs. Douglass having the final word in "A Farewell Epilogue to the Ladies."

No season, however short, was allowed to slip by unnoticed by the persistent Quakers and Presbyterians. They presented their usual petitions to the governor with so many signatures that "Neddie" Burd prophesied to his sister: "The Players must soon leave off here & will not be again permitted to act these two Years. They are Going to New York but it is believed that the Opposition will be strong enough to prevent their acting There." [9]

Once again, the American Company found itself in that now familiar predicament—caught between two fires.

· IX ·

INDIANS, ROYALTY,
AND FIREWORKS

(New York and Philadelphia, 1767-1770)

Upon their return to New York, in December, 1767, the players were pleasantly surprised when they encountered only token resistance from opponents of the drama in that community. The new theater had been completed. Located on the north side of John Street, it was of rough frame construction, the exterior painted the usual dull red. The building itself was set back some sixty feet from the street, and a crude covered passageway protected the carriage trade in inclement weather. Inside, the dressing rooms and green room were located beneath an unusually large stage. The auditorium contained the usual pit and gallery, but there was a double tier of boxes, enough seats so that a capacity house yielded receipts equivalent to $800.

Traveling overland from Philadelphia, the company encountered real-life tragedy. An account appeared in the *Mercury:* "one of the Stage Waggons, crossing the Ferry at kill van Kull, in a scow, some of the passengers seated themselves in the Waggon; but on approaching the shore the Waggon was by some means overturn'd into the River, by which accident two women (Mrs. Morris, belonging to the Play-House and her maid) were drown'd." [1]

Owen Morris was in mourning when the new John Street Theatre opened with *The Beaux' Stratagem* on December 7, 1767, and on this occasion, his customary part of "Scrub" was played by Thomas Wall. But one week was enough to mourn a wife, even one who was a beautiful and gifted actress, and when *Richard III* was played on December 14, Morris appeared as usual. This was one of the gala nights of the year, if not one of the most festive in the entire period of the colonial theater. Only a short while before, a group of Cherokee Indians, led by the noted Attakullakulla, or "Little Carpenter," had arrived from South Carolina seeking General Thomas Gage's assistance in mediating a peace treaty between their tribes and the Six Nations of the Iroquois. They were soon to leave for Albany, to participate in negotiations conducted by Sir William Johnson. When they heard there was a playhouse in town and expressed a desire to see a play, Gage ordered box seats for them. Douglass selected his program with care, realizing that upon this occasion, actions would speak louder than words. The ebullient *Richard III* was the primary attraction, followed by a pantomime ballet called *Harlequin's Vagaries*, the latter starring Lewis Hallam, Owen Morris, and Margaret Cheer. Douglass tested his ingenuity in exploiting the visit of the Indians; he billed the play as a command performance and referred to the visiting chieftain not only by his more familiar names but also as "The Great Warrior of Estator" and "The Raven King."

This shrewd advertising was effective. On the night of the play, "a great Concourse of People" tried to push their way into the building; the doorkeepers were forced to turn many away, as all available seats were quickly taken. A writer for the *New York Journal* seems to have paid more attention to the reactions of the savages than the action on the stage: "The Indians regarded the Play (which was *King Richard III*), with Seriousness and Attention, but as it cannot be supposed that they were sufficiently acquainted with the Language to understand the

Plot and Design, and enter into the Spirit of the Author, their Countenances and Behaviour were rather expressive of Surprise and Curiosity, than any other Passions. Some of them were much surprised and diverted at the Tricks of HARLEQUIN."

It seems that the music for this production was furnished by William Hulett, the dancer with the old Hallam Company, who now operated a music school in New York. Certainly, he was well acquainted with the new members of the company, for on December 3, he was joined by Stephen Woolls and Nancy Hallam at his benefit in Burns' Assembly Room, which was followed by a ball.[2]

Near capacity houses were not unusual after the departure of the Cherokees. But so many came to the theater in carriages that Douglass, in his newspaper advertisements, suggested a route to be followed through the streets in the vicinity of the playhouse, in effect, an early introduction of one-way streets. The interest by the gentry may have been stimulated by Governor Sir Henry Moore, who displayed the same interest in the New York theater that he had in the Jamaica playhouse. Not only had he readily granted the necessary permission to perform, but one production of *The Busy Body* was "By Command of Lady Moore." The three Masonic Lodges in New York also honored the Masons among the actors by requesting a performance of *Cymbeline*.

The appearance of unbridled gaiety and frivolity was only surface deep. The bitterness that had subsided with the repeal of the Stamp Act now burst into the open again with the passage of the Townshend Duties. Every issue of each newspaper urged the practice of frugality, and heavy attendance at the theater drew the fire of several commentators. Although Douglass, on December 30, staged the *Mourning Bride* "for the Benefit of the Debtors, in the New City-hall," one writer, hiding under the pseudonym of "Philander," constantly abused the playhouse and its tenants. He admittedly doubted the authenticity of the rumor that as much as £50 had been offered to reserve a box for the season, but that did not prevent him from publishing the whisper. To him, it appeared "that people were grown mad after plays," resulting in "a spirit of dissipation and extravagance." "R. S.," allying himself with "Philander," offered pungent commentaries on the customs of the players: "Some pretend that good moral instructions are to be learned at a play. I wish they would give us a list of these plays, for our actors don't seem to hit upon them; I wonder what father would recommend any comedy that has yet been acted, to his daughter for instruction or imitation; intrigue, cuckoldom, and imposing on parents and guardians are the main plots." [3]

It was a powerful argument, but after Philadelphia these attacks seemed comparatively mild, and Douglass and his American Company appear not to have been irritated. Few theatergoers took these critics seriously, and the destructive and often violent moods of the Stamp Act mobs were no longer so much in evidence.

There were some changes in the cast. On January 7, 1768, when *The Gamester* and *Catherine and Petruchio* (Garrick's version of *The Taming of the Shrew*) were played, Maria Storer made her first appearance by singing at the conclusion of the play. On January 28, a Mr. Raworth joined the company to play minor roles; by the infrequency of his appearances, he must have been one of the non-acting employees of the troupe. On March 24, Fanny Storer appeared for the first time. Mr. Allyn seems to have dropped into that obscurity from which he came.

At this time, the size and ability of the American Company were such that Douglass could stage any play presented by Covent Garden or Drury Lane in London. Even so, "A Gentleman" would frequently persuade the manager to allow him to assay the lead in a popular play. He was always anonymous in the playbills, for it ran counter to the rules of gentility that his name be linked publicly with the actors. This was an English custom adopted by devotees of the theater in the colonies and, no doubt, with Douglass' endorsement, for not only did the ambitious amateur usually pay for the privilege but he also "brought a good house" of his friends.

New plays were presented to New York audiences as soon as scripts became available, and, upon occasion, old forgotten farces would be revived. One old play, new to American audiences, was performed, Dryden's *All For Love, or The World Well Lost,* a variation on the Antony-Cleopatra theme. There were also two new farces, Colman's *Polly Honeycomb* and *Neck Or Nothing*, and a comedy, Murphy's *All in the Wrong*.

Gentlemen of the city, flattering their egos in imitation of the London gentry who demonstrated their influence by requesting the performance of a particular play or farce, sometimes deluged Douglass with requests. These "Bespeaks" were tolerated by managers, for usually they meant a good house and a heavy sale of box seats. Upon occasion, when there were conflicting solicitations, Douglass would tactfully append a note to the playbills explaining: "Mr. Douglass, in the most respectful Manner, begs Leave to acquaint the Gentlemen, who did him the Honour of a Note Yesterday Morning, desiring the *Honest Yorkshireman*, might be substituted in the Room of *Catherine and Petruchio*, that he could not make the Alteration without disobliging some Gentlemen, at whose Request it was given out." [4]

In early April, the Cherokees returned from Albany, but without their leader. After successfully negotiating a treaty with the Six Nations, "Little Carpenter" returned home by way of Fort Pitt, in an effort to effect similar pacts with the Delawares and Shawnees. His tribesmen had come down the Hudson to take ship passage for South Carolina. The play, *A Wonder! A Woman Keeps a Secret!* on April 7, became a secondary attraction to these stage-struck warriors. In "Return for the friendly Reception and civilities they have received in this city," the Indians offered to perform a war dance on the stage of the John Street Theatre at the conclusion of the regular performance. Apprehensive of the natural antipathy of any colonial towards any Indian in war dress, Douglass felt it incumbent to caution the audience: "It is humbly presumed, that no part of the Audience will forget the proper Decorum so essential to all public Assemblies, particularly on this Occasion, as the Persons who have condescended to contribute to their Entertainment are of Rank and Consequence in their own Country." No untoward incident occurred, and on the following Monday, the Cherokees sailed for South Carolina.

Individual dancing was seen less in New York this season than formerly. James Godwin and Mr. Mathews had severed their relations with the American Company before the actors left

Philadelphia. Group dancing by the cast became the fashion, and there were more musical numbers. Upon one occasion, a spectacle was built around the singing of "God Save the King," with Mr. Woolls carrying the melody, supported by a chorus of all the young female singers in the troupe. The singing of this song was, doubtless, a result of Douglass' visit to England, for "God Save the King" had become a favorite theatrical song in London when George III suffered his first mental illness in 1765 and was returned to affection in the hearts of his subjects. Such extravaganzas became necessary to offset the popularity of "the two Italian Brothers from Tunis," whose fireworks displays in John Jones's Ranelagh Gardens were attracting large numbers of spectators.

By this time, it had become evident that the sprightly Margaret Cheer was by far the most popular, and perhaps the best, actress in the company. When she became ill on the eve of Nancy Hallam's benefit, Douglass was forced to substitute *Love in a Village* for *The Clandestine Marriage*, for the former was the only comedy in the repertoire in which Miss Cheer did not play an important part—and this was before the day of understudies.

As spring faded into summer, and the temperature began to climb, Douglass issued frequent assurances that precautions had been taken to keep the house cool. Heat was only one irritant. Trivial rumors, including one that Stephen Wall planned to defer his benefit, presumably for a more favorable date, were considered important enough for public denials in the newspapers. Because of the suggestion of a whispering campaign against the actors, perhaps it is just as well that the season ended on June 2, 1768, with Mrs. Douglass' benefit, *The Earl of Essex* and *Fanny the Phantom*. The company either spent the summer in New York or made brief tours into the surrounding hinterlands. The former seems to be the more likely, as Mr. Woolls and Miss Wainwright were engaged by Ranelagh Gardens to appear in concerts every Monday and Thursday evening, to be followed by the fireworks of the "two Italian Brothers."

The John Street Theatre was reopened briefly in August when Douglass and Hallam appeared in a brief lecture series on

"Heads, Coats of Arms, Wigs, Horse Jockies, Sciences, Honesty, Flattery, Ladies Head Dresses, &c. &c." Following this kaleidoscopic display of erudition, the company set out for Philadelphia.[5]

The petition submitted by the Quakers to the governor the year before had proved impotent. Nevertheless, life had been dull in Philadelphia, especially for Alexander Mackrabie, who bemoaned the simplicity of his existence: "We have no plays or public diversions of any kind; not so much as a walk for the ladies. . . ." However, life held no such dismal prospects for one of the comedians. On August 29, 1768, the *Pennsylvania Gazette* carried exciting news: "Last week was married in Maryland, the Right Hon. Lord Rosehill, to Miss Margaret Cheer, a Lady much admired for her theatrical performances." This marriage was remarkable for several reasons. In the first place, Margaret Cheer seemed to be the first actress of the American stage to capture a British title; in the second place, the marriage did not last. Upon close examination, it appears that the man the petite actress married was an impostor—Burke's *Peerage* lists the wife of Lord Rosehill as Catherine Cameron. The most plausible explanation of this discrepancy between the newspaper report and the records is that this was a marriage of convenience; or perhaps, an annulment lies gathering dust in some forgotten court ledger. Whatever the answer, Miss Cheer's possible retirement from the stage came as something of a blow to the Philadelphia theatergoers, one of whom had declared just a few months earlier: "Miss Cheer never loses the sweetest accent, or faulters in the Clearness of Expression. . . . I am not alone, when I pronounce her one of the best Players in the Empire; she appears to me, from that Ease of Behaviour, which always shines through every Action, to have been among People of Fashion, for she well fits the highest Character she every assumes."

Her admirers were not forced to mourn her retirement for long. On September 19, the *Chronicle* carried a heartening announcement: "It is said the right Hon. Lady Rosehill (late Miss Cheer) has engaged to perform with Mr. Douglass, in the theatres of Philadelphia and New York, for the ensuing Winter, at a sum much above £10 per week, and a benefit. We hear that the theatre in Southwark will be opened (for one month only) on Wednesday the 21st instant, with a comedy." [6]

Despite this announcement the theater did not open until October 6, and rather than the announced comedy, the tragedy of *George Barnwell* was acted. For this opening performance, a gifted young storekeeper named Francis Hopkinson composed a prologue that was substantially a plea for toleration. Lewis Hallam recited the words implying that the moral influence of the theater might well be employed as a school for virtue:

> To bid reviving virtue raise her head,
> And far abroad her heav'nly virtue shed;
> The soul by bright examples to inspire,
> And kindle in each breast celestial fire;
> For injur'd innocence to waken fear;
> For suff'ring virtue swell the gen'rous tear;
> Vice to expose in each assum'd disguise,
> And bid the mist to vanish from your eyes,
> With keener passion, that you may detest
> Her hellish form, howe'er like virtue drest:
> The muse to cherish, genius to inspire,
> Bid fancy stretch the wing, and wit take fire—
> For these we come—for these we erect our Stage....

Appearances suggest that the American Company was undergoing severe financial reverses during the early part of this season in Philadelphia. Newspaper advertisements occupied a bare minimum of space, appearing only sporadically in the three papers then published in the city. It was not until November 15 that Margaret Cheer was listed in a playbill, and then she appeared as "Miss Cheer" rather than under her newly acquired title—perhaps an implication that her bridegroom either had abandoned her or had been exposed as a fraud. Fanny Storer had by this time left the stage, possibly to escape the advances of her amorous brother-in-law, had married a Mr. Metchler, and had sailed for England. A Mr. Byerly was the only new member of the company, a replacement for Patrick Malone, who had once again departed to seek his fortune in other parts. A Mr.

Darby was to begin a brief career on the last day of the season before retiring to a more mundane existence.

The two Italian brothers who had competed against the American Company in New York arrived in Philadelphia in early December. Rather than enter into a contest for the entertainment shillings of the town, Douglass joined forces with these pyrotechnical artists. Following the farce, the brothers appeared on the stage with their fireworks display, colorful wheels, fiery arches, sparkling fountains, "a Tornant with variegated Fire," and "many more curious pieces, too tedious to insert here." Douglass reminded his customers that, even though this exhibition was costing him heavily, he had "with pleasure, embraced the Opportunity of manifesting his Zeal & Attention" without an increase in prices. When this explosive entertainment was repeated to accompany the December 14, 1768, production of *Hamlet*, it might, indeed, be said that the stage was "full of sound and fury."

The final performance of the season, on December 30, was a gala affair. Nathaniel Lee's *Alexander the Great, or The Rival Queens*, although written in 1677, was played for the first time in America, followed by the farce, *Fanny the Phantom*. Ordinarily, this would have been a complete program, but on this night, Thomas Wall followed the farce with "a Critical Dissertation upon NOSES," and the evening was finally brought to a close with still another farce, *Neck Or Nothing*.

Just as the players were bringing their short Philadelphia season to a close, the General Assembly of Pennsylvania was holding its first sessions. In other towns, this would have swelled crowds for the playhouse, but in Philadelphia, the presence of the actors would only have reminded the legislators that perhaps something should be done about restricting the drama. Douglass left, assuring those in authority that he would not return to the city for at least a year, as he planned to go to South Carolina after a season in New York.

Even during this short period of acting, the company had enhanced its reputation among patrons of the theater. Lewis Hallam still clung tenaciously to his star billing, despite the presence of John Henry, who appears to have been an actor of at least equal, if not superior, abilities. But Hallam's techniques had improved; Alexander Graydon, who was critical of him, was forced to admit: "He was, however, at Philadelphia as much the soul of the Southwark Theatre as ever Garrick was of Drury lane; and if, as doctor Johnson allows, popularity in matters of taste is unquestionable evidence of merit, we cannot withhold a considerable portion of it from Mr. Hallam, notwithstanding his faults." [7]

In New York, musical presentations were still favored, with instrumental music furnished by William Hulett, who had recently opened a new school in Wall Street for instruction in the violin, German flute, and fencing. Stephen Woolls retained his laurels as the best male singer in the troupe, a position he was to claim "long after all voice had left him, and snuff and shuffle characterized his attempts." The leading female voices still belonged to Maria Storer, Nancy Hallam, and Miss Wainwright. Lewis Hallam, whose singing voice, at best, could have been only fair, held forth in such ambitious roles as Captain Macheath in *The Beggar's Opera*.

Plays and farces presented to New York audiences for the first time included Steele's *The Tender Husband*, Colman's *The Musical Lady*, Garrick's *The Guardian*, and Bickerstaff's latest comic opera, *The Padlock*. It was in the last that Hallam, as the drunken Mungo, put to good use his studies of Negro dialect in Jamaica.

This year saw more than the usual number of special performances. On St. Patrick's Day, the "GRAND KNOT, of the Friendly Brothers of St. Patrick" requested a special performance of *The Busy Body* and the obvious afterpiece, *The Brave Irishman*. In the playbills, Douglass judiciously listed only the subtitle rather than the full *Captain O'Blunder, or The Brave Irishman*. The Masons went the Irish one better. They persuaded the governor, quite possibly a member of the fraternity, to request a "Command" performance. The program of *The Tender Husband, or The Accomplished Fool* and *The Upholsterer, or What News?* was originally announced for March 20, but Passion Week fell during this period, and the play was rescheduled for March 27. One other special performance presents some grounds for speculation. On April 10, *Othello* was acted, the title role "attempted by a Gentleman . . . assisted by other Gentlemen, in the Characters of the Duke and the Senate of Venice." Their purpose was stated as "From a benevolent and generous Design of encouraging the Theatre, and relieving the Performers from some Embarrassments in which they are involved." These "Embarrassments," while not stated, were more than likely financial and may have resulted from the purchase of the new set of scenery advertised for this performance. Upon this, as on similar occasions, the boxes were laid into the pit, and box seat prices were charged for the whole. The Othello of this performance has been identified as Major James Moncrief, an officer of the British garrison stationed in New York who became a prominent amateur actor after the Revolution.

There was almost a week before the American Company was scheduled to leave, and some of the players seized upon this opportunity to do a little free-lancing. John Henry kept the theater open long enough to deliver a "moral, satirical, and entertaining Lecture, on Hearts," after which he rendered Hippesly's famed dance, the "Drunken Man," assisted by Maria Storer. Samuel Francis, who had postponed opening his "very genteel" and "pleasing" Vaux-Hall Gardens because of the theater, was repaid for his patience by the services of Stephen Woolls and Nancy Hallam for his opening night's concert.[8]

Shortly after July 1, the players journeyed up the Hudson to Albany to play a season limited to one month by the governor. No sooner had they arrived than Thomas Wall followed his usual practice of distributing handbills expressing his willingness to teach the guitar while a playhouse was being readied. There was no theater building in Albany, and the only structure of the necessary dimensions was the hospital, which Douglass obtained permission to use and fitted up with stage, boxes, and a gallery. On July 10, the players opened with *Venice Preserv'd* and announced their intention of playing on Mondays, Wednesdays, and Fridays thereafter. Other than the lowest advertised admission prices of any place in the colonies—Boxes, 6s., Pit, 4s., Gallery, 2s.—there is no further information as to their success or lack of it in this town.[9]

By early September, and despite Douglass' assurances of the preceding December that they would not return for a year, the American Company reappeared in Philadelphia. It is quite possible that they had planned to return to New York from Albany, but the death of Douglass' "great and honour'd Friend and Patron," Governor Sir Henry Moore, on September 11, 1769, would have made the appearance of the actors offensive and in bad taste. The demise of the fun-loving executive also made it more difficult to secure permission from the authorities in power. From outward appearances, it seemed that opposition to the drama had mellowed in Philadelphia. For one thing, the academy had launched a program of declamations based on the theater, although the plays were "read" rather than acted. The series had been inaugurated on May 29, 1769, for "the Lovers of Elocution," with the stately and ponderous "Demosthenes Seventh Oration" but had quickly slipped into the more popular readings of *Damon and Phillida, The Beggar's Opera, Love in a Village,* and *The Musical Lady,* leveling off on June 26 with Dean Swift's *Cantata.*

The Southwark Theatre had been reopened by Patrick Malone on August 11, nearly a month before the return of the American Company. Since deserting Douglass the year before, he had played with a troupe of theatrical malcontents then appearing in Annapolis. When the group had disbanded in that graveyard of dramatic organizations, he returned to Philadelphia, perhaps with the hope that he would be allowed to rejoin his former colleagues. While awaiting their arrival, he presented a one-man acrobatic exhibition in the theater. After a display of his agility on the slack wire, on which he performed a "Summerset," he entertained his audience with a hornpipe and an "Epilogue in Character."

For some reason, Malone was not allowed to join the company when it arrived in Philadelphia, although his talent on the slack wire would have fitted well within the programs they presented. They acted no plays, and the audiences at the Southwark witnessed the nearest thing to vaudeville presented in the eighteenth century. Hallam and Henry combined their talents to give the *Lecture on Heads,* with songs by Nancy Hallam during the intermissions. At the conclusion of the performance, the audience was invited on stage to gaze into the mysterious screen of a "camera obscura" that reflected images from across the room. This was the pattern of entertainment throughout September, light productions, sprinkled liberally with singing and dancing, and usually performed with the abbreviated cast of Lewis Hallam, John Henry, Mrs. Douglass, and Nancy Hallam. Mr. Broadbelt of the business staff was still pressed into service in emergencies, as was "A Gentleman" who could sing and dance. Difficulty with the machinery used in the pantomimes limited the number of light entertainments that could be offered. There was no apparent reason why the players were so restricted in their efforts. Quite possibly, Douglass' assurance that he would not return for a year had something to do with it, and an obvious conjecture is that the religious faction applied pressure to the chief executive to limit the scope of dramatic activities.

Whatever the reason, the American Company was experiencing the most difficult period of financial stress in its existence. On October 5, Douglass wrote a pathetic letter to Governor John Penn, in which he admitted his present circumstance "covers me with Shame, when the Situation of our Affairs, make so frequent Application absolutely necessary.

"I had flatter'd myself, that I shou'd not, for a Year to come, at least, have given your Honour any Trouble, but a Disappointment at Carolina, and the recent Loss of a great and honour'd Friend and Patron, whose Memory will ever be dear to the American Theatre, has made such a change in our Circumstances, that nothing but an Exertion of that Humanity, which you possess in so eminent a Degree, can save us from Destruction.

"Let my Situation speak for me, and, with your usual Goodness, do not think me too importunate if I sollicite your Honour for Permission to open the Theatre, for a short Time, this Winter, previous to my going to Annapolis, where I propose spending the Remainder of it.

"The Maid of the Mill, the Padlock, and some other Pieces not perform'd hitherto, on this Stage, will, I flatter myself, give your Honour some Entertainment.

"I shou'd not have made my Application in this Manner, but wou'd have waited on you myself, were not my feelings, upon this Occasion, too great, to permit me to say what I ought." [10]

This abject plea was effective, although it was not until a month later, on November 8, that the playhouse opened with *The Busy Body* and *The Padlock*. During the fall, highlights included the first American performance of the Kane O'Hara's new burletta, *Midas*, and the steady rise of Nancy Hallam to a position of leading actress. This young and beautiful girl was in great demand for singing appearances outside the theater, and on November 16 she appeared with Stephen Woolls in the Assembly Room in a vocal and instrumental concert, directed by a Mr. Gualdo, "After the Italian Method."

Attendance slacked off. Rather than the usual Monday, Wednesday, and Friday night performances, plays were now limited to a two-a-week schedule on Tuesdays and Thursdays. The behavior of those who did attend was open to censure. Douglass was so bold as to issue a reprimand: "The Orchestra, on Opera Nights, will be assisted by some musical persons, who, as they have no view but to contribute to the entertainment of the public, certainly claim a protection from any means of insult."

One novelty may have had a tendency to arouse the interest of the curious. Although frequently the stage saw a gentleman playing a part for his own amusement, *The Stratagem*, on December 12, 1769, marked the first occasion that a role was acted "by a young Gentlewoman, being her first appearance."

A theatrical season in Philadelphia would have seemed incomplete without some manifestation of displeasure by "the People called Quakers." On January 4, 1770, they presented their usual petition to Governor John Penn, chiding him for allowing the theater to remain unmolested contrary to law, along with "Remonstrances and Addresses of great Numbers of reputable Freemen." The governor paid so little heed to this and the usual castigations in the newspapers that, on July 19, 1770, the Society of Friends carried their appeal to the proprietors, Thomas and Richard Penn, deploring the indulgence of the governor in allowing "those Nurseries of Pride, Idleness, Extravagance and

Luxury, by which many of the People are already corrupted and debased."

As usual, the drama had its champions, and "Candidus" publicly avowed that he was "not ashamed to own, my admiration for dramatic performances hath induced me now and then to associate with some of the performers; from whose conversation I have often received both pleasure and advantages." Following this confession, he concluded with a defiant, "Who now dare call the Theatre a school of Vice. . . . ?"

Not even strong endorsements could stimulate flagging attendance, although Douglass taxed his genius in his attempts to attract additional customers. He presented more new plays than in previous seasons, including *The Siege of Damascus, Edward the Black Prince, or The Battle of Poictiers, The Tempest, or The Inchanted Island, The Funeral, or Grief A-La-Mode, Midas, The Good Natur'd Man,* and *Julius Caesar.*

Some concessions were made to the simpler and spiritual tastes of Philadelphia. Douglass reworked Congreve's *Love for Love* so that "The Beauties of the author are preserv'd, his Blemishes expung'd." The Dryden-Davenant version of Shakespeare's *The Tempest* was also revised, with the deletion of the "many indecent luxuriances which Dryden had introduced into it with the vitiated taste of the age in which he wrote." On January 18, a news item in the *Pennsylvania Journal* extolled this presentation as one of the top plays of the season: "The TEMPEST is to be acted To-morrow, written by Shakespeare, and alter'd by Dryden: It is one of those plays, in which *The Poet of Nature* has given an unbounded Scope to his created Immagination: he has not only form'd Beings of a different Species to Mankind, but endow'd them with Faculties adapted to their Characters—The Scenery, Machinery, and Decorations for this Representation, we are informed, have been prepared at very great Expence, and from the general Impatience among all Ranks of People for its Performance, it is imagined there will be a crowded Audience: at the Theatre To-morrow, will not only reflect Honour on our Taste, by patronizing one of the *Chef d'Oeuvres* of that Immortal Genius, but be some Compensation to the Players, for their bad Success this Season."

Their "bad Success" continued despite Douglass' efforts to fill empty benches with additional comforts and entertainments. February rains led to the construction of a "Foot Way" across the Common to allow ladies to walk to the playhouse without soiling their shoes. The huge John Henry demonstrated his athletic prowess by running twenty feet up a perpendicular scene in one Harlequin afterpiece. On holidays, merriment echoed from the theater walls. A group of British officers, celebrating St. George's Day on April 23, "met at a Tavern, stuffed roast Beef ond Plumb Pudding, and got drunk, *pour l'honneur de St. George;* wore Crosses, and finished the evening at the Play-House, where we made the People all Chorus 'God Save the King,' and 'Rule Britannia,' and 'Britons strike Home,' &c., and such like Nonsense; and, in short, conducted ourselves with all the Decency and Confusion usual on such Occasions."

In late May, Douglass was forced to fight fire with fire. Reverend George Whitefield was making his last American tour and, while in Philadelphia, so denounced the actors that the manager threatened to act Samuel Foote's *The Minor,* a biting comic satire on Methodism. A delighted and entranced Alexander Mackrabie witnessed the contest: "I believe I have never told you that we have got Whitefield among us. He preaches like a dragon, curses and blesses us all in one breath, and tells us he hopes to die in the pulpit. He abuses the players, who in turn advertised to perform *The Minor.* . . . the parsons petitioned the Governor against it, and the performance was dropt." This was the only time that the players had been forced to stand up to the redoubtable Whitefield, and, certainly, the first time they had been able to blunt his evangelical fervor.

On June 1, a new version of *Julius Caesar* was advertised as the last play of the season. The part of Antony was played by "a young Gentleman," making his first appearance on the stage. After this original anonymity, he became a regular member of the cast and appeared under his real name, Richard Goodman. He, like Samuel Greville, was a young law student enchanted with the theater. Despite his youth, Goodman was to gain his greatest fame playing old men in both eccentric and sophisticated comedy. The "young Gentlewoman" who had appeared incognito in *The Stratagem*, on December 12, 1769, was now revealed as Mary Richardson, who likewise became an accepted and valuable player in the troupe. One of the regular members appeared under a new name when Ann Storer was billed as Mrs. Henry, although there is nothing to suggest that a marriage to the amorous Irishman was ever solemnized before either clerical or secular authority. It was also about this time that Owen Morris remarried, once again to a beautiful and talented actress.

The year 1770 was that of the Boston Massacre, and it was soon apparent that "the spirit of Liberty breathes on every Act and on every Occasion." The selection of *Julius Caesar* was particularly apt at this time, even though a cynical Alexander Mackrabie noted: "Our Play-bills promise to exhibit to us the Noble Struggles for liberty of those renowned Romans, Brutus and Cassius, tho' poor Cassius was so deficient in his Latin as to call Publius Puppylies, throughout the whole Piece."

Douglass, harassed by evangelism and burdened with debt, prepared to leave for Virginia. Thomas Wall seized the interval before departure to present a "Rhapsody" of the lectures of George A. Stevens but took care to note in the bills that "no party, sect, or denomination is aimed at." There was time for only one presentation. By strenuous effort, Douglass secured finances to compensate for "our very bad Success this Season," and by the time of departure, the company was "getting very fast thro' our Difficulties." Haste was now important, and the need for money urgent as he was "oblig'd to carry the Company away directly to Williamsburg, that I may not lose the June Court." [11]

There was a need to mend fences and to re-establish the American Company in both Maryland and Virginia. Since he had last appeared in those colonies, a new company of comedians had toured the territory.

· X ·

THE NEW AMERICAN COMPANY

(*Williamsburg and Annapolis, 1768-1769*)

Although there had been no professional activity in the Williamsburg theater since 1763, the drama still stirred restlessly in Virginia, and sometimes manifested itself in unique surroundings. In 1767, the Reverend Mr. Warrington, rector of Elizabeth City Parish, had allowed the students of the "Rev. Mr. Warrington's School" to act the tragedy of *Cato*. Whether this was the famous Eaton School, of which Warrington was a trustee, or a parochial school is not clear in the newspaper account of the presentation. Camilla Warrington, daughter of the rector, recited a prologue that included these lines:

> If nothing please you else, you'll clap the zeal
> Of brats who pant to serve the common weal.

Five months previous to these juvenile capers, William Verling, who just half a year earlier had been appearing in Charleston with Douglass, arrived in Williamsburg. Engaging "the Great Room of the Rawleigh Tavern," he gave the *Lecture on*

Heads (which he probably pirated from Douglass) for two nights. He disappeared just as abruptly as he had appeared, but it is quite possible that he wandered through the colony, giving his lecture, and eventually wound up at Norfolk. Actors were not unknown in the Norfolk area at this time, for in January, 1768, the *Virginia Gazette* carried the bitter strictures of Margaret Bannerman against her husband Benjamin, who, she claimed, had put her out of their house and rented the same to "an actor and his wife for £40 a year."

This unidentified actor may have been one of those whom William Verling approached in organizing a new company of players, or he may have been Verling himself, who had just the year before married Elizabeth Conner, a Norfolk girl. In any event, a company of professional players was gathered together in this area, with Verling as prime mover and manager. For his feminine lead, he selected Henrietta Osborne, who had not journeyed to England as indicated by her announcement in Charleston. To provide terpsichorean entertainment, he contracted the services of James Verling Godwin, another truant from the American Company, who may have been a relative of Verling's. Other actors in this initial band were the former sailor Christopher Bromadge, Mr. and Mrs. Charles Parker, and George Walker. These last named actors may well have been former members of the little known company then acting in North Carolina under the direction of a Mr. Mills and starring a Henry Giffard. Possibly, the company had disbanded when Giffard announced his intentions of taking holy orders and petitioned Governor William Tryon to press his case with the church authorities. Although Tryon had been persuaded, his recommendation was unenthusiastic, and he cautioned the Bishop of London, "If your Lordship grants Mr. Giffard his petition you will take off the best player on the American stage."

Verling's troupe, calling themselves the Virginia Company, opened in Norfolk sometime before January, 1768. The only record of their activity in that port city is a notice of a benefit given Mrs. Osborne on January 19, at which she recited a prologue containing the lines:

For ten long years this motley life I've led. . . .
Yet though doom'd perpetually to roam,
Still when at Norfolk thought myself at home.[1]

Indications are that the group played in Norfolk until early
March. On March 17, a terse item appeared in the *Virginia Gazette* announcing: "The Theatre in this City will be opened on
Thursday the 31st instant." Permission was secured from George
Wythe, "the Worshipful the Mayor of Williamsburg," and "At
the old Theatre, near the Capitol," the company opened on
schedule with *Douglas* and the *Honest Yorkshireman*. The incidental dancing of James Godwin was featured as additional
entertainment.

A new actor, one Thomas Charlton, who appeared for the
first time in *Venice Preserv'd*, on April 8, was probably a cousin
or brother of Edward and Richard Charlton, the barbers and
peruke-makers of Williamsburg. Edward, at one time in the past,
had had a controlling interest in the theater and, during this season, assisted the Virginia Company by serving as their ticket
agent in Williamsburg. Two other new members had gained
some of their stage experience with the American Company,
Mrs. Dowthaitt and her daughter, who appeared first in minor
roles when *The Orphan* was played on April 15. Others who
eventually joined the company in Williamsburg were a Mr.
Leavie, Mr. Farrell, Mr. Mallory, and a Miss Yapp.

When Verling had played with Douglass in Charleston, he
had established himself as an able actor, and from his roles with
the Virginia Company, he was the most talented member of that
group. He did not, however, adopt the possessive attitude of
young Hallam but allowed other actors to alternate in male
leads. Henrietta Osborne was still the lovely temperamental actress of two years before and still retained her voice and figure.
James Godwin continued to present the same dances he had
performed with the American Company but now was given
better roles as an actor. The playbills suggest that all of the male
members of the cast were adequate, if not accomplished, dancers.
The Charles Parkers, man and wife, were better than average as
actors, as were Thomas Charlton and Christopher Bromadge.

Messrs. Walker, Farrell, and Leavie, Mrs. Dowthaitt, and the Misses Dowthaitt and Yapp seem to have been endowed with more enthusiasm than talent.

At this season of the year, it would appear that the troupe would be assured of sizable audiences, regardless of the dramatic abilities of the players. June court was approaching, a time when one traveler made the exaggerated estimate that there were between five and six thousand people in Williamsburg, a town whose permanent population probably never exceeded fifteen hundred. Waller, or Eastern, Street was no longer considered on the outskirts of town; the area in which the theater was located appears to have been considered an attractive business district. William Page advertised good lodgings for man or beast at his Blue Bell Tavern "opposite the play house." Thomas Brammer moved his store from Market Square "to a house opposite the play-house." Later in the year, gunsmith William Willess was to select a lot near the theater as a promising site for his shop.

The repertoire of the Virginia Company was essentially that of the American Company and followed the same basic pattern of presentation. In early May, George Washington was in town and followed his customary practice of attending the theater whenever possible. On May 2, he was apparently host to a theater party, for he recorded an expenditure of £1. 7s. 6d. for theater tickets on that date. There is no record of what he witnessed on this occasion, but apparently he experienced some pleasure, for on May 5, he was once again in the audience. It was well that he was for, within days, the heavy spring rains so cut down attendance that on May 12 it was announced: "Mr. Verling acquaints his friends, and the public, that his benefit, on account of the badness of the weather, is put off until next Friday; at which time their kind assistance will most sensibly oblige him."

Rains would have made little difference, on May 18, to the masculine patrons of the Waller Street Theatre. This was the night of Henrietta Osborne's benefit, *The Constant Couple*, in which she played the jolly blade, Sir Harry Wildair, as a "breeches part." Even without this display of feminine charms, this was the most pretentious program of the season. Mr. Parker waited until the intermission between the first and second acts to speak the prologue "in the Character of a Country Boy," while at the end of the second act, James Godwin led several of the male members of the cast in a dance called "The Coopers." Following the third act, Charles Parker entertained with a "Cantata." With the play over, Henrietta Osborne appeared once again, still dressed in male clothing. The bends and turns of a minuet, danced with Miss Yapp, outlined every detail of Mrs. Osborne's figure; the subsequent hornpipe by James Godwin must have seemed tame by comparison. In the farce that concluded the evening, the star, still dressed in breeches, appeared as the "First Courtier" in *The Anatomist*. Surely, Henrietta Osborne was the nearest thing to a burlesque "queen" to appear in eighteenth-century Williamsburg.

The benefits that followed were anticlimactic. Even when the Williamsburg Masons appeared in a body for Thomas Charlton's benefit of *The Miser* and *The Brave Irishman* on June 8, they were treated to no additional entertainment other than the special epilogue spoken by Mrs. Parker "in the Character of a Mason's Wife." When Miss Yapp selected *The Merchant of Venice* for her night, indications are that Verling interpreted Shylock as a serious and sympathetic character rather than the comic part so favored by Lewis Hallam. Henrietta Osborne portrayed what must have been a gay and light-hearted Portia.

The season wore on, and William Verling, James Godwin, and Henrietta Osborne became more and more the established mainstays of the company; Verling with his fine acting, Godwin with his nimble feet, and Mrs. Osborne with her versatility and physical charms. These, along with the Parkers and Charlton, formed the core of the troupe. This was particularly evident on June 3, in Mrs. Parker's benefit, *The Beggar's Opera*. Verling had never played the starring role of Captain Macheath, but he boldly attempted it. Mrs. Osborne played both Mrs. Peachum and Lucy Lockit, while Mr. Parker, who first appeared as Matt of the Mint, switched quickly into petticoats and reappeared as Mrs. Diana Trapes. In addition to playing the comparatively minor role of Filch, Godwin danced the popular "Drunken Peasant," assisted by Parker, who upon this occasion appeared as the Clown. The "Musick of the Opera" was conducted by Peter Pelham, the organist of Bruton Parish Church.[2]

The Virginia comedians left town sometime after June 8, although Christopher Bromadge remained behind, detained forcibly for unpaid debts. Sometime around the first of August, he was the recipient of a benefit acted for him "by some Gentlemen &c. in town." He appeared in person to speak the prologue, in which he indicated his financial distress:

> . . . I speak it to my cost;
> Pester'd with warrants, writs, and scire facias. . . .

Not even this benefit settled his pecuniary difficulties, but Bromadge did manage to leave town, although Edward and Richard Charlton were able to collect £9. 15s. from his bondsman. Thomas Charlton also defaulted on a bond, and indications are that the players quietly slipped out of town in the dead of night. They left behind not only a host of debts but also one very angry woman. Jane Vobe, at whose tavern "all the best people resorted," advertised for her runaway slave, Nancy, "a brisk genteel wench." As abductors of her servant, Mrs. Vobe accused "some of the comedians who have just left this town, with some of whom, as I have been informed, since she went off, she had some connections, and was seen very busy talking privately with some of them."

Following the benefit by the "Young Gentlemen" for Christopher Bromadge, the theater building was almost immediately put into use as a school, for it was "the only tolerable convenient place . . . at that time." This venture was not very successful, as Joseph M'Auslane, the new schoolmaster, publicly complained that "few scholars have offered." [3]

The Virginia Company of Comedians dropped out of sight and did not reappear for two months; in September, they played Alexandria. There was no formal playhouse in town, and it has been suggested that one of the local taverns served that purpose.

On September 20, Washington rode in from nearby Mount Vernon with "Mrs. Washington and ye two children. Went up to Alexandria to see the Inconstant, or Way to Win him acted." He spent the night in town so that he might see *Douglas* performed the following day. The company remained in Alexandria at least through October 6, for on that day, Washington purchased a pit ticket for his stepson John Parke Custis.

No records chronicle the wanderings of Verling and his troupe after they left Alexandria, but it is reasonable to assume they played such well established theater towns as Upper Marlborough and Chester in Maryland, and the smaller villages along the way. Either during their stay in Alexandria or shortly afterwards, Henrietta Osborne flew into another of her tantrums and quit Verling just as she had left Douglass some three years earlier. A brief notice in the *Virginia Gazette* is the clue:

> Williamsburg, Jan. 12, 1768
> I intend for Great Britain soon.
> Henrietta Osborne.[4]

Notwithstanding the loss of his talented leading lady, Verling carried his players to Annapolis. Now, however, they called themselves the New American Company, thereby hoping to be identified with Douglass' American Company of Comedians.

For some reason, extensive renovations must have been in order for the playhouse in Annapolis, for the actors advertised themselves as playing "at the New Theatre in Annapolis." The first playbill of the season carried the notice: "Upper Boxes are now preparing, the Passage to which, must be from the Stage; 'tis therefore hoped, such Ladies and Gentlemen as choose to fix on Their Seats, will come before the Play begins, as it is not possible they can be admitted after the Curtain is drawn up."

To replace Henrietta Osborne as leading lady, the services of Sarah Jones of Williamsburg had been acquired. The Dowthaitts had disappeared, but Patrick Malone and Mr. Darby, both lately of the American Company, had made their way south from Philadelphia to join the new group. Malone's wife began to make her appearances on the stage for the first time, something her talents had not permitted her to do with Douglass' company. Other new members who had joined just before or since the troupe left Williamsburg included Mr. and Mrs. William Burdett, Frederick Spencer, and a David Jefferson, the latter since alleged to have been everything from brother to grandfather of the great Joseph Jefferson of a later era.

Romeo and Juliet, on February 18, was the first play of the Annapolis season. Malone, at this time, demonstrated his usefulness by taking over some of the dancing chores from Godwin. One week later, when *The Beggar's Opera* was played, Mrs. Walker was tried in Mrs. Osborne's roles of Mrs. Peachum and Lucy Lockit, for which the indulgence of the audience was begged since it was "her First Appearance in them Characters." Her husband played a "breeches part" in reverse, donning female clothes for this operetta to play the part of Molly Brazen, a practice that Douglass had first inaugurated some ten years earlier.

Despite their makeshift operations and the addition of new and inexperienced personnel, the company seems to have prospered; the *Maryland Gazette* reported: "The Public may be assured, that the Company of Comedians, in this City, have gained great Applause by their last two Performances, *viz.* The Tragedies of *Douglass* and *Richard III.*" There were the usual stage-struck youths who persuaded Verling to allow them to appear incognito. On February 22, one of these "Gentlemen" had attempted Othello and, on April 3, the more difficult part of Hamlet. Another amateur duplicated this double effort but selected the less exacting roles of Damon in *Damon and Phillida* and Obediah Prim in *A Bold Stroke for a Wife.*

The company followed the customary practice of suspending operations for Passion Week but experienced disappointment when the meeting of the General Assembly was postponed until May 16. There was, however, some compensation in that the annual racing season, which always attracted the sporting element from some distance, was under way at this time in Annapolis.

Henrietta Osborne, that unpredictable of unpredictables, re-covered from her pique and rejoined the company on April 8, appearing in the title role of *Polly Honeycomb*, the farce that accompanied *Richard III* on William Verling's benefit night. Extra entertainment included a Mr. L'Argent in violin and harp-sichord solos and "several Tunes on the Musical Glasses." Ver-ling also appealed to the universal tendency of an audience to applaud child actors and starred Master Knapp, son of his ticket agent, in a Harlequin selection.

Although Verling emulated Douglass in varied techniques, he did not take the trouble to delete offensive passages from plays or to discipline his players as did the more astute manager of the American Company. As a result, one "Clarinda" penned an acid critique of the New American Company and brought into her sphere of censure the acting practices of the day. After a half-apologetic "You will be perhaps surprised that Female should attempt to reform those whom some of the other Sex have attempted, but without Success," she asked no forgiveness for her castigation of the actors:

"I live some Miles from Annapolis, but the Delight I place in seeing a Play, has drawn me frequently to your Theatre—The Money I expend in that Way justly entitles me to some Amuse-ment, and when I am disgusted, I think I have the right to com-plain, it being the Duty of every Actor to exert his utmost Abilities to render his Performance agreeable to the Audience. . . . before I mention those Things that have shock'd me, I will acknowledge the great Pleasure I have felt in Mrs. Osborne's performance of Juliet—Her feeling Manner of Acting, in my Opinion, made Amends for a Number of Incidents that were exceptionable, during the Representation of the Play—I staid in Town to go to the CONSTANT COUPLE—and tho' this Lady charmed me by her Acting, I own she struck my Admiration still more, to find it was in the Power of the same Woman, to express the delicate Sensibility of a Juliet—and the Levity of a Sir Harry Wildair—but all her Merit—had it been Ten Times greater, could not divest me of Resentment, when I observed a Violation of all Decorum, committed by one of the Actors.

"I have been informed . . . that if they take a Liberty of expressing, by Voice, or Gesture, their Resentment of being hissed, whether deservedly or not—such an Actor may think himself happy, if he is suffered to go on, upon making very great Concessions—and shall an Actor on this stage—insolently dare to tell an Audience not to applaud—what an Insult upon the understanding!—I wish myself, like Mrs. Osborne, in Breeches, to have made his Chastisement, a real one. . . . I have been told that this Gentleman has not denied, when he was publicly accused of it, that he did not always act as well as he could—What did this imply? Or did his Behaviour on Saturday, imply? but the most Sovereign Contempt for your City—Where, if I am rightly informed, the Manager has been heard to say, he has met with the greatest Encouragement and Indulgence.

"I cannot help mentioning a Thing that must always be disagreeable to a sensible Audience. It is the barefaced, illiberal, and very often indecent Insertions of some of his [the Manager's] Actors that play the low parts in comedy, or Farce, which is generally substituted for what they have either forgot, or perhaps, which is more likely, never perused—to be imperfect is so great a Fault, that the putting in their Ribaldry, is hardly a greater.

"I am afraid the Gentleman, who amused himself with playing HAMLET forgot to tell the Clowns, *to speak no more than was set down for them;* or if he did tell them, it was only in a Whisper.

"I would have these very witty—sprightly Gentlemen, when they personate Clowns, or Fools, known, that since the immortal Shakespeare, and Ben Jonson, we have hardly had an Author, that has presumed to draw such Characters—Conscious that it requires the most consumate Knowledge of human Nature, to put proper Words in their Mouths. . . . Then may we not naturally conclude, that it has been thought, by sensible Men, a difficult Undertaking, to draw such Characters as they ought to be; and, that it requires, at least, no common share of Understanding, to play the FOOL WELL."

There is nothing to suggest that these sharp strictures led to any amelioration in the stage manners of the actors. Benefits continued throughout the spring. When Patrick Malone chose *The Merchant of Venice* for his night, on April 25, Verling and Mrs. Osborne performed in the starring roles, but Malone had his moment in performing on the slack wire in the interval between the play and the farce. His exploits were incredible for a man of his age:

I. He vaults the Rope.
II. He lies on it at full Length.
III. He beats a Drum.
IV. He balances a Pyramid of Smoking Pipes on the Edge of a Drinking-Glass.
V. He balances the Pipes, and a Pyramid of Thirty Glasses of Jelly, in each Hand.
VI. He stands on his Head, on a small Jack-cord, and holds a Pistol in each Hand (which he will Fire, if agreeable to the Ladies.)

This night also was unique in that it marked the appearance of a "Gentleman" in something other than an acting role. One of the gentry selected this occasion to display his agility on the tight-rope.

Throughout the Annapolis run, Mrs. Osborne continued to delight the masculine segment of the audience with frequent appearances in male attire, playing the parts of Ranger in *The Suspicious Husband* and the Prince of Wales, "by desire," in *Henry IV*. Lest it be thought that Henrietta Osborne played nothing but male roles, it should be stated that she was a very competent actress and a most popular leading lady. Her appearances in "breeches parts" were the exception rather than the rule.

Each of the actors received two benefits; with the last performance on June 8, they disappeared just as suddenly as they had appeared in Virginia some eighteen months earlier. Malone returned to Philadelphia in the vain hope that Douglass would allow him to rejoin the American Company. Some of the actors probably settled in Annapolis, as Henrietta Osborne and William Verling seem to have done.[5]

An accumulation of debts led to the disbanding of the New American Company. In March, 1769, James Godwin was first to be hailed into court by Samuel Middleton, who charged him with "Trespass upon the Case," which, from the legal terminology of the day, would indicate a suit to recover property damage. Godwin seems to have finished the season in Annapolis and then fled town; the following year the sheriff was ordered to bring "his body before the Justices of our County Court." William Verling, as manager of the defunct company, was defendant in a number of law suits. Frances Frazier Adams, who kept a boarding house in Annapolis, sued for what must have been her bill, and Robert Jones initiated a suit for the wages due his wife Sarah, who had played the lead roles in the early part of the season. Debts that had been ignored in Williamsburg were pressed in the Anne Arundel County Court. Richard and Edward Charlton entered suits of "Trespass upon the Case" against Verling. One of the more interesting cases from a theatrical point of view was that brought by Sarah Hallam, the wife whom Lewis Hallam, Jr., had abandoned. She had settled in Williamsburg after separation from her husband some time after 1762. In her warrant, she named William Verling and Charles Parker as co-defendants, and the suit was to recover the sum of £20. 5s., "Which from her he Unjustly Detains." The sentimental tradition associated with the name of Sarah Hallam in Williamsburg would lead to an assumption that this sum was due her for acting with the company during the Williamsburg season. This hypothesis must be discarded when it is recalled that her sole appearance with Douglass' Company had been in a minor part. More likely, the occasion for the suit was less fanciful—conceivably a neglected board bill.

In the majority of the cases brought against him, Verling managed to clear himself because of the non-appearance of the plaintiffs, but in the suit brought by William Hardy, he was forced to pay £3. 5s. because Verling "Saith he cannot Deny the Action." Samuel Chase, the attorney representing the actor in these legal actions, was forced to bring his client into court to collect his own fee. Even then, Verling's resources were so nearly exhausted that Chase was forced to settle for the remaining two years and five months of service of Oliver Anderson, Verling's indentured servant.[6]

Even as Verling was struggling to disentangle himself from this web of debts, David Douglass was bringing his actors south to free himself of a similar affliction.

· XI ·

MARYLAND AND VIRGINIA

(Williamsburg, Fredericksburg, Norfolk, and Annapolis, 1770-1772)

Douglass arrived in Williamsburg in time for the June court, but except for the initial notice of his forthcoming arrival, there was little evidence of the company's activities in the press. The finances of the American Company were too depleted to allow newspaper advertising. The drum and billsticker, beating their way through the streets of the town, were the only forms of publicity the manager could afford at this time, other than "giving out" the next play at the end of each performance.

Joseph M'Auslane's school in the theater building had either failed or moved to other quarters. In April, Peter Gardiner had used the playhouse to exhibit his "curious set of Figures, richly dressed, four feet high, which shall appear upon the stage as if alive." These artificial comedians entertained Williamsburg audiences with the puppet plays *Babes in the Woods* and *Whittington and His Cat*.

The only newspaper reference to the arrival of the live comedians appeared in Purdie and Dixon's *Virginia Gazette* on June 14, 1770: "Yesterday Mr. Douglass with his company of comedians, arrived in town from Philadelphia; and, we hear, intend opening the theatre in this city, on Saturday, with the Beggar's Opera, and other entertainments."

Douglass had contracted with an agent to conduct an advance ticket sale. As early as May 24, some three weeks before the arrival of the American Company, George Washington noted in his ledger, "By 4 Play Tickets 30/." But, according to his diary, he did not use these on June 16 for *The Beggar's Opera*, as he recorded the purchase of two box seats for that evening. Throughout the next week, before his departure for Mount Vernon on June 22, he attended the theater on four other occasions.

The actors remained in Williamsburg until after August 13, 1770. On that date, Edward Charlton dressed the hair of the Douglasses, the Hallams, Owen Morris, and Mr. Parker. One unusual occurrence is noted here. Although Lewis Hallam had obviously separated from Sarah Hallam some years earlier, he paid for services rendered "Mrs. Hallam" by Charlton. Either the separation had been amiable, or young Hallam was traveling with a female companion to whom he lent his name for the sake of appearances.[1]

Shortly after Charlton dressed their hair, the comedians left for Annapolis, now claiming the distinction of "the genteelist town in North America." The Maryland run looked promising. Governor Horatio Sharpe, according to William Eddis, held a strong conviction that the stage, under proper supervision, could be "made subservient to the great interests of religion and virtue." Then, too, this was the racing season in the Maryland capital, and within a month, the General Assembly was to convene, both events calculated to swell appreciably the normal population of the community. There was no warning the actors were coming, merely a brief notice that they had arrived and their stay would be brief: "On Monday last, the SUSPICIOUS HUSBAND and THOMAS AND SALLY were performed, by the American Company of Comedians, at the Theatre in this City, to a polite Audience who testified great Satisfaction at their Entertainment. The Company's Engagement in Virginia will prevent them from performing here any longer than the end of next Month." An announcement in the same issue of the *Maryland Gazette* advised that the next two attractions would be *Cymbeline* and *Love in a Village;* this was the last occasion upon which Douglass saw fit to indulge in newspaper advertising during this stay in Annapolis.

The performance of *Cymbeline* drew encomiums from one of the local swains, and young Jonathan Boucher, Anglican rector of Annapolis, ventured so far into the worldly as to wax rapturous in a panegyric extoling the charms of Nancy Hallam. "X. Z." displayed a remarkable command of laudatory adjectives as he described the excellence of the American Company—but it is to be noted that he lavished his praise upon actresses only:

"I shall not at present expatiate on the Merits of the whole Performance but confine myself principally to one Object. The Actors are, indubitably, intitled to a very considerable Portion of Praise. But, by your Leave, Gentlemen (to speak in the Language of Hamlet), 'Here's Metal more attractive.' On finding that the part of Imogen was to be played by Miss Hallam, I instantly formed to myself, from my Predilection for her, the most sanguine Hope of Entertainment. But how was I ravished on Experiment! She exceeded my utmost Idea. Such delicacy of Manner! Such classical Strictures of Expression! The Musick of her Tongue! The *vox liquida,* how melting! Notwithstanding the Injuries it received from the horrid Ruggedness of the Roof, and the untoward Construction of the whole House; methought I heard once more the warbling of [Mrs. Theophilus] Cibber in my Ear. How true and thorough her Knowledge of the Character she personated! Her whole Form and Dimensions how happily convertible, and universally adapted to the Variety of her Part.

"A Friend of mine, who was present, was so deeply impressed by the bewitching Grace and Justness with which the Actress filled the whole Character, that, immediately on going Home,

Harlequin as Played by John Rich at Covent Garden
Courtesy of Harvard Theatre Collection

he threw out warm from the Heart, as well as Brain, the verses I inclose you.

"The House, however, was thin, I suppose for want of a sufficient Acquaintance with general, as well as particular Merits of the Performers. The characteristical Propriety of Mrs. Douglass cannot be but too striking to pass unnoticed. The fine Genius of that young Creature Miss [Maria] Storer unquestionably affords the most pleasing Prospect of an accomplished Actress. The discerning Part of an Audience that cheerfully pay the Tribute of Applause due to the solid Sense which is conspicuous in Mrs. Harman, as well as to her Perspicuity and Strength of Memory.

"The Sums lavished on a late Set, whose Merits were not of the transcendent Kind, in whatever Point of Light they are viewed, are still fresh in our Memories. And should these, their Successors, whose Deportment, Decency, and an unremitting Study to please, have ever confessedly marked, meet with Discountenance, methinks such a Conduct would not reflect the highest Honour either on our Taste or Spirit.

"The Merit of Mr. Douglass's Company is, notoriously in the Opinion of every Man of Sense in America, whose Opportunities give him a Title to Judge—take them for all in all—superior to that of any Company in *England,* except those of the Metropolis. The Dresses are remarkably elegant; the Dispatch of the Business of the Theatre uncommonly quick; and the Stillness and good Order preserved behind the Scenes, are Proofs of the greatest Attention and Respect paid to the Audience."

The attached verses, though unsigned, were written by the Reverend Boucher and he begged the "self-tutored PEALE" to immortalize Miss Hallam with his paints and canvas. Excerpts from his ode, "To Miss Hallam," imply that the young parson's admiration for the actress bordered on the secular:

> Hail, wond'rous Maid! I, grateful, hail
> Thy strange dramatic Pow'r
> To thee I owe, that Shakespeare's Tale
> Has charm'd my Ears once more.
>
> .   .   .   .

Say! Does she plead, as though she felt
Thy tender Tale of Woe?
Our Eyes, albeit unus'd to melt,
With Tears of Pity flow.

· · · · · · · · · · ·

She speaks!—What Elocution flows!
Ah! softer far her Strains
Than Fleeces of descending Snows,
Or gentlest vernal Rains.

Do solemn Measures slowly move?
Her looks inform the Strings:
Do Lydian Airs invite to Love?
We feel it as she sings.

Around her, see the Graces play,
See Venus' wanton Doves;
And, in her Eyes pellucid Ray,
See little laughing Loves.

Ye Gods! 'tis Cytherea's Face;
'Tis Dian's faultless Form;
But her's alone the nameless Grace
That ev'ry Heart can charm.

The "horrid Ruggedness of the Roof" was not the only flaw in the local playhouse. Douglass laid his plans for improving theatrical facilities in Annapolis by the construction of "a very handsome Theatre." The Anglican Church in the city was represented as "old and ordinary," and the land on which it stood was leased from the vestry by the manager of the theatrical company as a site on which to erect his new building. William Eddis, the new surveyor of customs for Annapolis, not only expressed his enthusiasm for the American Company, but on January 18, 1771, endorsed the method for financing the new playhouse: "My pleasure and my surprise were therefore excited in proportion, on finding performers in this country equal, at least, to those who sustain the best of the first characters in your most celebrated provincial theatres. Our governor ... patronizes the American Company; and as their present place of exhibition is in a small scale, and inconveniently situated, a subscription, by his example, has been rapidly completed to erect a new theatre, on a commodious, if not an elegant plan. The manager is to deliver tickets for two seasons, to the amount of the respective subscriptions, and it is imagined, that the money received at the doors, from non-subscribers, will enable him to conduct the business without difficulty; and when the limited number of performances is completed, the intire property is to be vested in him. This will be a valuable addition to our catalogue of amusements. The building is already in a state of forwardness, and the day of opening is anxiously awaited." [2] The very fact that Douglass was able to build a theater at all, albeit by subscriptions, implies that his major financial difficulties had been solved.

Leaving Annapolis, as planned, to meet prior commitments in Virginia and to allow time for the construction of the new building, Douglass and his comedians, for the next eighteen months, traveled between Williamsburg and Annapolis, playing short engagements in the smaller communities along the way. In January, 1771, they were at Dumfries, Virginia, perhaps playing in the new sixty by twenty-eight foot Assembly Room for which bids had been solicited two years earlier. In this village, on January 23, George Washington saw *The Recruiting Officer*, and upon his return six days later, he purchased two tickets in the pit. From his notation, "By Esps. at the Play 6s. 3d.," it would seem he spent something for refreshments, possibly at the makeshift bar sometimes set up in theaters of the day. [3]

By late March, the comedians were in Williamsburg. On April 19, Hudson Muse wrote his brother from Northumberland County: "In a few days after I got to Virginia, I set out for Wmsbrg, where I was detained for 11 days, tho' I spent the time very agreeably, at the plays every night, & really must join Mr. Ennalls & Mr. Basset in thinking Miss Hallam super fine. But must confess her luster was much sullied by the number of Beauties that appeared at that court. The house was crowded every night, & the gentlemen who have generally attended that place agree there was treble the number of fine Ladys that was ever seen in the town before—for my part I think it would be impossible for a man to have fixed upon a partner for life, the choice was too general to have fixed on one. About the latter end of this month, I intend down again. & perhaps shall make out another trip as the players are to be there again, and its an amusement I am so very fond of."

The American Company acted in Williamsburg and its environs until late May. While Washington was in Williamsburg this month, he, almost as a matter of course, attended the playhouse whenever the opportunity presented itself. On May 2, 3, and 8, he was in the audience and, on the last occasion, acted as host to a theater party, dining earlier in the evening with "Colo. Fairfax and some Gentlemen," with his expenditure for play tickets on this night totalling 37s. 6d.[4]

An announcement on May 16 stated that the company would appear near the end of the month in Fredericksburg, where they were to perform every Monday, Wednesday, and Friday evening. This was but a continuance of Douglass' shrewd practice of following the crowds, for the annual fair was to be held in Fredericksburg during June. The company opened there no later than Tuesday, May 28, when they presented *The Provok'd Husband*, followed on successive nights by *Hamlet* and *All in the Wrong*. The cast at this time was essentially the same as it had been for the past two years, with the exception of John Henry, who had been sent to England to recruit new actors and acquire new scenes for the opening of the new Annapolis Theatre. In Fredericksburg, the actors obviously played in a courtroom or warehouse, as only pit seats were advertised. Washington was in town visiting relatives and, after dining with his brother-in-law on July 24, spent the rest of the evening at the playhouse.[5]

From Fredericksburg to Annapolis, the logical route for a troupe of strolling players would be by way of Dumfries, Alexandria, Piscataway, Port Tobacco, and Upper Marlborough. Playing short engagements in each of these towns on the return to the Maryland capital, Douglass timed his arrival so as to appear in Annapolis in time for the September racing season and the meeting of the General Assembly on October 1.

The new theater was near completion. Built of brick, it was probably the finest playhouse in the colonies, notwithstanding the claims made for the Southwark Theatre in Philadelphia. In June, Douglass had made a hurried visit to Annapolis to check on the progress of the construction and stimulate the payment of pledges. An advertisement in the *Maryland Gazette*, on June 13, had promised greater entertainment facilities with the completion of the

NEW THEATRE

Mr. Douglass begs Leave to acquaint the Gentlemen, who have subscribed to the new Theatre in Annapolis, that all the Materials for the Building are now purchased, and the Workmen engaged to complete it by the First of September: He assures them, that nothing will be wanting on his Part, nor on the Parts of the Gentlemen who have undertaken to superintend the Work, to render it as commodious and elegant as any Theatre in America. He has sent to London to engage some Performers, and expects them, and a new Set of Scenes, painted by Mr. Doll, in a few Weeks. In short, the Publick, whose Favours he most gratefully acknowledges, will, he flatters himself, be convinced by the efforts he makes to entertain them, that he has a proper Sense of their Goodness, and an unremitting Desire to make every Return in his Power, for the Obligations he is under to them.

He would esteem it as a very great Favour, if the Gentlemen who have neglected to pay their Subscription Money, will be good enough to send it as soon as possible, as the Sum collected, it is by no means sufficient to answer the necessary Demands that will very soon be made.

The new theater, located on West Street next to Reynolds' Tavern, was still unfinished when it opened on September 9,

1771, with *The Roman Father* and *The Mayor of Garrat*. The first night drew "a numerous and brilliant Audience, who expressed the greatest Satisfaction not only at the performance, but with the House, which is thought to be as elegant and commodious, for its Size, as any Theatre in America." Douglass, quite properly, spoke the prologue, and the epilogue was recited by Ann Storer Henry; one or both may have been written by Jonathan Boucher. Douglass' appeal to the audience was ponderous in style and sprinkled with classical allusions, but in the blithesome epilogue, Mrs. Henry begged the customers "for the unfinish'd State of our House make Allowance," before candidly admitting:

> And a Sinner, I am, for no Woman ere breathing
> Turn'd Actress, but strait she was reckon'd a Heathen:
> And how then in Conscience, can I, a forlorn One,
> Be thought any other, for i'Faith, I was born One.

The promised new scenery was not displayed on opening night. The *Jenny*, bringing John Henry from England, did not drop anchor in Norfolk until September 11. He had been unable to employ actors, for in London, at this time, "tolerable actors" were "very scarce." The new backdrops had arrived by November 2; on that date William Eddis commented: "Our new theatre, of which I gave you an account in a former letter, was opened to a numerous audience the week preceding the races. The structure is not inelegant, but, in my opinion, on too narrow a scale for its length; the boxes are commodious, and neatly decorated; the pit and gallery are calculated to hold a number of people without incommoding each other; the stage is well adapted for dramatic and pantomimical exhibitions; and several of the scenes reflect great credit on the ability of the painter. I have before observed that the performers are considerably above mediocrity; therefore little doubt can be entertained of their preserving the public favour, and reaping a plenteous harvest."

The elegance of the new theater, contrasted with the drabness of the church, was disturbing to the Reverend Jonathan Boucher, and although he harbored no enmity towards the actors, his published lament ran:

> Here in Annapolis alone,
> God has the meanest House in Town.

Jeremiads were lost in the sounds of gaiety; this was the racing season and the theater was at its sparkling best. Among those attracted by the racing was the Squire of Mount Vernon, and on four of the nine nights Washington spent in Annapolis, he attended performances in the playhouse. Undoubtedly, he inspected what was then the talk of the town, the portrait of Nancy Hallam that the local artist, Charles Willson Peale, had painted in response to the lyric appeal of the year before. She had been portrayed as Imogen in a scene from *Cymbeline* in which the beautiful and unfortunate girl, disguised as the boy Fidele, emerges from a forest cave, with fearfully uplifted eyes, into the astonished presence of Bellarius and his royal wards. Peale retained the picture as an exhibition piece in his studio and later hung it in his museum. This combination of Nancy Hallam on canvas and in the flesh led "Paladour" to range into the rhapsodic in the "Poet's Corner" of the *Maryland Gazette:*

> SAY, HALLAM, to the wond'rous Art
> What Tribute shall I pay?
> Say, wilt thou, from a feeling Heart,
> Accept this votive Lay?
>
> .   .   .   .
>
> From earliest Youth; with Rapture, oft
> I've turn'd great Shakespear's Page;
> Pleas'd, when he's gay, and sooth'd, when soft,
> Or kindled at his Rage.
>
> Yet not till now, till taught by Thee,
> Conceiv'd I Half in his Pow'r!
> I read, admiring now I see,
> I only not adore.
>
> .   .   .   .

Methinks I see his smiling Shade,
And hear thusly him Proclaim,
"In Western Worlds, to this fair Maid,
I trust my spreading Fame."

Peale, likewise, was praised in metrical composition by a local minstrel:

Thy Pencil has so well the Scene convey'd,
Thought seems but an unnecessary Aid;

followed by a plea to apply his talents to another feminine member of the company:

Another Scene still claim's thy Pencil's Aid;
Storer in Ariel. Enchanting Maid!

Apparently feeling that one portrait of an actress of the American Company was enough, Peale disregarded this request, depriving Maria Storer of her opportunity for immortality on canvas.

Maria Storer of the fairy-like figure and the excellent singing voice charmed the audience almost as much as did Nancy Hallam. Another of the actresses also had her following among the faithful; the second Mrs. Owen Morris, "a tall and elegant woman," was much admired for her "very spirited" acting.[6]

Annapolis audiences had little time to compare the beauty and talents of the actresses. After a short season, the company swung back to Williamsburg, opening in the Virginia capital in late October with Richard Cumberland's new action-filled comedy *The West Indian* and *The Musical Lady*. George Washington arrived in town about the same time, presumably to record the land he claimed under the provisions of the Dinwiddie Proclamation of 1754 as a reward for past military service. As usual, he combined business with pleasure and attended the theater on five of the ten nights he spent in Williamsburg. He returned to Mount Vernon five days too soon to have witnessed the first Virginia performance of *King Lear* on November 12, 1771. The many evening entertainments scheduled for this session of the General Court forced the company to present their plays in the afternoon, and it seems likely that it was Douglass who superintended the spectacular fireworks display on the afternoon of November 1.

Soon after the first of January, 1772, the comedians journeyed to Norfolk for a short stay, but they assured their Williamsburg patrons that they would return in time for the spring meeting of the General Assembly and would remain through the April court; this, however, would mark their last appearance in Virginia for some time, as the American Company would be forced to return northward to fulfill previous commitments. There is no record of the plays presented in Norfolk, but they were performed in a theater converted from an abandoned pottery near the river on Main Street.

George Washington was in Williamsburg when Douglass and his players returned and was in the theater on March 12. His stay in town extended from March 2 through April 19, but with politics bordering on the turbulent, he appeared at the theater upon only three occasions, probably witnessing the presentations of Cumberland's *The Brothers* and Hugh Kelly's *False Delicacy*. Certainly, he saw the hit play of the season on March 26, Kelly's *A School for Libertines, or A Word to the Wise*, the only program that encouraged comment from the *Virginia Gazette:* "Mr. Kelly's new Comedy, *A Word to the Wise*, was performed at our Theatre last Thursday, to a very crowded and splendid Audience. It was received both Nights with the warmest Marks of Approbation; the Sentiments with which this excellent Piece is replete were greatly, and deservedly applauded; and the Audience, while they did Justice to the Merit of the Author, did no less Honour to their own refined Taste. If the Comick Writers would pursue Mr. Kelly's plan, and present us only with moral Plays, the Stage would become (what it ought to be) a School of Politeness and Virtue.

"Truth indeed, obliges us to confess that for several Years past, most of the new Plays that have come under our Observation have had a moral Tendency, but there is not enough of them to supply the Theatre with a Variety of Exhibitions sufficient to engage the Attention of the Public; and the most desirable Enjoyments by too frequent a Repetition, become insipid."

Other new plays were put into rehearsal and a new actress made a brief appearance with the company. She was Mrs. Stamper, who played several major roles and, upon one occasion, was advertised as a singer. She failed to realize her promise, for she rarely appeared in important parts after the comedians left Williamsburg. Rehearsals of the latest plays from London were going well, and, on May 7, the *Gazette* carried this item: "We are authorized to announce that the new Comedy of THE FASHIONABLE LOVER, now acting at the Theatres Royal in Drury Lane and Edinburgh, with the utmost Applause, will shortly appear in our Theatre. Such is the Industry of the American Company, that though the Piece has not been above ten Days in the Country, it has been rehearsed more than once, and is already, we hear, fit for Representation." This performance of Cumberland's newest play drew customers from as far away as Yorktown and led William Reynolds to comment: "I am much obliged to you for the Fashble Lover which I have had an opportunity of seeing presented on our Williamsburg Stage but dont think it by any means equal to his West Indian."

The company, as the April court began to draw to its close, began to make preparations for moving. On April 30, 1772, David Douglass advertised his carriage for sale, "a Genteel Phaeton," complete with four sets of harness. Although it was announced that it would be "some Years" before the possible return of the American Company, neither the players nor the townspeople recognized this as the last occasion upon which the American Company or any other troupe of professional actors would appear in colonial Williamsburg. Four months were spent on the road before the comedians reappeared in Annapolis. Possibly, Richmond was included in their itinerary, for it boasted a theater by that date.[7]

They opened in Annapolis' West Street Theatre on September 1 with Kelly's *A Word to the Wise* and Garrick's *Lethe*. New scenery, painted by Richards, the London artist, was featured in the initial advertising. Practices for the reservation of box seats were revealed in the bills of the day: "Places in the

Boxes may be had at the Theatre, where a Book is kept for that Purpose. Ladies and Gentlemen who take Places will please to send their Servants at Five o'Clock, and they shall be put in Possession of them." On opening night, the "brilliant and judicious Assembly" crowding the playhouse expressed their satisfaction with "The Alterations and Improvements since last Season, [which] have made this Theatre the most commodious and elegant of any, that we know of, in America." Lewis Hallam's prologue, "written by a Gentleman in this City" (probably William Eddis), appealed to both England and her colonies to allay their growing bitterness towards one another:

> A nobler Subject now inspires my Breast,
> In ev'ry gen'rous, honest Mind, confest,
> I feel the ardent Passion fire my Heart;
> Exempt from tragic Pomp, or servile Art.
> Long may blest Concord here maintain her Sway,
> And radiant Science gild each rising Day;
> Whilst Patriots plead, without one private View,
> And glorious Liberty alone pursue!
> So shall the Mother Isles with Joy approve,
> And aid their Offspring with parental Love!

As Hallam finished his prologue and retired backstage, "the Curtain drew up, the new Scenes painted by Mr. Richards presented themselves to us, and exhibited a View of a superb Apartment, at the end of a fine Colonade of Pilars of the Ionic Order, which, by the happy Disposition of the Lights, had a most pleasing Effect." The play itself "was received with the greatest Marks of Approbation."

There was a nostalgic note in the program of September 28. A special benefit, "by Particular Desire," was staged for Henrietta Osborne, now retired in Annapolis and devoting her energies to her store near the market-house. On this occasion, there was only one role for Mrs. Osborne—Sir Harry Wildair in *The Constant Couple*. It was an appropriate swan song, for never again was her name to appear in the cast of a play presented on the colonial stage.

George Washington arrived in the Maryland capital too late to see Mrs. Osborne in the part she had made famous. He, along with his stepson, John Parke Custis, did not arrive for the Annapolis races until early October. In addition to his usual run of poor luck at the race track, where he lost bets totaling £1. 6*s.*, he incurred additional expense through his attendance at the playhouse upon at least four occasions. Almost certainly, he attended the special race, on October 8, run for "The American Theatrical Company's Purse of Fifty Pounds, free for any horse, Mare or Gelding to carry nine Stone. Heats 4 Miles." And unless he placed his bet on Mr. Water's "Nettle," he lost once again. Winner or loser, he did attend the performance of *The West Indian* and *The Padlock* that evening at the theater.[8]

The Annapolis theatrical season lasted well past the middle of October. With the closing of the West Street playhouse, the comedians made their way back to Philadelphia, their financial status much improved over what it had been two years before.

· XII ·

THE LAST TOUR OF
THE AMERICAN COMPANY

*(Philadelphia, New York, Annapolis,
and Charleston, 1772-1774)*

Insofar as drama in general was concerned, opposition
in Philadelphia had waned into complacency. Antipathy was reserved for professional drama; a stout line of demarcation had
been drawn between the amateur and professional actor. No
outcry against the evils of the theater had been raised when the
students of Joseph Rathell's school gave a public performance
of *Cato* in 1771. In fact, when facilities at the school proved
inadequate to accommodate the crowd, Rathell rented the Assembly Room and scheduled a second performance on April 18,
adding entertainments that included a musical interlude and
charging half a crown to aid in defraying expenses. Presbyterians
raised no objection when the students of the grammar school of
Princeton College performed a "dramatick Piece, in Latin, be-

fore a numerous and learned Audience" as an exercise to demonstrate their proficiency in the language.[1]

On October 28, 1772, Douglass opened the Southwark Theatre with *A Word to the Wise*, coupled with *The Padlock* as an afterpiece. Mrs. Owen Morris was the only new member of the cast and, even now, was unveiling the eccentricity that was to characterize her later life. The opening night's program was well received by the theatergoers of Philadelphia, with "Philo Theatricus" publishing a lengthy critique of the actors, the play, and the audience. The efforts of Lewis Hallam as Mungo in *The Padlock* were thought worthy; Miss Hallam was "as much a Woman of Fashion as we have seen on any stage"; and the other actresses, "besides their pleasing Figures, were genteel, elegant, and fashionable in their Deportment." Only Thomas Wall was subjected to adverse criticism, and an apology was found for him in that "we verily believe that Mr. Wall does as well as he can, and therefore we must by no Means censure him."

A Word to the Wise received the same favorable response it had evoked in Williamsburg and Annapolis, and in this critic's opinion, "Comedy, we think is the best acting Sermon of Morality, we have heard and we sincerely congratulate the Friends of the Theatre, upon the Chastity and Purity of our modern Comedies; where Vice, if held up to the public View at all, is shewn in so deformed, so ludicrous a Light, that to see it, is sufficient to make us abhor and detest it; and where Virtue appears dignified, by Sentiments that do Honour to Humanity, and is beheld in every Light that can excite our Admiration. . . . We flatter ourselves that the little dirty commonplace Aspersions, with which the illiberal Hand of Ignorance has so frequently larded it, will vanish. . . ."

More caustic strictures were directed towards the behavior of the audience, and violent censure was directed at the conduct of "some Ruffians in the Gallery, who so frequently interrupted the Performance, and in the most interesting Scenes, [and who] deserve the severest Reprehension—they are too despicable to argue with, otherwise they might be told that, because they pay three Shillings for their Admittance into a Public Assembly, they are not, therefore, warranted to commit repeated Outrages, upon that part of the Audience who go there really to see the Play, and be instructed and entertained; or to interrupt the Actors who are doing their best to please them. They might be informed, that, tho' they have an undoubted Right to every Species of Entertainment, promised them in the Bills, they have not the smallest Title to any Thing else, and that if they call for a Song, or a Prologue, of which no Notice is given in the Bills, the Actors have an equal Demand upon them for an extraordinary Price for a Compliance with their Request—which of those vociferous Gentlemen, if a Carpenter, Mason, or Taylor, will do more Work than he bargains for without adequate Compensation?—Are not the Players in the same Predicament?—But to dismiss the Subject, the Directors of the Theatre are thus publicly desired to engage a Number of Constables, and dispose them in different Parts of the Gallery, who upon the smallest Disturbance, for the Future, may be authorized, by any Magistrate, and there are always enough in the House, to apprehend, and carry to the Work-House, such Rioters, by which Means, Peace will be restored, and a few Examples deter others from the like Outrages." This public scolding quieted the "Gallery Gods," but only briefly. At the time, no one seemed to realize that the disruption of the performance was a reflection of the general political unrest, and the rowdy element had taken their cue from the English Whigs. When *A Word to the Wise* was first played in London's Drury Lane in March, 1770, the performance was broken up by groans and hisses merely because Hugh Kelly was suspected of writing for the king's party.

There was some feeling that the mischief makers had gained entrance to the theater with counterfeit tickets, and when the performance of Arthur Murphy's *The Way to Keep Him* was advertised for November 23, the playbills carried the tag, "Those who are possessed of *Gallery Tickets*, bought for any of the preceding Plays, are requested to bring them in this Night, as a new Set is made out, and none of the old ones will be admitted afterwards." Smouldering resentment at British retaliation for the burning of the *Gaspée*, fired by reactivated committees of correspondence, hung heavy in the winter air. It burst forth into violence in a riot outside the gallery door on the night of December 9, "when the Doorkeepers were greatly abused in the Execution of their Office." Two of the trouble makers were seized and carted away to the workhouse by the constables. This was but a lull, for some of the group returned to the darkened theater after the evening's performance and exercised their wrath in acts of vandalism. Five days later, a notice appeared in the *Pennsylvania Packet:*

TEN POUNDS REWARD
A Burglary

Whereas a number of evil disposed persons, in the night between the ninth and tenth instant (December) burglariously and feloniously broke open the gallery door of the Theatre, tore off and carried away the iron spikes which divide the galleries from the upper boxes; and had they not been then detected and put to flight by the servants of the Theatre, who dwell in the house, would, there is reason to imagine, have completed their malicious designs. In order therefore, that the perpetrators may be brought to justice, the above reward is offered to whoever will discover any of the persons concerned in the said burglary, to be paid on their conviction.

DAVID DOUGLASS

Nothing indicates that the vandals were ever apprehended.

The right-minded faction shunned violence, and although their anti-theater barbs had become less frequent, one writer directed a potent query to the actors: "Are not all the meaner passions of the soul in you extinct, and when you throw off these garments of the flesh, will you not appear before the father of spirits with that boldness which goodness alone inspires, confident that you have fully answered the purposes, for which he sent you into life?" [2]

Despite the physical frenzy of the habitués of the cheaper seats and the literary scorn of the more devout, the Philadelphia season of 1772-73 was a success. Such popular favorites as *The Roman Father, Love in a Village, The West Indian,* and *The Mourning Bride* found favor, as did selections from Shakespeare. Lewis Hallam now made only infrequent appearances in singing roles and seems to have channeled his musical talents into other endeavors. He did not appear in such plays as *Love in a Village* and *The School for Fathers,* but the bills noted that "the orchestra [is] to be conducted by Mr. Hallam." Personnel changes had taken place. Samuel Greville had become disenchanted with the stage and had sought greener pastures; a Mr. Dermot replaced him. Mr. Johnson was a new name appearing on the bills, but he was listed so seldom that it must be concluded that he was but a backstage employee pressed into service for those plays that demanded a large cast. On January 30, 1773, a "Monsieur Francis" was announced as a new dancer "from the Theatre in Amsterdam." Five days later, Mrs. Stamper made her final and only appearance since Williamsburg and was now billed as a singer "from the Theatre Royal in Edinburgh." Francis, whose real name was Francis Mentges, later became an officer in the American army during the Revolution.

Similarly, there were innovations among the regular members of the cast. John Henry was now developing Shylock as one of his better roles, while the second Mrs. Morris, whose height and stately carriage made her ideal for the part, played Portia. She also assumed some of the more mature characters formerly acted by Margaret Cheer. Mrs. Douglass was ill during a large part of this Philadelphia season and appeared intermittently. Nancy Hallam now played practically all of the younger heroines, while Maria Storer scampered about the stage in such roles as "Ariel, an Airy Sprite." Yet, there were never enough actors to fill the casting demands of some productions. When *Henry IV* was staged on January 11, 1773, three actors were forced to appear in double roles, in addition to parts in the farce, Coffey's *The Devil to Pay, or The Wives Metamorphosed.*

Despite the popularity of the newer plays from London, there were frequent requests for old favorites. At times, solicitations were so insistent that Douglass was forced to insert a statement in the newspapers that he would get to them as quickly as possible. Additional machinery and scenes were now and then introduced for such innovations as the "Grand Masque" of *Neptune and Amphitrite*. Religious opposition had evidently faded into such a state of tranquility that Nancy Hallam even dared play an occasional breeches part—never before performed in Philadelphia.

The presentation of George Cockling's *The Conquest of Canada, or The Siege of Quebec*, on February 17, 1773, was the most spectacular production in the twenty-one year existence of the American Company. The playwright had been stationed in Boston for a number of years as a government official, and his play, first published in London in 1766, saw its first Philadelphia edition December 9, 1772. Douglass was besieged with many requests for this martial drama, including those from the two "Gentlemen" listed in the cast. Soldiers and sailors from the local garrison and naval vessels appeared on stage through the courtesy of their commanding officers. No farce was scheduled as Douglass assured his patrons that: "It will be taken as a favour, if the Town, for that night, will dispense with a Farce; as the Stage will be much crowded with the Artillery, Boats, &c. necessary for the representation of the piece; and with the Men from both Corps, whose assistance the Commanding Officers are glad enough to indulge us with."

So well was this extravaganza received that it was repeated twice, but on later occasions, there was no mention of the authentic properties or temporary actors furnished by the naval and military forces; indeed, it is very likely they were absent, for a farce was added in the subsequent performances. This play, with its North American background, revived memories of Thomas Godfrey and his *Prince of Parthia*. Less than a month later, in a poem "On the Death of Mr. Thomas Godfrey," an unknown admirer lamented, "His Roses fade, his Lillies bloom no more," but still stoutly maintained that "While Genius blossoms Godfrey still shall live."

Less than two weeks later, another new play was acted for the first time on an American stage, a dramatic romance by Thomas Arne and David Garrick called *Cymon*, which, although not so pretentious in display as *The Conquest of Canada*, did feature a

"Procession of the Different Orders of Chivalry; and the Shepherds of Arcadia, with a Sett of Transparent Scenes."

On March 8, when *The Fashionable Lover* was presented as the first benefit of the season, the Masons honored Mr. and Mrs. Douglass. Stephen Woolls sang "The Mason's Anthem," and Douglass costumed himself "in the Character of a Master Mason" to speak the prologue. When, on March 24, *The Recruiting Officer* was presented on behalf of Messrs. Byerley, Parker, and Johnson, Mrs. Morris was cast in the role of Sylvia "by particular Desire." Evidently, there was some doubt expressed as to her ability to handle the part, for the playbill carried the courteous but defiant explanation: "Mrs. Morris, in respect to those few Ladies and Gentlemen, who through kindness to her, have advised her not to play the part of *Sylvia*, begs leave to assure them, that she performs it now, in compliance with the request of many Friends of the Theatre, and with a fixed rule amongst Performers, to lend each other every help they can, in the time of Benefits."

The last benefit in Philadelphia, *The Wonder! A Woman Keeps a Secret!* was given for John and Ann Henry on March 29. Unusually heavy spring rains had caused the cancellation of so many programs that, upon this occasion, the bills carried the assurance that the play would be performed despite unfavorable weather. Two more nights of playing brought the season to a close, and the company prepared to make the journey to New York. John Henry, now treasurer of the company, ran a card in the local papers calling upon all creditors to the company to present their bills for payment—in itself, an indication that the finances of the troupe were better than they had been for some time.[3]

By April 12, New York newspapers were advising that the John Street Theatre would open April 14 and that the season would last no longer than the end of May. As usual, Thomas Wall utilized his time away from the playhouse to increase his income and announced his services as a music teacher, this time as an instructor on the mandolin rather than the guitar.

The first play of the season was so well received that braggadocio swaggered in the playbills. When *The Way to Keep Him* and *Catherine and Petruchio* were acted on April 23, pomposity tinged the announcement: "Those who neglect attending the Theatre this Evening, will lose the most finish'd Nights Entertainment the American Theatre ever produced."

Douglass was, however, providing New York theatergoers with full value for the price of admission. Not only were they presented with the usual play and farce, but, quite often, there were such additional attractions as "Balancing, Tumbling, and Slack-Rope"—sometimes without previous mention in the bills. Yet, even this was not always sure to please the boisterous element in the gallery. As in Philadelphia, the manager was forced to resort to stringent measures, and on May 2, he included a threat along with a reprimand: "The repeated Insults, which some mischievous Persons in the Gallery have given, not only to the Stage and Orchestra, but to the other Parts of the Audience, call loudly for Reprehension; and since they have been more than once, ineffectually admonish'd of the Impropriety of such a Conduct in a public Assembly, they are now (for the last Time) inform'd, that unless the more regular and better dispos'd People, who frequent that Part of the Theatre, will interfere, either by turning out the Offenders, or pointing them out to the Constables, who attend there on purpose, that they may be brought to justice, *The Gallery for the future must be shut up*." Inasmuch as there was no further mention of disturbances in this section of the playhouse, it may be assumed that this threat was effective.

William Hulett was still operating his dancing school and, no doubt, providing music for the theater. Still a favorite with the actors, he was possibly responsible for persuading the Misses Hallam and Storer to lend their talents to a concert given for a Mr. Zedwitz on May 11. Nancy Hallam sang two of the more popular numbers of the day, "Vain is Beauty's gawdy Flower" and "The Soldier tired of War's Alarms," while tiny Maria Storer appeared in a duet with Hulett's ten-year-old son.

On May 10, 1773, *The Gamester* and *The Padlock* were the selections for the evening. A young, but frail, Josiah Quincy, who was returning to Boston from South Carolina, was in New

York long enough to savor the entertainment offered by "the nursery of vice" that was denied him in Massachusetts. The occasion was unusual enough to lead him to note in his journal: "Went to the playhouse, saw the Gamester and Padlock performed. The players make an indifferent picture in tragedy. They make a better in comedy. Hallam has merit in every character he acts. Mr. Woolls in the character of Don Diego, and Mrs. Morris in that of Ursula, I thought, acted superlatively. I was, however, much gratified upon the whole, and I believe if I had staid in town a month I should go to the theatre every acting night. But as a citizen and friend to the morals and happiness of society, I should strive hard against the admission, and much more the establishment of a play-house of any state of which I was a member."

The new farce, *Cross Purposes,* was presented for the first time on a colonial stage on May 27, 1773, as an afterpiece for *Hamlet.* It was hailed as "altogether a laughable lively production, and, from the temporary satire upon the reigning follies and vices of the times, will probably have a run." New Yorkers were particularly interested in this comedy, for the author, William O'Brien, had formerly resided in their city for several years. One out-of-town visitor took advantage of this program to visit the New York theater for the first time. He was that inveterate theatergoer, George Washington, who had journeyed to New York to establish his stepson, John Parke Custis, as a student in King's College.[4]

Notwithstanding Douglass' earlier assertion that the company would remain in the city no longer than the end of May, they continued playing on through the summer. The season was not without sorrow. One of the few remaining members of the original Douglass Company was lost to the stage when Mrs. Harman died, after a lingering illness of several months. In early June, the local papers carried her obituary: "On Thursday last died in the 43d year of her age, Mrs. Catherine Maria Harman, grand daughter to the celebrated Colley Cibber, Esq.; *poet laureate,* she was a just actress, possessed with much merit in low comedy and dressed all of her characters with infinite propriety, but her figure prevented her from succeeding in tragedy, and in genteel comedy. In private life, she was sensible, humane and benevolent, her little fortune she has left to Miss Cheer, and her obsequies were on Saturday night attended by a very genteel procession to the cemetery of the Old English [Trinity] Church."

With the passing of one familiar figure from the stage, another made a brief return appearance. Margaret Cheer was given a benefit on June 21, playing The Lady in the first American production of Milton's *Comus* and Kitty in *High Life Below Stairs*. After appearing as Queen Elizabeth, in Douglass' benefit of *Richard III* on June 24, her subsequent dramatic activities were limited. Evidently, none of the actresses would relinquish their roles to the former Lady Rosehill, and she was reduced to making one last effort by speaking the Mason's prologue when the fraternity honored John Henry and Thomas Wall for their benefit on St. John's Day, June 25. Once again, she returned to obscurity. Mrs. Henry also disappeared, but only temporarily, and possibly because of an accouchement.

Despite an occasional diatribe against the drama by "Cato," who declared the theater to be little more than a harlot's market place, the American Company prospered in New York. More and more, additional entertainments were featured on the programs. On one occasion, "Some pieces of Musick" were offered by the band of the Royal Welsh Fusiliers. On those days when there was no performance at the John Street playhouse, and Thomas Wall was not occupied with mandolin lessons, he gave illustrated (by paintings and drawings) lectures in "Mr. Hull's Long Room."

After the last of the personal benefits was played, *George Barnwell* and *Edgar and Emmeline* were presented on July 26, for the benefit of the proposed hospital in New York, "in return for the many favours they [the actors] have received from the inhabitants of this place." To justify this source of income, it was "hoped by the friends of the Hospital that the Moral of the play to be acted will have some influence with even those who are otherwise no friends to the Theatre." The provost of King College, the Reverend Doctor Myles Cooper, composed a rather innocuous prologue, whose delivery by Lewis Hallam was "graceful and animated." One of the largest crowds of the season was in attendance, and the newspapers took particular care to call attention to the generosity of the company, testifying that "almost all" of the actors and non-acting personnel of the theater relinquished all claims to financial rewards.

The players lingered in New York long enough to try out one new play: Oliver Goldsmith's latest comedy, *She Stoops to Conquer, or The Mistakes of a Night*, on the night of August 2, 1773. To titillate the interest of the more critical, it was announced that the play had been designed "to recover the expiring art of writing true English comedy." "The Humour," ran the advertisements, "is irresistible ... and the incidents that appear improbable are, in general, the natural Effects of the Thoughtless sallies of a young frolicksome country squire." Serving as a vehicle for the introduction of one George Hughes to the colonial stage, the performance drew enthusiastic reviews. Its success was "on our stage unexampled, Mr. Hallam and every other Actor exerted all their comic powers, and appeared thrice themselves on this occasion." Douglass was not present to witness this triumph; already, he had sailed for Charleston to complete the necessary arrangements for soliciting subscriptions and constructing a new theater there. After a repeat performance of *She Stoops to Conquer,* on August 5, the company made its preparations to travel. John Henry, acting as manager in the absence of Douglass, left New York ahead of the other actors, hurrying to Annapolis to ready the West Street Theatre.[5]

Perhaps it was because the Maryland capital was thronged with visitors attracted by the fall racing season that the American Company saw fit to engage in little local advertising. Among those arriving to see the horses run was George Washington, who had no way of knowing that, at the time, he was seeing the American Company for the last time as a unit. Of the six days he was in Annapolis, three nights were spent at the theater, and his expenditures of £3. 6s. for play tickets almost equaled the £3. 16s. he lost at the race course and the card tables. The 1773 season in Annapolis opened around the first of September and continued through the second week of October. Local poets focused their attentions upon Maria Storer, and "Philomenos" sang the praises of her sweet voice:

> While now she wakes that living lay,
> And fills the enraptur'd soul.
> I feel my beating heart obey,
> And own her lost controul.
> Sweet Marmonist! prolong the strain
> The melody of heav'n;
> And soothe with songs, the tender pain,
> Thy tender songs have giv'n————

One bit of whimsy amused Mrs. Douglass during the company's stay in Annapolis; she had the singular experience of reading her own obituary which appeared in a number of newspapers: "Last Week died at Philadelphia, Mrs. Douglass, Wife of Mr. David Douglass, Manager of the American Company of Comedians, Mother of Mr. Lewis Hallam, and Mrs. Mattocks, of Covent Garden Theatre, and Aunt of Miss Hallam; a Lady who by her excellent Performances upon the Stage, and irreproachable Manners in private Life, had recommended herself to the Friendship and Affection of many of the principal Families on the Continent and in the West Indies." This report, originating in James Rivington's New York *Gazetteer*, was soon followed by a retraction, stating that the original story "was found to be erroneous; for by late Advices from Annapolis in Maryland, where the American Company of Comedians is now performing, that Lady was in good Health, and Acting on the Stage with her usual Applause."

Douglass completed his mission in Charleston, "having secured the Patronage of the Gentlemen of that City. which will enable him to build and open an elegant Theatre before Christmas." On August 30, he sailed for Philadelphia aboard the *Sea-Nymph*. By October 9, he had rejoined his players in Annapolis, although his sudden illness led to a postponement of *The Tempest*, originally scheduled for that date. *Jane Shore* and *The Irish Widow* were substituted, with the playbills stating that printed scripts of *The Irish Widow* could be purchased either of John Henry or "at the Offices where the Tickets are sold." The night following the last play of the season, Thomas Wall kept the West Street Theatre open long enough to present the new lecture he had tried out on the New York audiences.[6]

After Annapolis, the players took the road for Philadelphia. One historian of Baltimore asserts they stopped over in that city for a short season, playing in the converted warehouse that stood at the corner of Baltimore and Frederick streets. Although the time interval may have allowed them a stay of no more than a week, there seems to be no documentary support for this conclusion.

As soon as the actors arrived in Philadelphia, and while the Southwark Theatre was being readied, Thomas Wall hired "the Long Room in Videll's Alley" and advertised his lectures. When the Southwark opened on November 1, with the *School for Fathers* and *Love-A-La-Mode*, the public were informed that "the House will be open for a Fortnight only, as the Company proposes, about that time, embarking for South Carolina."

Abbreviated as the season was, it was still long enough to allow dissension to rip the ranks of the American Company and to allow long-smouldering envy and peevishness to burst into the open. On November 3, the day *The Earl of Essex* was scheduled to be acted, Thomas Wall received a note, scrawled across the bottom of one of the old handbills advertising guitar lessons, which Wall had originally distributed in Albany. The message contained the warning:

Philadelphia

Moses Franks presents his Compliments to Mr. Wall and out of regard informs him that there is a Number of Gentlemen intend hissing Mr. Byerly, and insisting on Mr. Walls Perform[ing] the Part of Sir Walter Raleigh. Mr. Byerlys performance not being much Admir'd in this City dont let them know that I gave this hint to you.

Saturday, Nova. 3.

To avoid possible trouble, Byerley was removed from the cast, but Wall was not given the part. Sir Walter Raleigh was played by the newcomer, George Hughes. The change so upset the temperamental Byerley that he sulked for the next twelve days, and his name was not listed in the playbills during this period of internal turmoil. There was one happy, though nostalgic, note; Miss Wainwright came out of her retirement of six years to make a brief reappearance with her old companions.

Hamlet, played on November 8, was introduced by an original prologue written by William Eddis, in which "the sweets of Liberty" were extoled, reflecting the spirit of the times. A prologue the following week touched off a dispute that ended in high dudgeon, with harsh words passed both in public and privately. It had all started innocently enough with the announcement: "Mr. Douglass begs leave to assure the town, that the Play on Saturday was by him really, absolutely, and *bona fide,* intended to be the last performance of the American Company this season, but having been much solicited for the WEST-INDIAN, and the vessel in which the Company [will] embark for Carolina, having been delayed a day longer than was expected, he with pleasure, embraces the opportunity of complying with the wishes of an audience, to whom he owes every possible mark of attention, respect and gratitude."

Richard Goodman had been the original choice to speak the special prologue on this occasion, but at the last moment, Lewis Hallam either was given, or demanded, that privilege. Not only was the prologue taken from him, but Goodman was replaced by John Henry in the part of Major O'Flaherty. So infuriated was the displaced actor, and so contrary was this maneuver to the established custom of the theater, that Douglass concluded that cancellation was the only solution and issued a handbill with the explanation: "Mr. Douglass having been informed that there is a Probability of a Disturbance happening in the House this Evening, occasioned by a Dispute between Mr. Goodman and Mr. Henry concerning the part of Major O'Flaherty, thinks it a Duty incumbent upon him to do all he can to prevent it, and the only Method that suggests itself to him, is to give up the

Play entirely, for this season, for should any Mischief happen, he would think himself accountable for the Consequences."

Within hours, another broadside was being distributed through the streets of Philadelphia: "The Town's Compliments to Mr. Douglass—are sorry that his apprehension of a Disturbance in the House, should preclude them from the Pleasure they were expecting this Evening at the Representation of the West-Indian —Therefore desire, nay insist, that the Play shall go forward."

This attempt to stamp out the brush fire of internal discord availed nothing, and, two days later, a card signed by John Henry appeared in the *Pennsylvania Journal:* "JOHN HENRY most respectfully assures the Town, that he has too great a deference for their opinion to wish to do anything contrary to it. He should, had the Play gone on, have, previous to the drawing up of the curtain, addressed the Audience and submitted himself entirely to their judgment: But Mr. Douglass's concern for the peace of the Theatre prevented him from having an opportunity of evincing that respect he has for the Public, and of confusing those falsehoods that, he understands, have been propagated against him. . . ." In the long run, John Henry lost the dispute, for when *The West Indian* was acted in Charleston the following April, the part of Major O'Flaherty was played by Richard Goodman.[7]

This caviling and display of injured pride could well have played a part in the decision of several actors to break with the company before they sailed for South Carolina. Thomas Wall, finding lecturing and music teaching perhaps more lucrative than acting, was no longer listed among the players. Francis Mentges had tired of the roving life of the comedian and opened an academy in the long room of the Fountain Tavern on Chestnut Street, where he taught dancing after both the French and the German manner. And, almost immediately after the last play in Philadelphia, Mary Richardson married a Mr. Hamilton of Maryland and retired from the stage.

The remaining actors sailed for Charleston on the *Sea-Nymph,* the brigantine advertising "genteel accommodations for passengers." Arriving in the South Carolina city on Thursday, November 25, they discovered the theater still unfinished, although originally its completion had been promised for early November, but its progress was such that they could begin acting before Christmas. There is relatively little information about this new theater other than that it was located on Church Street, on the lot where the Anglican Church formerly stood.

No sooner was it known that the players were in town than "A Plain Dealer" let fly a rhyming blast at the governor for granting the necessary permission, with the dire prediction "Sure he Heaven will never win." This slight and unusual ripple of discontent was of little consequence, and the new theater was scheduled to open on December 20, although a rash of last-minute details forced a two-day postponement. When the play-house did open on December 22, the occasion was considered to be of such note that the newspapers of New York, Philadelphia, and Williamsburg all republished the local account of the first night: "On Wednesday last, the new theatre in this town was opened with Mr. Kelly's WORD TO THE WISE, and HIGH LIFE BELOW STAIRS, with an occasional prologue and epilogue spoken by Mr. Hallam and Mrs. Douglass. The performance gave universal satisfaction; Mr. Hallam in particular, in Captain Cormer, displayed his extraordinary theatrical talents, in a most spirited manner. Indeed all the performers did great justice to their characters; but that Gentleman's superior abilities were so remarkably striking, that we could not pass them over unnoticed. The house is elegantly finished, and supposed, for the size, to be the most commodious on the continent. The scenes, which are new and well designed, the dresses, the music, and what had a very pleasing effect, the disposition of the lights, all contributed to the satisfaction of the audience, who expressed the highest approbation of their entertainment." The new lighting arrangements may well have accentuated the new costumes described as "a Set of most superb Habits having been just imported from London . . . at an immense Expense."

With the waning of this first flush of enthusiasm, the season settled into routine. As in the past, Stephen Woolls and the Misses Hallam, Wainwright, and Storer assisted Peter Valton in a concert. And, on June 1, when the *Sea-Nymph* once again dropped her hook in Charleston harbor, Ann Storer Henry, who had not acted with the company since they left New York, rejoined her husband and companions.

But even routine has a way of reversing itself. These were troubled times, and disgruntled persons, bitter and angry over recent measures of the British Parliament, were looking for things with which to find fault. For the first time, Charleston evidenced a spirit of antipathy towards the theater. A "foolish female," signing herself "Cleopatra," declared the theater to be the "Devil's Synagogue" but, after a visit to the playhouse, was forced to change her mind and admit that it was not so evil as she had thought. A more serious complaint was registered with the "Grand Jurors at the last Session for this District," in a resolution declaring the theater to be "unfit for the present low Estate of the Province," decrying the unnecessary expenditures for pleasure, and condemning the drama as "a Means of promoting the frequent Robberies that are committed and of Vice and Obscenity." Fortunately, it was voted down.

This swelling spirit of solemnity and demands to eliminate frivolities by no means dampened the enthusiasm of Charleston's devotees of the theater. During the annual festivities celebrating the repeal of the Stamp Act, the Light Infantry Company and the local regiment of Foot Militia staged a review, following which the officers went in a body to witness the performance of *The Recruiting Officer* and *The Oracle*, acted in response to their special request. Naturally, the inevitable "Gentleman for his Amusement" made his appearance during the season, this time playing the lead in *The West Indian*. Just as inevitably and just as naturally, the Masons had their night, although this occasion assumed the form of a charity performance. *Cato* and *The Reprisal* were the selections chosen "For the Benefit of the Charity-Fund of the Union-Kilwinning Lodge, appropriated to the Relief of the Members of the Society of Free Masons, their Wives, Children and Orphans, when in distress." The program, of course, included the usual Masonic songs, epilogues, and prologues.

Although *Douglas* and *The Devil to Pay*, on May 16, were advertised as "the Last Play for These Three Years," they were followed on May 19 by *King John* and *The Guardian*. Thus ended a season that saw a total of fifty-eight plays presented, and the fact that twenty were of a musical nature indicated this to be one of the gayest seasons in the history of the company—despite the gravity of the times. Not only had the Charlestonians regularly filled the auditorium night after night, but the audience had sometimes spilled over onto the stage. This had made it virtually impossible "that the Performers can do their Characters that Justice their Duty to the Publick requires," and Douglass was forced to establish a firm rule that no one was to enter the theater by the stage door. With the closing of the playhouse, the *South Carolina Gazette* evaluated the season in glowing terms: "Warmly countenanced and Supported by the Publick, the Manager and his Company were excited to the most strenuous Efforts to render their Entertainments worthy of so respectable a Patronage.

"If it is considered how late it was in the Season before the House could be opened, the Variety of Scenery and Decorations necessary to a regular Theatre, the Number of Plays represented and that almost every Piece required particular Preparations, it must be confessed that the Exertions of the American Company have been uncommon and justly entitles them to those Marks of Public Favour that have for so many Years stampt Merit in their Performances.

"The Choice of Plays hath been allowed to be very judicious, the Director having selected from the most approved English Poets such Pieces as possess in the highest Degree the *Utile Dulce*, and while they entertain, improve the Mind by conveying the most useful Lessons of Morality and Virtue." [8]

The season over, the company disbanded for the summer. Most of the members scattered, to reassemble in New York in the fall. After playing New York and Philadelphia in 1775-76, they promised to return to Charleston "with a Theatrical Force hitherto unknown in America."

Actors and actresses sailed off as transportation became available. Nancy Hallam embarked for Sandwich, England, to be followed shortly by Hallam and Stephen Woolls, who sailed in the *Eagle* for Falmouth. The *Union* carried John and Ann Henry, accompanied by Maria Storer, overseas, while the faithful *Sea-Nymph* bore the Owen Morrises and Miss Wainwright back to Philadelphia. Douglass and his wife were the last to leave, taking passage on the schooner *Rose* for New York on June 20. Only Richard Goodman remained in Charleston. Combining his talents with those of a Mr. Allen, "from the Theatre-Royal in Edinburgh," they began, on July 6, a series of lectures centered on that delightful eighteenth-century exposition in phrenology, Stevens' *Lecture on Heads*. Soon thereafter, the Church Street Theatre was advertised for rent for a two-year period, the proceeds to be used by the Charity fund of the Union-Kilwinning Lodge.[9]

The Douglasses, along with several of the lesser members of the troupe, arrived in New York on June 30, with "all the necessary Apparatus for performing in this city during the ensuing winter." Sometime after this, Mrs. Douglass was in Philadelphia where, it was reported, she died "of a hurt she received in the theatre." Her interment in the Presbyterian cemetery at the corner of Fourth and Arch streets was attended by all the ladies of the neighborhood, an implication that Presbyterian antagonism against the players was ebbing.

In the fall, despite the loss of Mrs. Douglass, the tumultuous times, and the ever-widening breach between England and her colonies, the players prepared to open a full season in New York. New faces were to be added to the cast. Thomas Wignell, a cousin of Lewis Hallam's and a former player of David Garrick's Drury Lane Company, had been persuaded to come to the colonies as a member of the American Company. He had arrived in New York and was in a local hairdresser's chair when word came that meant the end of the American colonial theater. The Continental Congress, meeting in Philadelphia, had, on October 20, 1774, passed a resolution that read: "We will, in our several stations, encourage frugality, economy, and industry ... and will discountenance and discourage every species of extravagance and dissipation, especially all horse-racing, and all kinds of gaming, cock-fighting, exhibition of shews, plays, and other expensive diversions and entertainments." This edict, in addition to the temper of the times, boded ill for the comedians. Shortly after receiving a letter from Peyton Randolph, President of the

Continental Congress, informing him of this action, Douglass initiated preparations to seek the friendlier atmosphere of "the island of Jamaica, and they will not return to the continent, until its tranquility is restored."

On February 2, 1775, Douglass and his actors were aboard the *Sally* when that vessel sailed for Jamaica, "where they intend exerting their justly applauded Talents for the entertainment of the Ladies and Gentlemen of that polite and opulent island." On July 1, 1775, they gave their first performance of the season in Jamaica, opening the program with a special prologue written for the occasion by Benjamin Moreley, surgeon-general of the island, in which were included the lines:

> The Muse alarm'd at the loud tempest's roar,
> Seeks an asylum on this peaceful shore.[10]

So ended the era of the professional theater in colonial America which, singularly enough, began and ended on a ship called the *Sally*.

· XIII ·

EPILOGUE

___

The limitations of the colonial theater are obvious. It was derivative in nature; it produced practically no playwrights; and its stylized acting ignored the more natural innovations introduced to the English stage by David Garrick. But it did bring a lively and vigorous entertainment from the Old World to the New and demonstrated that a tiny colonial capital, such as Williamsburg or Annapolis, could sustain one of the important ornaments of civilized life, a repertory theater. To call the colonial theater derivative is not to damn it—indeed, all colonial cultures are, by their very natures, derivative.

Yet, there were subtle perquisites unrecognized until brought into the focus of historical perspective. Murray and Kean, Lewis Hallam, Sr., David Douglass, William Verling, and even Robert Upton played significant and important roles in the imposition of culture on colonial America, and they were responsible for more than just establishing the theater as a segment of the leisure-time activities of the Americans. Alhough they never would have believed it at the time, the activities of the comedians, by thrusting ingrown religious and moralistic prejudices into the public domain, gradually weakened them so that, by 1792, even Puritan Massachusetts repealed its anti-theater law of 1750. On the other hand, it is doubtful that the drama itself was ever the great moral influence that it claimed to be or that its champions claimed for it. It was purely and simply an instrument of entertainment, and any cultural gains were merely by-products, not primary objectives. Its leveling influence lay in the fact that the theater provided the same entertainment for all, while its seating arrangements, segregating patrons in box, pit, and gallery symbolized those social distinctions customary in the eighteenth century.

Equally important is the suggestion that the peregrinations of the players became a mirror of public opinion, even reflecting what might be seen as sectional differences between the northern and the southern colonies, differences sometimes grounded in religious mores. Always, there seemed to be a ground swell of opposition in the North, while the southern audiences, for the most part, welcomed the arrival of the players. And it is an interesting commentary that there was never a reported riot or unusual disturbance in the playhouses of Williamsburg, Annapolis, or Charleston before the Revolution. Perhaps this was because so many "fine Ladyes" attended the southern theater, while, in the North, the mechanics and artisans, never noted for genteel deportment, were able to afford the price of admission to the playhouses. These differences, in turn, make it difficult to discover a pervasive theme. If one exists, it must fall within the bounds of that ingenuity so skilfully exercised by theater managers in the varying shades of adversity in every community. Struggle, perhaps, is the best word that sums up the one ever-present element—struggle against religious zealots, against moralists, but, more than anything else, a struggle for survival. This was especially true in the lean years following the Seven Years' War, when depression blighted the economy, and during that period immediately preceding the Revolution, when passions played about the periphery of rebellion.

The actors, by presenting the latest plays of the London stage, in addition to the old favorites, gathered up a portion of the cultural lag that existed between England and her colonies. For instance, Goldsmith's *She Stoops to Conquer* was played in Philadelphia in 1773, the same year it was first presented in London. When Charles Dibdin provided a popular new score for Isaac Bickerstaff's comic opera, *The Padlock*, it appeared on the New York stage within eight months of its original presentation at Drury Lane. The majority of the plays, despite the virtuous content claimed for them by Douglass, were reflections of the English taste, perhaps best analyzed in George Farquhar's statement: "A play without a beau, cully, cuckold or coquette, is as poor an entertainment to some palates, as their Sunday's dinner could be without beef and pudding." Since the beginning of the century, there had been attempts to cleanse the stage of obscenity, and, though a news item of 1766 datelined London noted, "In a tragedy lately rejected at one of our playhouses there were no less than three rapes, four murders, a forgery, and an incest," nevertheless by the time they reached the colonies they had been notably reformed. The versions of Restoration comedies that survived were so altered that their authors would have had difficulty recognizing their literary efforts.[1]

Despite the performances of new plays written for the London stage, William Shakespeare was the most popular playwright with American playgoers. Again, this was a reflection of English tastes, the overseas transplanting of the Georgian revival of Shakespeare, of which someone has said:

> After one hundred and thirty years' nap,
> Enter Shakespeare with a loud clap.

In the twenty-four years before the Revolution, fourteen of his plays were performed at least 180 times, and, in the light of the paucity of information, it would be reasonable to guess the total to be at least 500. Shakespeare was performed in the altered versions played on the London stage. Of the fourteen plays, only two seem to have been presented in anything like their original form, and even those two were cut to fit into an abbreviated playing time. Although it was felt that Shakespeare's greatest forte lay in his facility "to interest the minds of an audience," managers did not hesitate to insert "vile and degrading interpolations," so that "little of the creative powers of Shakespeare is to be seen in it."

On the American stage, *Richard III* and *Romeo and Juliet* were the two Shakespeare favorites and were presented more than any contemporary tragedy. David Garrick's alterations of the Bard's works seem to have been most favored by the American comedians, even though it has been said of them that they were "sometimes the reverse of creditable." His adaptation of *The Taming of the Shrew*, retitled *Catherine and Petruchio*, was often selected as an afterpiece to accompany *Romeo and Juliet*, which, of course, featured the popular and gaudy funeral procession to the tomb of the Capulets.[2]

After Shakespeare's works, the most popular play in the colonies was George Lillo's *George Barnwell*, sometimes said to have been the first honest attempt to correct, from the stage, the vices and weaknesses of mankind. This piece, depicting the temptations of a young man to steal and murder because of his infatuation for an unscrupulous woman, brought domestic middle-class tragedy into fashion, and one lady was quoted in the *Gentleman's Magazine* as saying that "none but a prostitute could find fault with this tragedy." In the colonies, it was always a wise selection in those communities that exhibited hostility towards the stage, and, following English custom, it was nearly always presented during the Christmas and Easter seasons for the edification of apprentices.[3]

George Farquhar was the author of the two most popular comedies presented on the colonial stage, *The Recruiting Officer*, followed in popularity by *The Beaux' Stratagem*. The witty *Recruiting Officer* contains lines that border on the indecent, but the gaiety and rollicking good humor make partial amends for what may be lacking in propriety. Written in 1705, when all England was blazing with martial spirit and while the playwright himself was on a recruiting party, the play was in demand in America during those crises in which the colonies were threatened with involvement in the military activities of the Empire.[4]

The Beggar's Opera was, by far, the most popular musical piece in a day when musicals were popular. Written by the genial humorist John Gay, this "Newgate Pastoral" was a long-time favorite with London audiences. Through the adventures of a highwayman, Captain Macheath, Gay satirized Italian opera, court modes, marriage customs of the aristocracy, and, especially, the political life of the age of Sir Robert Walpole. It is to be suspected, however, that colonial audiences overlooked the mordant satire and agreed with Dr. Johnson's evaluation, "There is in it so much of real London life, so much brilliant wit, and such a variety of airs, which, from early association of ideas engage, soothe, and enliven the mind, that no performance which the theatre exhibits delights me more." [5]

Although not listed among the most popular, Addison's *Cato* must be included in any discussion of plays presented during the colonial period. Not only was it performed by professionals, especially when they felt it necessary to illustrate the noble aims of the theater, but it was also a favorite with amateurs. This tragedy, combining neoclassic correctness with Whig politics, is built around the theme of Cato's stand for liberty, against the suspected domination of Caesar, and his choice of death rather than submission. This exercise in dramatic form, with little more than lifeless abstractions as characters, was ideally suited for amateur exercises in that it was "more properly a succession of declamatory scenes than a tragedy; elegantly written, perfectly moral, and correctly in nature . . . we listen to the sentiments, we admire the beauty of the language and we are delighted with the morality they convey." Although he did not especially like the play, Douglass scheduled it on those occasions when he was under heavy fire by the moralists. Douglass was always a man to pay attention to the temper of the times. Perhaps the best illustration of this was his increased playing of *The Suspicious Husband* during the crisis preceding the outbreak of the Revolution, especially after an anecdote appeared in the papers that the play was based on the suspected infidelity of the queen of George I. [6]

Almost every program of the colonial stage included a main attraction followed by an afterpiece. Afterpieces originally were used as "Crutches to our weakest Plays" and were not presented with the better pieces, as they would "dishonor our best Authors, in such bad company." Once introduced, however, their popularity was so great that they became a regular feature of each night's entertainment. Usually, they were farces, built around a singular situation or a case of mistaken identity, and sometimes musical productions of two or three acts. They were always light and designed to end the evening in a burst of gaiety. The favorite afterpiece in America, as in England, was the pantomime. Though not quite the same thing as *commedia dell'arte*, English panto-mime, as developed by John Rich, combined the stock characters and situations of the harlequinade with elements from classic myths, folk tales, or contemporary events. They leaned heavily on scenic display, spectacle, dance, and acrobatics, and they were often cited as evidence of the low taste of audiences. The basic cast of the harlequinade included Harlequin, the lover of Colum-bine; Pantaloon, her father; and the Clown, the bumbling servant of Harlequin. Pantaloon constantly attempted to interfere with the courtship of Harlequin and Columbine, and out of this stock situation developed a flurry of tricks and feats of agility.[7]

Among those fringe benefits to American culture offered by the colonial theater were musical interludes and similar entertain-ments that often set catchy lyrics to classical tunes (notably com-positions of Arne and Handel), thereby subtly tuning the Ameri-can ear to good music. Several actors who developed on the colonial stage were rated by competent critics as the equals of many favorites of the London theaters. The professional theater popularized the presentation of plays in schools and encouraged the art of public speaking, the latter flourishing to a remarkable degree in the revolutionary generation.

The literary influence of the colonial theater cannot be meas-ured, especially since it encouraged so few to turn to playwriting, but it has been claimed that two of the most famous utterances of the revolutionary era came from the story of *Cato*. Patrick Henry's defiant "Give me liberty or give me death," and Nathan Hale's pathetic "I regret that I have but one life to lose for my country," were echoes, it is said, of lines from that play.[8]

"The Arts," Benjamin Franklin once wrote, "delight to travel westward. After the first cares for the necessities of life are over, we shall come to think of the embellishments." This observation, by a sage who was always wise beyond his years, sums up the importance of the colonial theater more succinctly than could any other statement. The players brought the dramatic arts westward, preparing the way for future embellishments in the shape of a native theater after the shackles of colonialism were broken. Yet, the colonial theater was an example of the pace and strength of colonial America, struggling against almost insurmountable odds and always growing stronger through experience.

The 1774 resolution of the Continental Congress did not kill the theater in America—it merely suspended it during a period of war and surging emotions. The barely perceptible thread of plays presented by the military of both armies lent the drama just enough vigor to survive the American Revolution. A stronger and more evident thread existed in Jamaica, where the players had always enjoyed a hospitable reception. There, the American Company combined its talents with the troupe that had been entertaining the islanders since 1772. By the late fall of 1775, the Kingston theater boasted "a passable set of actors," and four years later, it was operating under the direct management of Lewis Hallam.

But the old American Company faded to only a memory as the actors and actresses followed their individual stars after their flight from New York in 1775. Upon his return to Jamaica, David Douglass retired from the stage. With William Aikman, a loyalist of Scotch descent from Charleston, he returned to his original profession of printer. Together they founded the *Jamaica Mercury and Kingston Advertiser*, later renamed *The Royal Gazette*. In 1779, he was appointed to the post of Master of Revels; the prerogatives of his position granted him control over the players, gave him a seat on the stage at every performance, and allowed him the proceeds of one benefit a year. This same year, Douglass and Aikman were appointed "Printers to the King's Most Excellent Majesty for Jamaica and Its Dependencies." In April, 1778, Douglass remarried; his new wife, the former Mary Peters, proved herself more productive in a family way than the former Mrs. Hallam by bearing him two children. The old manager prospered in Jamaica, more so than he ever had as a theatrical entrepreneur in the mainland colonies. He became a justice, an officer in the militia, and a member of the Council, accumulating a fortune estimated at £25,000. By August 9, 1789, when he died of a "Complaint of ye Bowels," he was termed a "gentleman," a designation he could never have hoped to attain as an actor on the American colonial stage.[9]

Lewis Hallam was too much the actor to forsake the stage, although he confined his activities primarily to the theater in Jamaica until 1783. He experienced one personal tragedy during this period—the death of his physician son, Lewis, Jr. Of the two sons born to Lewis and Sarah Hallam, apparently this younger Lewis had spent most of his life in Jamaica, possibly living with his mother's people after Lewis and Sarah separated. A local newspaper carried his obituary: "Kingston, September 23rd, 1780: On Monday night last, after a painful illness of twenty-one days, departed this life Mr. L. D. Hallam, Jr., in the 19th year of his age. The loss of this amiable and worthy young man is deeply regretted by every person that was connected with him in friendship or business: in friendship he was steady, disinterested and honorable; in his medical capacity, ingenious, faithful and industrious. With most heartfelt concern, one who knew him well, feels the influence of his virtues, in deploring that they exist no more."

In 1785, Lewis Hallam formed a partnership with John Henry, with whom he was at constant odds. Incompatibility finally forced the dissolution of this association, and Hallam joined forces with John Hodgkinson; William Dunlap later became a third partner. Hallam retired from the managerial field in 1797 to become a salaried actor. He had faded fast. As early as 1787, a New York newspaper had criticized his dissipated abilities with the observation, "His battered looks, and shrunk carcass looks the debilitated rake but the soul, the animation, the fire, had left the withered body," and a contemporary could put up but a weak defense for the former idol by admitting Hallam "preserved only the wreck of his former capacity, but still was a various and elegant actor."

Prevented by his early marriage to Sarah, who was still living, from taking another wife, Hallam lived in conjugal fashion with a Miss Tuke, apparently with the understanding of legal marriage at the death of Sarah. Peter Early, a young law student in Philadelphia, wrote of the eventful fulfillment of this promise in 1793: "Lewis Hallam and Miss Tuke were married on Monday evening last by the right reverend Bishop White. O ye Gods and God-desses what a feast the dry boned old Devil must have had. The old wretch has been long under restraint by reason of a wife, from who he has been parted many years. However, to his great satisfaction no doubt she died about four weeks ago in Virginia & the damned Hypocrite was so affected with the intelligence that he could not act for two nights after. The result is that in about a month's time after her death, he married Miss Tuke. Damn the old Scrawny boned wretch how I should like to cuckle [cuckold] him. I'll [warr]ant he's had many a tip of [Tuke] before he was married."

Lewis Hallam's second wife was no better than he deserved. She drank heavily and quarreled continuously with other members of the cast; several disputes between the managers were "owing to her bad conduct." It was shortly after his second marriage that Hallam brought his second son, Mirvan, northward from Virginia, where he had been brought up by his mother in Williamsburg. There is no indication of his age at this time, although he had married some time before he left Virginia. Mirvan made his stage debut playing a role in *The West Indian* in New York during 1793. By 1797, his father planned to establish him as a manager in Jamaica, as soon as he could gain control of the West Indian theaters. This ambitious scheme never materialized, and although Mirvan continued his stage career, his talent was so limited that he added little luster to the family name.[10]

Lewis Hallam died in 1808. Cantankerous, parsimonious, querulous, crafty, and irritable, he was still able and talented within the demands of the eighteenth-century theater and, as such, must be given his just due as the first great actor of the American stage.

From available evidence, John Henry was just as good a performer as Lewis Hallam, possibly better, but had been held down in the early part of his career by the latter, who always referred to him as "a splendid amateur actor." Henry did not remain in Jamaica throughout the American Revolution; the years 1779-80 were spent acting in London's Drury Lane where, among other parts, he played Othello. In 1794, tiring of his arrangement with the irascible Hallam, he sold out to his partner for $10,000, although he was still regularly employed as an actor.

Ann Storer Henry is believed to have borne Henry one son who eventually became a ship captain. Wearying of the dissolute Henry, she left him and promptly married an actor of mediocre talent, by the name of Hogg, who was twenty-four years her junior. As Ann Henry Hogg, she appeared on the New York stage as late as 1798. Several children were born of this union who, after the death of their parents, abandoned their porcine surname and replaced it with that of Biddle, under which they figured prominently on the American stage for two generations.

John Henry was never long without a Storer. In 1781, Maria played in the same company with Henry and remained with him the rest of his life. In 1785, she appeared in a concert in Charleston as "Miss Maria Storer, that celebrated Disciple of Calliope," but, after 1787, she billed herself as Maria Henry. She bore him a daughter, of whom little is known other than that in later years she eloped and died shortly afterwards. In the twilight of his life, John Henry's huge body was wracked with consumption, and death came to him aboard a small coastal vessel bound for Rhode Island. Maria was with him in these last moments, and the shock of witnessing his body buried unceremoniously on a sand bar weakened the fabric of her mind. She returned to Philadelphia, sent for Henry's body, and, soon after seeing it decently interred, died insane, April 25, 1795.

Many members of the old American Company of Comedians played together in the islands during the war. One playbill from Kingston, in 1781, listed these names in the cast: Lewis Hallam, John Henry, Richard Goodman, Owen Morris, Mr. Dermot, Stephen Woolls, Mrs. Morris, Maria Storer, and Margaret Cheer. At times, even the nomadic James Verling Godwin seems to have appeared with them. George Hughes, who had joined the company late in their American tour, recast his histrionic abilities and became a successful auctioneer.[11]

Margaret Cheer, no longer involved with the pretensions of nobility, eloped with a Mr. Long, her father's coachman. She came out of retirement in 1793, but the blossom had faded and her reception was so poor that she abandoned the stage permanently. She died as Mrs. Long, in Jamaica, in 1800.[12]

Miss Wainwright is said to have first married a Mr. Miranda while in the West Indies and, after his death, the actor Isaac Morales. She apparently played on the Jamaican stage for some time, and there are reports indicating her later return to Philadelphia.[13]

The only clue to the eventful fate of Adam Hallam, Lewis' brother, is that a person by that name was listed as a shoemaker in the New York Directory for 1798. Nancy Hallam was listed as a "spinster" in Jamaica in 1775 when, on May 15, she married John Raynard, the organist of the Kingston Parish Church. As Mrs. Raynard she was to become the leading lady of the company in Kingston.[14]

Owen Morris lived to become the patriarch of the American stage, dying in New York, in 1808, at the age of ninety. His wife survived him many years and was a great favorite both as an actress and a singer, her songs "When William" and "I've Kissed and I Have Prattled" often being "rapturously encored." Her reputation for eccentricity seems deserved; her adherence to those fashions that had been popular in her youth—a long-trained dress, high-heel shoes, a high turban-like headdress, and a white cravat—was a costume that drew the attention of adults on the street, as well as the ridicule of small boys. She died around 1829.[15]

Samuel Greville, the first native American professional player, established himself as a practitioner of medicine in Charleston. He was married in 1773 and died the following year.[16]

Anna Tomlinson, of the early days of the Douglass Company, appeared with her daughter, Jane, on the New York stage during the American Revolution in the "Theatre Royal," operated by British officers who had "come, to Minister to Minds diseas'd." [17]

Thomas Wall stuck to his lecture circuit in the colonies. His dissertations on heads and noses were abandoned in favor of the more fabulous demonstrations of electricity. Even before Douglass sailed for Jamaica, Wall was appearing in Maryland with his new entertainment. Eight months later, he was using a room at

Gabriel Maupin's in Williamsburg, lecturing on the wonders of his element, advertised "For promoting religion, morality, useful knowledge, the instructions of the curious, and for the benefit of persons afflicted with paralytic disorders." It was Wall who attempted the first efforts to reinstate the theater in the later stages of the American Revolution, in 1782-83, as co-manager with Adam Lindsay, a tavern-keeper of Baltimore, and with a supporting player who was listed as "Mr. Shakespear." [18]

One person who appeared on the early American stage and found little success there, but who gained the most responsible position in later years, was Walter Murray. In 1766, he was listed as a member of the Council in Quebec, and at that time, Lieutenant Governor Guy Carleton had noted in a dispatch that Murray had, in the past, "acted as a strolling player." [19]

There is little evidence of William Verling's later life. One clue appears in the *Virginia Gazette*, October 10, 1787: "We hear from Petersburg that the new-emissioned company of comedians, under the old veteran, V------s, shortly intends to show new and old faces in a new stile, at the old theatre in this city. And however strange it may appear, 'tis said they are chiefly from Old and New England, and e'en part of the Old and New American Company."

In Williamsburg, only Sarah Hallam remained as a last reminder that the now decaying village had once been a proud theater town. Her estranged husband may have contributed some money for the support of young Mirvan, but there is evidence that Sarah operated a boarding house as early as 1770. If she did receive financial support from Lewis Hallam, it seems likely that it was discontinued in 1774 when he left for Jamaica; possibly, it was for this reason that she advertised, on August 19, 1775, the establishment of a dancing school. The school, or other enterprises, prospered for, by 1783, she owned two slaves. Despite her earlier connections with the stage, although it was primarily through marriage, she was very popular among the ladies of Williamsburg in her declining years. Reports indicate that she operated her dancing academy until her death on November 27, 1793.[20]

The buildings that Douglass had constructed as theaters met

many and varied fates. The John Street Theatre in New York and the Southwark in Philadelphia were operated, during the Revolution, by British officers who followed their usual custom of forming a theatrical group to relieve the boredom of garrison duty. Even in Boston, the redcoats forced the drama down constricted Puritan throats by converting Faneuil Hall into a playhouse.

In 1775, the vestry of St. Anne's Parish in Annapolis decided "to take down the organ, pack same in proper boxes as the Reverend Mr. Lendrum and Vestry agree that in the ruined condition of the Church Building, the Play House be fitted up for a Place of divine Worship and that the clerk erect a pulpit therein." For the next seven years the walls of the theater echoed back the notes of sober hymns, rather than the lilting lyrics of a Miss Hallam, Wainwright, or Storer. A vested rector now intoned the Holy Scriptures on the spot where Henrietta Osborne once gamboled in a breeches part.

The Church Street Theatre in Charleston survived two sieges and a military occupation, but it burned in 1782 and was not rebuilt on that spot.

In Williamsburg, where it all began, the playhouse stood as late as 1775. Five years later, the property "whereon the Old Play House lately stood" was sold, and in January, 1787, the last vestiges disappeared when the foundation bricks were sold to James Moir, brick mason and carpenter.

With the playhouse gone, Virginians could only manifest their interest in the drama by reading plays to one another—just as they had done a hundred years before.[21]

NOTES

CHAPTER I

1. For accounts of early Spanish and French dramatic efforts, see Carlos Eduardo Castañeda, "The First American Play," *The Catholic World*, CXXXIV (January, 1932), 429-37; Louise S. Hasbrouck, *Mexico from Cortes to Carranza* (New York, 1918), 163-64; Hubert Howe Bancroft, "The History of Arizona and New Mexico, 1530-1888," *The Works of Hubert Howe Bancroft* (San Francisco, 1882-1890), XVII, 127; Fred Lewis Gay, "The First American Play," *The Nation*, LXXXVIII (February, 1909), 136; Margaret M. Cameron, "Play-Acting in Canada during the French Regime," *Canadian Historical Review*, XI (March, 1930), 9-19; Reuben Gold Thwaites, ed., *The Jesuit Relations and Allied Documents: Travels and Explorations of the Jesuit Missionaries in New France, 1610-1791* (Cleveland, 1896-1901), XVIII, 85-87, 251; XXXVI, 149; XLVI, 103; XLV, 107; XXXVII, 95.

2. Sheldon Cheney, *The Theater: Three Thousand Years of Drama, Acting and Stagecraft* (New York, 1935), p. 285; Dixon Ryan Fox, "The Development of the American Theater," *New York History*, XVII (January, 1936), 23; "Diary of Samuel Sewall, 1700-1714," Massachusetts Historical Society *Proceedings*, 5th series, V (Boston, 1877), 103-4; "Letter Book of Samuel Sewall," Massachusetts Historical Society *Collections*, 6th series, II (Boston, 1886), 29-30.

3. "Indentures of Apprentices, 1718-1727," *Collections of the New-York Historical Society for 1909* (New York, 1909), pp. 113-14, 122, 127, 130. Apprentice indentures in other colonies were similarly worded.

4. Louis B. Wright, *The Atlantic Frontier: Colonial American Civilization, 1607-1763* (New York, 1947), pp. 243-44; William S. Dye, "Penn-

sylvania Versus the Theater," *Pennsylvania Magazine of History and Biography*, LV (1931), 337; John Blair Linn, ed., *Charter to William Penn and the Laws of the Province of Pennsylvania from 1682 to 1801* (Harrisburg, 1896), II, 4; James T. Mitchell and Henry Flanders, comps., *The Statutes at Large of Pennsylvania from 1682 to 1801* (Harrisburg, 1896), II, 24.

5. George C. D. Odell, *Annals of the New York Stage* (New York, 1927), I, 3-4; Arthur Hornblow, *History of the Theater in America: From Its Beginning to the Present Time* (Philadelphia, 1919), I, 30.

6. *Historical Magazine*, IX (April, 1865), 118.

7. Richardson Wright, *Revels in Jamaica, 1682-1838* (New York, 1937), pp. 8-9; [Anthony Aston], *The Fool's Opera; or, The Taste of the Age. Written by Mat Medley. And Performed by His Company in Oxford. to Which is Prefix'd, A Sketch of the Author's Life, Written by Himself* (London, 1731), pp. 20, 21; Charles Dibdin, *A Complete History of the Stage* (London, 1800), IV, 413. Upon his return to England in 1704, Aston became a strolling player, noted for his declamatory prowess. He often traveled alone, and in contemporary newspaper notices (pasted in the end pieces of the Harvard Theatre Collection's copy of *The Fool's Opera*), he boasted that "Disputation will be maintain'd against any or all, who are whimsical enough to oppose him in the Premises." Aston died sometime after 1749.

8. Odell, *Annals of the New York Stage*, I, 8; Arthur Hobson Quinn, *A History of the American Drama from the Beginning to the Civil War* (New York, 1923), p. 6; Oral S. Coad, "The First American Play," *The Nation*, CVII (August 17, 1918), 182-83. A copy of Hunter's play is in the Huntington Library, San Marino, California.

CHAPTER II

1. Sir A. W. Ward, *Shakespeare and the Makers of Virginia* (London, 1919), pp. 11, 21; Edward D. Neill, *History of the Virginia Company with Letters to and from the First Colony Never Before Printed* (Albany, 1869), pp. 61-64; Edward D. Neill, *Virginia Calorum; the Colony Under the Rule of Charles the First and Second, A.D. 1625-1685* (Albany, 1886), p. 16; Crashaw quoted in George C. D. Odell, *Annals of the New York Stage* (New York, 1927), I, 3.

2. Samuel Pepys, *The Diary of Samuel Pepys, transcribed by the Rev. Mynors Bright from the Shorthand Manuscript in the Pepysian Library at Magdalene College*, edited by Henry B. Wheatley (New York, 1946), I, 330; Alfred Harbage, *Cavalier Drama* (New York, 1936), pp. 115, 268; R. C. Bald, "Sir William Berkeley's *The Lost Lady*," *Transactions of the Bibliographical Society*, 4th series, XVII, 395-426.

3. Delemere quoted in Louis B. Wright, *The First Gentlemen of Virginia: Intellectual Qualities of the Early Colonial Ruling Class* (San Marino, 1940), pp. 151-52; John Spencer Bassett, ed., *The Writings of Colonel William Byrd of Westover in Virginia, Esqr.* (New York, 1901), pp. 341-42; *Virginia Magazine of History and Biography*, X (April,

1903), 403, 405; Louis B. Wright and Marion Tinling, eds., *The Secret Diary of William Byrd of Westover, 1709-1712* (Richmond, 1941), pp. 109-10; Gilbert Chinard, ed., *A Huguenot Exile in Virginia* (New York, 1934), p. 158.

4. J[ames] F. B[arnes], Jr., "Discovery of Old Daguerreotype Establishes Place of Presentation of Ye Bare and Ye Cub," *William and Mary Literary Magazine*, XXXIII, No. 2 (n.d.), 118-19; Jennings Cropper Wise, *Ye Kingdome of Accawmacke, of the Eastern Shore of Virginia in the Seventeenth Century* (Richmond, 1911), pp. 325-26.

5. Lyon Gardiner Tyler, *Williamsburg, the Old Colonial Capital* (Richmond, 1907), p. 224; Hugh Jones, *The Present State of Virginia* (London, 1724), p. 32.

6. "Historical and Genealogical Notes," *William and Mary Quarterly*, XXII (July, 1913), 68-69; Tyler, *Williamsburg*, p. 224; "Proceedings of the Vistors of William and Mary College, 1716," *Virginia Magazine of History and Biography*, IV (October, 1896), 169; York County Records, Orders, Wills, York County Courthouse, Yorktown, Virginia, XV, 52-54. There is the possibility that indenture as used here is in the sense of a contract, but from the wording of the original document, such does not appear to be the case. It is stated in the articles of agreement that the Staggs had been "bound to the sd. Wm. Levingstone to Serve him in the colony of Virga. in the Arts, Professions...." This is also indicated by the agreement in that the remuneration due the Staggs was made retroactive to the date of original indenture.

7. York County Records, Deeds, Bonds, III, 202, 204-6, 343, 384, 398; James W. Knight, "Archeological Report, Block 29, Area 9 (Northwest Corner of Colonial Lot 164), October, 1947," a manuscript report filed in the Department of Research, Colonial Williamsburg, Inc., p. 3; *Virginia Gazette* (Williamsburg), December 9, 1745. Robert H. Land in his excellent article, "The First Williamsburg Theater," *William and Mary Quarterly*, 3rd series, V (July, 1948), 362, lists the payment made by Levingston as £45. The release, however, states that the consideration was "45 of the good & lawfull money of England." On November 19, John Clayton noted that he had received from Levingston the "within named forty five Shillings Currt. money being the Consideration for the Three Lotts within mentioned...." The reconstruction of the theater is based on the advertisement in the *Gazette* of December 9, 1745, calling for alterations and repairs to the building necessary for its conversion to a courthouse.

8. R. A. Brock, ed., *The Official Letters of Alexander Spotswood, Lieutenant-Governor of the Colony of Virginia, 1710-1722* (Richmond, 1935), p. 284. A play seems particularly appropriate as a celebration of the birthday of George I, because that monarch had this year ordered the Great Hall at Hampton Court to be converted into a theater as a method of patronizing English actors during the off-season summer months (John Doran, *Annals of the English Stage: From Thomas Betterton to Edmund Kean* [London, 1899], II, 132).

9. York County Records, Orders, Wills, XVI, 10, 38, and Wills and Inventories, XVIII, 164; *Virginia Gazette*, January 13, May 19, 1738;

Land, "The First Williamsburg Theater," *WMQ*, pp. 364-65. Land based this assumption on the fact that Levingston was involved in administering the wills of Ives and Hurlston.

10. York County Records, Orders, Wills, XV, 587, 612; XVI, 38, 42, 222, 230, 692; Jones, *Present State of Virginia*, p. 31.

11. York County Records, Orders, Wills, XV, 144, 156, 317, 357, 393, 584, 590, 692; XVI, 10, 26, 38, 61, 74, 75, 95, 110, 122, 132, 222, 230, 236; York County Records, Deeds, VII, 46; H. R. McIlwaine and Wilmer L. Hall, eds., *Executive Journals of the Council of Colonial Virginia* (Richmond, 1925-45), IV, xxxix; William Waller Hening, ed., *The Statutes at Large: Being a Collection of All the Laws of Virginia* (New York and Philadelphia, 1823), IV, 273; *William and Mary Quarterly*, XXII (January, 1913), 68-69; photocopy Spotsylvania County Deed Book A, 1720-29 (Part 2), Virginia State Library, Richmond, Virginia. The name Robert Faldo is frequently used as a legal pseudonym throughout the York County Records. After Levingston's death, his widow seems to have followed her husband's professions of medicine and purveyor of refreshment. When William Byrd visited the then new village of Fredericksburg in October, 1732, he noted "Mrs. Levistone, who Acts here in the Double Capacity of a Doctress and Coffee Woman. And were this a populous City, she is qualify'd to exercise 2 other callings" (Bassett, ed., *Writings of William Byrd*, pp. 373-74).

12. William Hugh Grove manuscript diary, 1731-32, Alderman Library, University of Virginia, Charlottesville, Virginia; Robert "King" Carter Letterbooks, 1727-29, typescript copy in the Department of Research, Colonial Williamsburg, Inc., Book II, 138, 144; Book III, 204-5; Book IV, 232; Book V, 263, 273. In February, 1736, William Prentiss received a "Letter of Administration" as executor for the estate of Charles Stagg, as he appeared to be the "greatest Creditor." In May of that same year, Stagg's estate was appraised at £211.13.2, which did not include one old blind Negro and two books on dancing. However, debt claims of at least £149.18.5 were proved against the estate. (York County Records, Wills and Inventories, XIX, 263-64.)

13. Governor William Gooch to his brother, May 26, 1735, Letters of Governor William Gooch, Virginia, 1727-51, typescripts in the Department of Research, Colonial Williamsburg, Inc., pp. 43-44; William Byrd to Sir John Randolph, January 21, 1735, *Virginia Magazine of History and Biography*, IX (January, 1902), 240-41; York County Records, Deeds, Bonds, VI, 153. That the part of Squire Marplot was played by Dr. Potter is based on the above letter of Governor Gooch, who describes him as being able to understand and compose music, a playwright, "and a very pleasant merry fellow." Dr. Potter's first name was determined through an advertisement in the *Virginia Gazette* of April 22, 1737, offering a reward for information of those persons who had broken into and robbed his wine cellar. At this time Dr. Potter was suspected by the Virginians of having murdered his wife before leaving England. There is some evidence (*Virginia Gazette*, September 4, 1746) that he later moved to Spotsylvania County. The reference to "Oldfield" is to Anne Oldfield, reigning beauty of the English stage from around 1700

to her death in 1730 when she was buried in Westminster Abbey. There is a strong possibility that Byrd had seen her in the first London production of *The Busy Body* in 1709.

14. Thomas P. Graffenried, *History of the de Graffenried Family from 1191 A.D. to 1925* (New York, 1925), pp. 150-51; York County Records, Deeds, Bonds, III, 343; William Byrd to John Randolph, January 25, 1735, *Virginia Magazine of History and Biography*, IX (January, 1902), 241; *Virginia Gazette*, February 25, 1738, to April 20, 1739. Christopher de Graffenried owned two lots in Williamsburg, but one (No. 235) as shown on the town plat in Tyler's *Williamsburg* possessed no access to the street and was not a good location as a residence. The other lot (No. 175) was next to the Governor's Palace, particularly desirable for a town house (York County Records, Deeds, Bonds, V, 398). It is interesting to note that Tscharner de Graffenried, son of Christopher and Barbara, advertised in 1745 for a runaway servant who "pretends to teach dancing" (*Virginia Gazette*, September 26, 1745). William Dering not only taught dancing in Williamsburg but traveled around the countryside instructing the children of plantation owners in the intricacies of the dance. A "Dance day" was held at periodic intervals at designated homes where a number of his pupils would gather for instruction. He was on friendly terms with Byrd, and after 1741 Dering was signing "Gent." after his name (Maude H. Woodfin and Marion Tinling, eds., *Another Secret Diary of William Byrd of Westover, 1739-1741: With Letters & Literary Exercises, 1696-1726* [Richmond, 1942], pp. 82, 186; York County Records, Wills and Inventories, XIX, 350).

15. *American Weekly Mercury* (Philadelphia), August 26, 1736; *Virginia Gazette*, September 10-17, 1736; "The Statutes of William and Mary Codified in 1736," *William and Mary Quarterly*, 2nd series, XXIV (April, 1914), 288; Charles Dibdin, *A Complete History of the Stage* (London, 1800), IV, 34; Thomas Jone to Elizabeth Jones, September 17, 1736, and Elizabeth Holloway to Elizabeth Jones, October 23, 1736, Joseph Jones Papers, Manuscript Division, Library of Congress.

16. *Virginia Gazette*, April 21, 1738; *Boston Gazette*, May 29, 1738.

17. York County Records, Deeds, V, 153-54; VIII, 107-9; *Virginia Gazette*, December 19, 1745; (Purdie & Dixon), October 10, 1766; McIlwaine and Hall, eds., *Executive Journals of the Council of Colonial Virginia*, V, 490-91.

CHAPTER III

1. "Pickle Herring was the lineal descendant of Vice in the old Morality Plays" (William S. Dye, "Pennsylvania Versus the Theater," *Pennsylvania Magazine of History and Biography*, LV [1931], 351); James Logan quoted in Thomas Clark Pollock, *The Philadelphia Stage in the Eighteenth Century* (Philadelphia, 1933), p. 4; *American Weekly Mercury*, May 7, 1724, and October 26, 1729; Richardson Wright, *Hawkers and Walkers in Early America: Strolling Peddlers, Lawyers, Doctors, Players and Others, From the Beginning to the Civil War* (Philadelphia, 1927), p. 204.

2. George Freedley, "An Early Performance of Romeo and Juliet in New York," *Bulletin of the New York Public Library*, 40 (1936), 494; *New York Gazette*, March 23, 1730; August 30, 1731; September 8, December 11, 1732; October 8-15, 1733; *New England and Boston Gazette*, January 1, 1733; Oral S. Coad, "American Theatre in the 18th Century," *South Atlantic Quarterly*, XVII (July, 1918), 190-91; Alliston Brown, *A History of the New York Stage: From the First Performance in 1732 to 1903* (New York, 1903), I, 10; Isaac Newton Stokes, *The Iconography of Manhattan Island, 1498-1909* (New York, 1928), IV, 356.

3. *New York Weekly Journal*, April 15, 1734; February 5, 1739; July 24, 1749; *New York Gazette*, February 6-20, 1739; *New York Gazette Revived in the Weekly Post Boy*, September 7, 1747 (hereafter cited as the *New York Weekly Post Boy*).

4. "For the benefit of" was added to advertisements to distinguish professional from amateur concerts (O. G. Sonneck, *Early Concert Life in America (1731-1800)* [New York, 1949], p. 13); *South Carolina Gazette* (Charleston), January 22 to February 22, 1735. At this time the rate of exchange for South Carolina currency was 76 to 10.

5. *South Carolina Gazette*, May 3, 1735, to January 31, 1736. "Silvia's" prologue is in the *Gentleman's Magazine*, IV (May, 1736), 288.

6. *South Carolina Gazette*, February 21, 1736, to May 28, 1737; Eola Willis, *The Charleston Stage in the XVIII Century* (Columbia, 1924), p. 33; Carl Bridenbaugh, *Cities in the Wilderness: The First Century of Urban Life in America, 1625-1742* (New York, 1938), p. 441; Sonneck, *Early Concert-Life in America*, p. 14; David Duncan Wallace, *South Carolina: A Short History* (Chapel Hill, 1951), p. 211.

7. *Pennsylvania Gazette* (Philadelphia), December 30, 1742, to March 17, 1743; November 23, 1749, to March 27, 1750; Edward Shippen quoted in Carl and Jessica Bridenbaugh, *Rebels and Gentlemen: Philadelphia in the Age of Franklin* (New York, 1942), pp. 98, 137; manuscript diary of John Smith, Ridgeway Branch of the Free Library of Philadelphia; John F. Watson, *Annals of Philadelphia and Pennsylvania, In the Olden Time; Being a Collection of Memoirs, Anecdotes and Incidents of the City and Its Inhabitants, And of the Earliest Settlements of the Inland Part of Pennsylvania, From the Days of the Founders* (Philadelphia, 1844), I, 102; *Minutes of the Common Council of Philadelphia, 1704-1776* (Philadelphia, 1852), p. 523.

8. The property of Rip Van Dam had been sold just two months earlier by the executors of his estate. *New York Weekly Post Boy*, November 6, 1749, to July 23, 1750; *Pennsylvania Gazette*, March 6, 1750; Charles P. Daly, *First Theatre in America* (New York, 1896), pp. 48-49.

9. *New York Weekly Post Boy*, September 10, 1750, to August 26, 1751; William Dunlap, *History of the American Theatre* (New York, 1832), p. 17.

10. *New York Weekly Post Boy*, December 26, 1751, to March 2, 1752.

11. Mons. Denoyer was a featured dancer at London's Drury Lane in 1738. *Pennsylvania Gazette*, October 26, 1745; *Virginia Gazette*, December 19, 1745; August 29, 1751, to April 17, 1752; York County Records,

Deeds, V, 627; Lyon G. Tyler, ed., "Diary of John Blair," *William and Mary Quarterly*, VII, 15; VIII, 147; Virginia Gazette Day Book, manuscript in Alderman Library, University of Virginia, photocopy in Department of Research, Colonial Williamsburg, Inc., *passim*.

12. Robert Hunt Land, "The Theatre in Colonial Virginia" (Unpublished M.A. thesis, University of Virginia, 1936), p. 24; *Virginia Gazette*, April 30, 1752; Paul Leicester Ford, *Washington and the Theatre* (New York, 1899), p. 9.

13. Andrew Burnaby, *Travels Through the Middle Settlements in the Years 1759 and 1760 with Observations upon the State of the Colonies* (2nd ed.; London, 1776), p. 70; *Maryland Gazette* (Annapolis), April 12, 1749, to December 4, 1751; Charles Durang, *The Philadelphia Stage: From 1749 to 1821*, First Series, Chapter III, run serially in the Philadelphia *Sunday Dispatch* between 1854 and 1856. There were two additional series following the one cited above. Used in this study was the copy in a bound scrapbook in the Harvard Theatre Collection, Houghton Library, Harvard University. As there is no pagination, citations will be by chapter number. Durang, like Dunlap, claims that the greater part of his information came from Lewis Hallam, Jr., when the latter was an old man.

14. *Maryland Gazette*, June 18, to December 21, 1752; Durang, *Philadelphia Stage*, Chapter III. Durang claims that Lewis Hallam, Jr., stated that Wynell and Herbert were "loaned" to Murray-Kean by the elder Hallam. This seems unlikely as their names are not in evidence in subsequent playbills of the Hallam Company.

CHAPTER IV

1. Edward Long, *The History of Jamaica* (London, 1774), II, 283; Richardson Wright, *Revels in Jamaica, 1682-1838* (New York, 1937), pp. 6, 26; Charles Leslie, *History of Jamaica* (1740), quoted in Glenn Hughes, *A History of the American Theater* (New York, 1928), p. 22; John C. Fitzpatrick, ed., *The Diaries of George Washington, 1748-1799* (New York, 1925), I, 25; Paul Leicester Ford, *Washington and the Theatre* (New York, 1899), p. 7; Bayle Bernard, "Early Days of the American Stage, Being a Selection from the Papers of One of Its Managers," *Tallis's Dramatic Magazine* (March, 1851), pp. 14-41. Bernard states that his information came from Owen Morris, a member of Moody's company in Jamaica, and later a player with David Douglass' American Company.

2. *Daily Post* (London), September 3, 1731; *Daily Advertiser* (London), August 22, 1731; August 26, September 12, 1737; *Kentish Post* quoted in Sybil Rosenfeld, *Strolling Players & Drama in the Provinces, 1660-1765* (Cambridge, 1939), pp. 225-26; Thomas Davies, *Dramatic Miscellanies: Consisting of Critical Observations of Several Plays of Shakespeare: With a Review of His Principal Characters, and Those of Various Eminent Writers as Represented by Mr. Garrick, and Other Celebrated Comedians, with Anecdotes of Dramatic Poets, Actors, &c.* (London, 1785), I, 7-9, 178-79; John Doran, *Annals of the English Stage:*

From Thomas Betterton to Edmund Kean (London, 1899), II, 5-6, 67-68; *Proceedings at the Sessions of the Peace, and Oyer and Terminer, For the City of London, and County of Middlesex, on Wednesday the 10th, Thursday the 11th, Friday the 12th, Saturday the 13th, and Monday the 15th of December, 1735, In the Ninth Year of His MAJESTY'S Reign, Being the First Sessions in the Mayoralty of the Right Honourable JOHN WILLIAMS, Knt. Lord-Mayor of the City of London, in the Year 1735* (London, 1735), pp. 14-16; *Pennsylvania Gazette*, July 31, 1735; *New York Gazette*, August 11, 1735.

3. John Gibson to Mrs. John Ross, August 16, 1740, Gibson-Maynadier Papers, Maryland Historical Society, Baltimore, Maryland; *Daily Advertiser* (London), August 26, September 12, September 15, 1737; September 26, 1738; August 28, 1740; Charles Beecher Hogan, "The New Wells, Goodman's Fields, 1739-1752," *Theatre Notebook*, III (July-September, 1949), 69-71; Rev. J. Genest, *Some Account of the English Stage, 1660-1830* (Bath, 1832), V, 223-25.

4. Tate Wilkinson, *Memoirs of His Own Life* (York, 1790), II, 92; George O. Seilhamer, *History of the American Theatre: Before the Revolution* (Philadelphia, 1888), I, 144; William Dunlap, *History of the American Theatre* (New York, 1832), pp. 4-6; Oral S. Coad, "American Theatre in the 18th Century," *South Atlantic Quarterly*, XVII (July, 1916), 195; V. C. Clinton-Baddeley, *All Right on the Night* (London, 1954), p. 169; John Hodgkinson, *A Narrative of His Connections with the Old American Company, From the Fifth September, 1792, to the Thirty-first of March 1797* (New York, 1797), p. 15; *Daily Journal* (London), August 4, 1732; Joseph N. Ireland, *Records of the New York Stage, from 1750 to 1860* (New York, 1866), I, 46; Thomas Gilliland, *The Dramatic Mirror: Containing the History of the Stage, from the Earliest Period to the Present Time: Including a Biographical Account of All the Dramatic Writers, from 1660. And Also of the Most Distinguished Performers, From the Days of Shakespeare to 1807: And a History of the Theatre in England, Ireland and Scotland* (London, 1808), I, 181; Hogan, "New Wells," *Theatre Notebook*, p. 72.

5. William Dunlap, *Diary of William Dunlap (1766-1839): The Memoirs of a Dramatist, Theatrical Manager, Painter, Critic, Novelist and Historian*, edited by Dorothy C. Barck (New York, 1930), I, 352; Hodgkinson, *Narrative*, p. 15; Wilkinson, *Memoirs*, III, 204; Oral S. Coad, "Stage and Players in Eighteenth Century America," *The Journal of English and Germanic Philology*, XIX (April, 1920), 202; James J. Lynch, *Box, Pit and Gallery: Stage and Society in Johnson's London* (Berkeley, 1953), p. 124; *New York Gazette and Weekly Mercury*, July 12, 1753 (hereafter cited as *New York Mercury*); Charles Durang, *The Philadelphia Stage: From 1749 to 1821*, First Series, Chapter II (Philadelphia *Sunday Dispatch*, 1854-56); Dunlap, *History of the American Theatre*, p. 7.

6. *Virginia Gazette*, June 12-July 3, 1752; George C. D. Odell, *Annals of the New York Stage* (New York, 1927), I, 61; *William and Mary Quarterly*, VIII (April, 1900), 237; George Gilmer to T. P. Walker, June 30, 1752, Gilmer to Walter King, November 30, 1752, Gilmer Let-

ter Book in possession of Mrs. Elizabeth Brock and lent to the Virginia Historical Society, Richmond, Virginia; H. R. McIlwaine, ed., *Journals of the House of Burgesses of Virginia (1619-1776)* (Richmond, 1905-15), VII, 78, 86; H. R. McIlwaine, ed., *Legislative Journals of the Council of Colonial Virginia* (Richmond, 1918-19), II, 1701-3; H. R. McIlwaine and Wilmer L. Hall, eds., *Executive Journals of the Council of Colonial Virginia* (Richmond, 1925-45), V, 404. Although Hallam declared thirteen months later that the company's date of debarkation in Virginia was June 28, 1752 (*New York Mercury*, July 2, 1753), Miss Mary A. Stephenson in her report on "The Second Theater" (Research Department, Colonial Williamsburg, Inc.) has determined through an exhaustive search of the *Virginia Gazette* that the only *Sally* entering either the York or James rivers during 1752 arrived on June 2.

7. The average dimensions of colonial theaters were computed from the following measurements: Williamsburg (1718)—86 feet by 32 feet (James W. Knight, "Archeological Report, Block 29, Area 9 [Northwest Corner of Colonial Lot 164], October, 1947," MS Department of Research, Colonial Williamsburg, Inc.); Southwark of Philadelphia (1766)—95 feet by 50 feet (Durang, *Philadelphia Theatre*, Chapter III); Chapel Street of New York (1761)—90 feet by 50 feet (*New York Gazette*, April 12, 1764); Charleston (1763)—75 feet by 35 feet (*South Carolina Gazette*, November 3, 1765); Halifax, North Carolina (1769)—60 feet by 30 feet. These figures of the Halifax theater are at best approximate for they were scaled from C. J. Sauthier, *Plan of the Town of Halifax in Halifax County, North Carolina, Survey'd & Drawn in June 1769 by C. J. Sauthier;* York County Records, Deeds, V, 493-99; *Virginia Gazette*, May 20, 1737; July 24, August 21, December 22, 1752; George Gilmer to Walter King, November 30, 1752, Gilmer Letter Book, Virginia Historical Society; Durang, *Philadelphia Theatre*, Chapter II; *Maryland Gazette*, September 6, 1770; Alexander Graydon, *Memoirs of His Own Time with Reminiscences of the Men and Events of the Revolution*, edited by John Stockton Littell (Philadelphia, 1846), p. 88; John F. Watson, *Annals of Philadelphia and Pennsylvania . . . ,* I, 473; George Saunders, *A Treatise on Theatres* (London, 1790), pp. 26, 83; *Pennsylvania Packet* (Philadelphia), December 14, 1772; *New York Mercury*, February 1, May 3, 1762; Montague Summers, *The Restoration Theater* (New York, 1924), pp. 39, 270-78; Wilkinson, *Memoirs*, II, 33; Theatre Royal Account Book, 1779, New-York Historical Society, New York; Odell, *Annals of the New York Stage*, I, 206. There is little evidence that footlights were used in the American colonial theater; but there is always the possibility, for toward the end of the era newspapers were commenting on the "pleasing effect" of the "Disposition of the Lights" (W. J. Lawrence, "Early American Playgoing," *The Theatre*, XXIV [December, 1916], 404; *New York Mercury*, February 21, 1774).

8. "Clap-trap" means just that. In eighteenth-century theatrical parlance it was a trick, or "trap," employed by actors and managers to gain the applause of the audience. *Virginia Gazette*, August 21-September 22, 1752; Durang, *Philadelphia Stage*, Chapters II, III; John Hill, *The Actor: A Treatise on the Art of Playing: Interspersed with Theatrical Anec-*

dotes, Critical Remarks on Plays, and Occasional Observations on Audi-ences (London, 1750), p. 315; Dunlap, *History of the American Theatre,* p. 9; Coad, "Stage and Players in Eighteenth Century America," *JEGP,* p. 202; *William and Mary Quarterly,* III (April, 1895), 252; Tyler, *Williamsburg,* p. 230; George Gilmer to Walter King, November 14, 1752, Gilmer Letter Book, Virginia Historical Society.

9. McIlwaine, ed., *Legislative Journals,* V, 412-15; *Virginia Gazette,* November 10-17, 1752; *Maryland Gazette,* December 14, 1752; *Pennsylvania Journal and Weekly Advertiser* (Philadelphia), January 16, 1753; *Pennsylvania Gazette,* January 16, 1753.

10. *Virginia Gazette,* December 8, 1752; *Pennsylvania Gazette,* February 20, 1753; Manuscript Account Book of Alexander Craig, Research Department, Colonial Williamsburg, Inc.; *New York Mercury,* July 2, 1753; York County Records, Deeds, V, 553-55; Orders and Judgments, 1752-1754, pp. 207-13, 254-9, 277-78, 281-82.

CHAPTER V

1. In 1738 a story in a Philadelphia newspaper described the initiation of a youth into the Masons, stating "Some of the Company then diverted themselves at a Play called *Snap-Dragon,* holding their heads over the Pan, that their Countenances, from the blue reflexion of the Flames might appear ghastly and hideous" (*Pennsylvania Gazette,* February 7, 1738; for a more modern meaning see Marion Brown, *The Southern Cookbook* [Chapel Hill, 1951], p. 351); *National Advocate* (New York), September 1, 1821; Theodore Sedgewick, *A Memoir of the Life of William Livingston* (New York, 1833), p. 102; *New York Mercury,* July 2-September 17, 1753; Mathew Clarkson to John Griffith, July 17, 1753, Miscellaneous Manuscript Collection, New-York Historical Society.

2. *New York Weekly Post-Boy,* September 17, 1753; *New York Mercury,* August 6-October 1, 1753; Philip Schuyler to Abraham Ten Broock, September 21, 1753, Benson J. Lossing, *The Life and Times of Philip Schuyler* (New York, 1860), I, 68-69; *Daily Post* (London), August 25, 1731; Rev. J. Genest, *Some Account of the English Stage, 1660-1830* (Bath, 1832), V, 308-10; O. G. Sonneck, *Early Concert Life in America (1731-1800)* (New York, 1949), p. 159; Charles Durang, *The Philadelphia Stage: from 1749 to 1821,* First Series, Chapter IV (Philadelphia *Sunday Dispatch,* 1854-56; Jonathan Boucher, *Reminiscences of an American Loyalist, 1735-1789,* edited by Jonathan Bouchier (Boston, 1925), p. 13.

3. *New York Mercury,* October 22, 1753, to March 25, 1754; *New York Weekly Post-Boy,* November 19, 1753; *Maryland Gazette,* February 7, 1754.

4. Carl and Jessica Bridenbaugh, *Rebels and Gentlemen: Philadelphia in the Age of Franklin* (New York, 1942), p. 138; Durang, *Philadelphia Stage,* Chapter III; William Dunlap, *History of the American Theatre* (New York, 1832), pp. 15-16; Alliston Brown, *History of the New York Stage: From the First Performance in 1732 to 1903* (New York, 1903), I, 5; *Pennsylvania Journal,* May 3-June 7, 1753.

5. Dunlap, *History of the American Theatre*, p. 17; *Pennsylvania Gazette*, January 29-June 6, 1754; *New York Mercury*, April 29, 1754; Durang, *Philadelphia Stage*, Chapter IV; playbills in the collection of the Pennsylvania Historical Society, Philadelphia, Pa.

6. *Pennsylvania Gazette*, June 6-June 27, 1754; *Pennsylvania Journal*, August 8, 1754; Bridenbaugh, *Rebels and Gentlemen*, p. 139; Charles Beecher Hogan, "The New Wells, Goodman's Fields, 1739-1752," *Theatre Notebook*, III, 70-71; Durang, *Philadelphia Stage*, Chapter IV; Dunlap, *History of the American Theatre*, p. 18.

7. Durang, *Philadelphia Stage*, Chapter IV; Dunlap, *History of the American Theatre*, p. 18; Arthur Hornblow, *History of the Theater in America: From Its Beginning to the Present Time* (Philadelphia, 1919), I, 96; *South Carolina Gazette*, October 3, 1754, to January 9, 1755.

8. Bayle Bernard, "Early Days of the American Stage..., *Tallis's Dramatic Magazine* (March, 1851), p. 140; Richardson Wright, *Revels in Jamaica, 1682-1838* (New York, 1937), pp. 39-41; *New York Mercury*, October 6, 1758.

CHAPTER VI

1. Richardson Wright, *Revels in Jamaica, 1682-1838* (New York, 1937), pp. 28, 40-45, 341; William Dunlap, *History of the American Theatre* (New York, 1832), pp. 35, 81; Alexander Graydon, *Memoirs of His Own Time with Reminiscences of the Men and Events of the Revolution*, edited by John Stockton Littell (Philadelphia, 1846), pp. 76-77; Joseph N. Ireland, *Records of the New York Stage from 1750 to 1860* (New York, 1866), I, 20-21; Charles Durang, *Philadelphia Stage From 1749 to 1821*, First Series, Chapter XII (Philadelphia *Sunday Dispatch*, 1854-56); William Dunlap, *Diary of William Dunlap (1766-1839); The Memoirs of a Dramatist, Theatrical Manager, Painter, Critic, Novelist and Historian*, edited by Dorothy C. Barck (New York, 1930), I, 146. This is the only reference to Nancy Hallam by this name. As the famous Miss Hallam of later years, she has usually been assigned the name of Sarah Hallam, actually the wife of Lewis Hallam, Jr., who, except for one recorded performance, had no connection with the stage other than through marriage.

2. *New York Mercury*, January 1-February 5, 1759; Arthur Hornblow, *History of the Theater in America: From Its Beginning to the Present Time* (Philadelphia, 1919), I, 101-2; Dunlap, *History of the American Theatre*, p. 18; Virginia D. Harrington, *New York Merchants on the Eve of the Revolution* (New York, 1935), p. 309; Clarence S. Brigham, *Journals and Journeymen: A Contribution to the History of Early American Newspapers* (Philadelphia, 1950), p. 201.

3. *New York Mercury*, January 1-February 5, 1759; Bayle Bernard, "Early Days of the American Stage...," *Tallis's Dramatic Magazine* (June, 1851), p. 241; Lorenzo Sabine, *Biographical Sketches of Loyalists in the American Revolution* (Boston, 1894), II, 20; Dunlap, *History of the American Theatre*, p. 22.

4. In later years William Williams studied architecture in London. Returning to Philadelphia, he advertised that he was now "carrying on

the business of House Carpentry in the most useful and ornamental manner" (*Pennsylvania Packet*, February 1, 1773). Samuel Hazard and others, eds., *Pennsylvania Archives* (Philadelphia and Harrisburg, 1852-1949), 1st series, II, 659-60; *Pennsylvania Gazette*, January 20, June 14, 1759; *American Magazine and Monthly Chronicle* (1758) quoted in Carl and Jessica Bridenbaugh, *Rebels and Gentlemen: Philadelphia in the Age of Franklin* (New York, 1942), p. 139; John F. Watson, *Annals of Philadelphia and Pennsylvania*... (Philadelphia, 1844), I, 472; William S. Dye, "Pennsylvania Versus the Theater," *Pennsylvania Magazine of History and Biography*, LV (1931), 335; manuscript petition, May 22, 1759, Pennsylvania Historical Society; James T. Mitchell and Henry Flanders, comps., *The Statutes at Large of Pennsylvania from 1682 to 1801* (Harrisburg, 1896), V, 446-47; *Minutes of the Common Council of Philadelphia, 1704-1776*, VIII, 339-42.

5. *Pennsylvania Gazette*, June 21, 1759 to January 10, 1760; *Pennsylvania Journal*, June 28-December 27, 1759; Hornblow, *History of the Theater in America*, I, 101; Graydon, *Memoirs*, p. 88.

6. Elihu Riley, *Annapolis "Ye Antient Capital of Maryland"* (Annapolis, 1901), p. 4; *Maryland Gazette*, March 6-May 15, 1760.

7. Andrew Burnaby, *Travels Through the Middle Settlements in the Years 1759 and 1760*... (2nd ed.; London, 1776), p. 64; *Maryland Gazette*, May 15-June 26, 1760.

8. William Allason Miscellaneous Papers, Virginia State Library; Lyon Gardiner Tyler, *Williamsburg, the Old Colonial Capital* (Richmond, 1907), p. 230; Thomas Dibdin, *Reminiscences* (London, 1827), I, 7; Burnaby, *Travels*, p. 36; York County Records, Orders and Judgments, 1752-54, pp. 337-38; *Virginia Gazette*, February 10, 1758; Paul Leicester Ford, *Washington and the Theatre* (New York, 1899), p. 19; Alexander Craig Manuscript Account Book, Research Department, Colonial Williamsburg, Inc.; *Virginia Gazette* (Purdie & Dixon), April 14, 1768; William Allason to Robert Allason, June 11, 1761, William Allason Letterbook, 1757-1770, Allason Papers, Virginia State Library; York County Records, Land Causes, 1746-59, pp. 135-58, 203 *passim*.

9. *Newport Mercury*, August 11, 1761, quoted in Charles Blake, *An Historical Account of the Providence Stage* (Providence, 1868), p. 19.

CHAPTER VII

1. Boston did not always maintain such a rigid front against things theatrical. In 1732 the play *George Barnwell* was printed in the local *New England Weekly Journal* in a series of weekly installments. William W. Clapp, *A Record of the Boston Stage* (Boston, 1853), p. 2; *The Charter and General Laws of the Colony and Province of Massachusetts Bay, to Which is Added an Appendix, Tending to Explain the Spirit, Progress and Jurisprudence of the State; Especially in a Moral and Political View* (Boston, 1814), p. 346; *Maryland Gazette*, March 27, 1760; Anne Rowe Cunningham, ed., *Letters and Diary of John Rowe, Boston Merchant, 1759-1762, 1764-1779* (Boston, 1903), pp. 77, 197, 200; *Discord*

and Civil Wars: Being a Portion of the Journal Kept by Lieutenant Williams of His Majesty's Twenty-Third Regiment While Stationed in British North America (Buffalo, 1954), p. 14.

2. *Bull's Memoir of Rhode Island,* quoted in Charles Blake, *An Historical Account of the Providence Stage* (Providence, 1868), p. 20; *New York Mercury,* November 9, 1761; Bayle Bernard, "Early Days of the American Stage...," *Tallis's Dramatic Magazine* (June, 1851), pp. 235-238.

3. Alliston Brown, *History of the New York Stage From the First Performance in 1732 to 1903* (New York, 1903), I, 6; *New York Gazette,* November 26-December 31, 1761; *New York Mercury,* December 28, 1761, to May 3, 1762.

4. Blake, *Providence Stage,* pp. 19, 29-32; Bernard, "Early Days of the American Stage," *TDM,* p. 238; Gertrude Selwyn, *Providence in Colonial Times* (Providence, 1912), p. 305; Arthur Hornblow, *History of the Theater in America: From Its Beginnings to the Present Time* (Philadelphia, 1919), I, 24, 118.

5. *South Carolina Gazette,* November 5, 1763, to March 31, 1764; Paul Leicester Ford, *Washington and the Theatre* (New York, 1899), p. 19; Julian Boyd, ed., *The Papers of Thomas Jefferson* (Princeton, 1950-), I, 7; Edward A. Wyatt IV, "Three Petersburg Theaters," *William and Mary Quarterly,* 2nd series, XXI (April, 1941), 84; Arthur Kyle Davis, *Three Centuries of an Old Virginia Town* (Petersburg, 1912), p. 9; *Georgia Gazette* (Savannah), November 17-December 29, 1763; Alexander Garden to David Colden, February 1, 1764, *Letters and Papers of Cadwallader Colden: Collections of the New-York Historical Society for the Year 1922* (New York, 1923), p. 281; Carl Bridenbaugh, *Myths and Realities: Societies of the Colonial South* (Baton Rouge, 1952), p. 99; Eola Willis, *The Charleston Stage in the XVIII Century* (Columbia, 1924), p. 44.

6. *South Carolina and American General Gazette* (Charleston), October 31, 1765; *South Carolina Gazette,* October 31, 1765; Wesley Swanson, "Wings and Backdrops," *The Drama,* XVIII (October, 1927), 6; *Pennsylvania Chronicle,* April 12, 1770; Edwin Duerr, "Charles Ciceri, and the Background of American Stage Design," *Theatre Arts Monthly,* XVI (December, 1932), 988; Richard Southern, *The Georgian Playhouse* (London, 1948), pp. 20-21; George C. D. Odell, *Annals of the New York Stage* (New York, 1927), I, 139-40; Oral S. Coad, "Stage and Players in 18th Century America," *The Journal of English and Germanic Philology,* XIX (April, 1920), 205; Allardyce Nicoll, *The Development of the Theatre: A Study of Theatrical Art from the Beginnings to the Present Day* (New York, 1927), p. 64. Not until the 1790's did London theaters use a new set of scenery for each play.

7. *South Carolina and American General Gazette,* October 31, 1765, to May 30, 1766; *South Carolina Gazette and Country Journal* (Charleston), March 4 to May 6, 1766; V. C. Clinton-Baddeley, *All Right on the Night* (London, 1954), pp. 160-61; *South Carolina Gazette,* December 1, 1766.

CHAPTER VIII

1. *New York Gazette*, April 2, 1764, May 12, 1766; *New York Mercury*, February 25-March 4, 1765; May 5, 1766; Joseph N. Ireland, *Records of the New York Stage, from 1750 to 1860* (New York, 1866), I, 41; Edmund S. and Helen M. Morgan, *The Stamp Act Crisis: Prologue to Revolution* (Chapel Hill, 1953), pp. 162, 195-96, 197; G. D. Scull, ed., *The Montresor Journals: Collections of the New-York Historical Society for 1881* (New York, 1882), pp. 357, 362, 364, 370-75; *Maryland Gazette*, May 22, 1766; *Georgia Gazette*, July 2, 1766; *Pennsylvania Gazette*, May 8, 1766.

2. Letter of Dr. Smith copied from the Minutes of the Trustees, July 12, 1763, Playbill of Drury Lane, Pennsylvania Historical Society; *Pennsylvania Gazette*, July 12, 1766.

3. John F. Watson, *Annals of Philadelphia and Pennsylvania* ... (Philadelphia, 1844), I, 473.

4. *Pennsylvania Chronicle*, November 6, 1766; *Pennsylvania Gazette*, November 27, 1766, to January 29, 1767; *Pennsylvania Journal*, January 1-January 29, 1767; Robert Hamilton Ball, "Samuel Greville, First Player," *Princeton Alumni Weekly*, XXX (1929), 117-24; Edward Burd to Sarah Burd, January 24, 1767, Lewis Burd Walker, ed., *The Burd Papers: Selections from Letters Written by Edward Burd, 1763-1823* (n.p., 1899), pp. 13-14; Alexander Mackrabie to Philip Francis, January 22, 1767, Beata Francis and Eliza Keary, eds., *The Francis Letters by Sir Philip Francis and Other Members of His Family* (New York, n.d.), I, 102.

5. *Pennsylvania Gazette*, January 29-March 5, 1767; *Pennsylvania Journal*, February 2-March 26, 1767; *Pennsylvania Chronicle*, February 9-May 4, 1767.

6. *Pennsylvania Gazette*, February 12-April 16, 1767; *Pennsylvania Journal*, February 19-July 2, 1767; *Pennsylvania Chronicle*, April 2-July 6, 1767; Joseph Jackson Collection, University of Pennsylvania Library, Philadelphia, Pa.; Harry Dichter and Elliot Shapiro, *Early American Sheet Music: Its Lure and Its Lore, 1768-1889* (New York, 1941), p. 17; John McPherson quoted in Carl and Jessica Bridenbaugh, *Rebels and Gentlemen: Philadelphia in the Age of Franklin* (New York, 1942), pp. 127-28; George O. Seilhamer, *History of the American Theatre: Before the Revolution* (Philadelphia, 1888), I, 185; Arthur Hornblow, *History of the Theater in America: From Its Beginning to the Present Time* (Philadelphia, 1919), I, 122-23; Richard Moody, *America Takes the Stage: Romanticism in American Drama and Theatre, 1750-1900* (Bloomington, 1955), pp. 188-89. The only other recorded performance of *The Prince of Parthia* was on March 26, 1915, when it was acted by the Zelosophic Society of the University of Pennsylvania, and it is said to have proved a very actable play (Arthur Hobson Quinn, *A History of the American Drama from the Beginning to the Civil War* [New York, 1923], pp. 16-17).

7. *New York Journal*, March 7-August 6, 1767.

8. Richardson Wright, *Revels in Jamaica, 1682-1838* (New York, 1937), pp. 51-52; *Newport Mercury*, August 31, 1767.

9. *Pennsylvania Chronicle*, September 21-November 28, 1767; *Pennsylvania Journal*, September 24-November 23, 1767; Alexander Mackrabie to Philip Francis, October 8, 1767, *Francis Letters*, I, 77; Edward Burd to Sarah Burd, November 17, 1767, *Burd Papers*, p. 18.

CHAPTER IX

1. Dunlap indicates that he is recalling the appearance of the theater from memory. It would be wise to keep in mind that his estimate of an equivalent of $800 was made in the 1830's. William Dunlap, *History of the American Theatre* (New York, 1843), p. 28; *New York Mercury*, December 14, 1767.

2. *New York Mercury*, December 3-17, 1767; *Georgia Gazette*, January 20, 1768.

3. *New York Journal*, December 17, 1767, to January 28, 1768; *New York Mercury*, December 28, 1767.

4. *New York Journal*, January 7-April 14, 1768; *Georgia Gazette*, May 18, 1768.

5. *New York Journal*, May 12-August 25, 1768; *New York Mercury*, June 27-August 22, 1768.

6. Alexander Mackrabie to Mrs. Philip Francis, March 9, 1768, Beata Francis and Eliza Keary, eds., *The Francis Letters by Sir Philip Francis and Other Members of His Family* (New York, n.d.), I, 91; *Pennsylvania Gazette*, August 29, 1768; *Pennsylvania Chronicle*, January 22, August 29, October 6, 1768; *Virginia Gazette*, September 22-October 6, 1768; Sir Bernard Burke, *Genealogical and Heraldic History of the Peerage, Baronage, and Knightage* (97th ed.; London, 1939), II, 1865.

7. *Pennsylvania Journal*, October 6-December 29, 1768; Thomas Clark Pollock, *The Philadelphia Stage in the Eighteenth Century* (Philadelphia, 1933), pp. 11-12; Richardson Wright, *Revels in Jamaica, 1682-1838* (New York, 1937), p. 52; *Pennsylvania Chronicle*, December 12, 1768; Alexander Graydon, *Memoirs of His Own Time with Reminiscences of the Men and Events of the Revolution*, edited by John Stockton Littell (Philadelphia, 1846), p. 88.

8. The Mr. Parker who was playing with the comedians in New York during this season sometimes has been identified with the Mr. Parker who played with the New American Company. This was impossible, for both Mr. Parkers were playing this season, one in New York, the other in Annapolis. *New York Mercury*, January 2-July 3, 1769; *New York Gazette*, January 9, 1769; *New York Journal*, January 9-June 29, 1769; Joseph N. Ireland, *Records of the New York Stage, from 1750 to 1860* (New York, 1866), I, 55.

9. Wall's original handbill in the Department of Research, Colonial Williamsburg, Inc.; *New York Mercury*, July 3, 1769.

10. Although there were several versions of the camera obscura in operation at this time, the one described below seems to have been the

best model for audience viewing; its principles had been known since 1686. It was a wooden box with a projecting tube in which a combination of a convex and a concave lens had been fitted. The image was first thrown upwards upon an inclined mirror and then reflected upwards to a paper screen on top of the box. A similar device is still operating and may be seen (for a fee) in Edinburgh, Scotland. *Pennsylvania Chronicle*, May 29-June 26, 1769; David Douglass to John Penn, quoted in Pollock, *Philadelphia Stage*, pp. 26, 128.

11. *Pennsylvania Journal*, November 16, 1769, to May 31, 1770; *Pennsylvania Chronicle*, December 11, 1769, to June 4, 1770; manuscript petitions, January 4, July 19, 1770, Society Miscellaneous Collections, Pennsylvania Historical Society; Alexander Mackrabie to Philip Francis, June 2, 1770, *Pennsylvania Magazine of History and Biography*, XIV (1891), 491; Alexander Mackrabie to Philip Francis, April 24, June 9, 1770, *Francis Letters*, I, 113, 118; undated letter of David Douglass, William Bradford Papers, Pennsylvania Historical Society. There is some evidence suggesting, despite a discrepancy in dates, that Owen Morris returned to Virginia and there married Elizabeth Walker of Norfolk. The records list two people by those names being married November 26, 1770. There is also the possibility that they may have lived together, with Elizabeth Walker using the name of Mrs. Morris, until they returned to Virginia to have the nuptial rites performed in that colony (*Lower Norfolk County Virginia Antiquary*, IV [1890], 63).

CHAPTER X

1. *Virginia Gazette* (Purdie & Dixon), May 21, 1767; January 8-February 4, 1768; (Rind), February 4, 1768; George D. Willard, *History of the Providence Stage, 1762-1891* (Providence, 1891), p. 18; William Tryon to the Bishop of London, June 15, 1768, William L. Saunders, ed., *Colonial Records of North Carolina* (Raleigh, 1886-90), VIII, 786-89. The notice of Verling's marriage to Elizabeth Connor is in *Lower Norfolk County Virginia Antiquary*, IV (1890), 56. C. J. Sauthier, *Plan of the Town of Halifax in Halifax County, North Carolina, Survey'd & Drawn in June 1769 by C. J. Sauthier* shows a playhouse at this date, along with a Gaol, Court House, "Hampe House," and Tobacco House. The Henry Giffard mentioned may well have been the son of the Mrs. Henry Giffard who appeared on the stage of Drury Lane, and the Henry Giffard who at one time was the manager of a theater in Goodman's Fields (*Daily Advertiser* [London], February 1, 1738; October 23, 1772).

2. *Virginia Gazette* (Purdie & Dixon), March 17-December 22, 1768; (Rind), March 17-July 28, 1768; York County Records, Judgments and Orders, pp. 337-38; original playbills, April 15, May 18, June 3, June 8, [1768], Research Department, Colonial Williamsburg, Inc.; J. Franklin Jameson, ed., "Journal of a French Traveller in the Colonies, 1765," *American Historical Review*, XXV (July, 1921), 724; John C. Fitzpatrick, ed., *The Diaries of George Washington, 1748-1799* (New York, 1925), II, 267-68, 267n.

3. *Virginia Gazette* (Purdie & Dixon), August 31, 1768; September 7, 1769; York County Records, Order Book, 1768-70, pp. 10, 43, 57, 59, 67, 177, 415, 427; Jameson, ed., "Journal of a French Traveller," *AHR*, p. 741. In addition to Christopher Bromadge, cases for debt were brought against William Verling, Thomas Charlton, James Godwin, George Walker, and Sarah Jones, although the latter actress did not appear in playbills until after the company arrived in Annapolis.

4. Mary C. Powell, *The History of Old Alexandria* (Richmond, 1928), p. 138; Washington, *Diaries*, I, 292; Paul Leicester Ford, *Washington and the Theatre* (New York, 1899), p. 20; *Virginia Gazette* (Purdie & Dixon), January 12-26, 1769.

5. *Maryland Gazette*, February 16-April 27, 1769. Although there is no evidence that these actors played with the New American Company on its Virginia tour, it seems likely that they did, as they also had their day in the York County Court. William Burdett, Frederick Spencer, and David Jefferson were all sued for the recovery of debt (York County Records, Orders and Judgments, 1768-70, pp. 16, 483, 484, 503).

6. Anne Arundel County Judgments, Hall of Records, Annapolis, Maryland, EB No. 1, 163; EB No. 2, IX, 95-96, 97-99, 101-3, 99-100, 106, 123, 426-27.

CHAPTER XI

1. *Virginia Gazette* (Purdie & Dixon), April 13-June 14, 1769; John C. Fitzpatrick, ed., *The Diaries of George Washington, 1748-1799* (New York, 1925), I, 379n., 384, 384n.; manuscript Account Book of Edward Charlton, 1769-73, Galt Manuscripts, Research Department, Colonial Williamsburg, Inc.

2. Jonathan Boucher, *Reminiscences of an American Loyalist, 1735-1789*, edited by Jonathan Bouchier (Boston, 1925), pp. 5, 66; *Maryland Gazette*, August 30-September 6, 1770; William Eddis, *Letters from America, Historical and Descriptive; Comprising Occurrences from 1799 to 1777, Inclusive* (London, 1792), pp. 93-95.

3. *Virginia Gazette* (Rind), March 16, 1769; Washington, *Diaries*, II, 5.

4. Hudson Muse to Thomas Muse, April 19, 1771, *William and Mary Quarterly*, II (April, 1894), 240-41; Washington, *Diaries*, II, 17, 17n.

5. Washington, *Diaries*, II, 27; *Virginia Gazette* (Purdie & Dixon), May 16, 1771; playbill, May 28, 1771, Research Department, Colonial Williamsburg, Inc.

6. *Maryland Gazette*, June 13-November 7, 1771; Boucher, *Reminiscences*, p. 66; Elinor Frere to Hatley Norton, March, 1769, Frances Norton Mason, ed., *John Norton & Sons, Merchants of London and Virginia: Being the Papers from their Counting House for the Years 1750 to 1795* (Richmond, 1932), p. 90; Eddis, *Letters from America,* p. 108; Washington, *Diaries*, II, 35, 35n.; Charles Coleman Sellers, *Portraits and Miniatures by Charles Willson Peale* (Philadelphia, 1952), p. 96; William B. Wood, *Personal Recollections of the Stage* (Philadelphia, 1855), pp. 25, 28; William Dunlap, *History of the American Theatre*

(New York, 1832), p. 82. In 1854 the Peale portrait of Nancy Hallam was sold to one "Baird" for $5.50. After many years of gathering dust in an obscure attic it was discovered, through the efforts of Dr. E. P. Alexander, and purchased (for a much larger sum than that paid by "Baird") by Colonial Williamsburg, Inc.

7. *Virginia Gazette* (Purdie & Dixon), October 17-November 7, 1771, January 2-May 7, 1772; Washington, *Diaries*, II, 39-40, 57-58; Thomas B. Rowland, "Norfolk Theatres of the Olden Time," *Lower Norfolk County Virginia Antiquary*, II (1898), 102; William Reynolds to George F. Norton, May 23, 1772, William Reynolds Letterbooks, Library of Congress; Martin Staples Shockley, "The Richmond Theater," *Virginia Magazine of History and Biography*, LX (July, 1952), 422.

8. *Maryland Gazette*, August 27-October 8, 1772; *Virginia Gazette* (Rind), October 22, 1772; Washington, *Diaries*, II, 82-83, 82n.

CHAPTER XII

1. Carl and Jessica Bridenbaugh, *Rebels and Gentlemen: Philadelphia in the Age of Franklin* (New York, 1942), pp. 142-43; *Virginia Gazette* (Purdie & Dixon), October 29, 1772.

2. *Pennsylvania Packet and General Advertiser* (Philadelphia), October 26-December 14, 1772; *Pennsylvania Journal*, October 28, 1772; *Pennsylvania Chronicle*, October 31-December 26, 1772; Mrs. Mary Durang's manuscript description of the second Mrs. Morris, Harvard Theatre Collection.

3. *Pennsylvania Journal*, February 3, 1772, to March 31, 1773; *Pennsylvania Packet*, December 7, 1772, to March 8, 1773; *Pennsylvania Chronicle*, January 25-March 29, 1773; Charles Durang, *Philadelphia Stage: From 1749 to 1821*, First Series, Chapter VIII (Philadelphia *Sunday Dispatch*, 1854-56); Joseph Jackson Collection, University of Pennsylvania.

4. *New York Mercury*, April 12-May 2, 1773; *New York Journal*, April 22, 1773; *New York Gazetteer*, May 6-May 27, 1773; Josiah Quincy, *Memoir of the Life of Josiah Quincy, Junior, of Massachusetts Bay, 1744-1775* (3rd ed.; Boston, 1875), p. 105; John C. Fitzpatrick, ed., *The Diaries of George Washington, 1748-1799* (New York, 1925), II, 113.

5. *New York Gazetteer*, June 3-August 5, 1773; *New York Mercury*, June 7-August 5, 1773; *New York Journal*, June 17-July 29, 1773. The success of *She Stoops to Conquer* was considered newsworthy enough to be reported in the newspapers in other colonies where the players had performed.

6. Washington, in later years, was to see individual members of the company on the stage, including John Henry, Lewis Hallam, and the Owen Morrises. Washington, *Diaries*, II, 125, 125n.; *Maryland Gazette*, October 7-October 14, 1773; *New York Gazetteer*, August 26-September 23, 1773; *New York Journal*, September 30, 1773; *Virginia Gazette* (Purdie & Dixon), September 16-October 14, 1773; playbill, n.d., Research Department, Colonial Williamsburg, Inc.

7. Thomas J. Scharf, *The Chronicles of Baltimore: Being a Complete History of "Baltimore Town," and Baltimore City from the Earliest to the Present Time* (Baltimore, 1874), pp. 112-13; *Pennsylvania Packet*, August 30-November 22, 1773; *Pennsylvania Journal*, November 3-December 1, 1773; *Pennsylvania Gazette*, November 3, 1773; original handbill quoted in Thomas Clark Pollock, *The Philadelphia Stage in the Eighteenth Century* (Philadelphia, 1933), pp. 31, 32; original playbill, n.d., Research Department, Colonial Williamsburg, Inc.; *South Carolina and American General Gazette*, April 22, 1774.

8. *Pennsylvania Journal*, November 10, 1773; *South Carolina Gazette and Country-Journal* (Charleston), August 14, 1773, to June 7, 1774; *South Carolina Gazette*, November 29, 1773, to May 30, 1774; *New York Gazetteer*, February 24, 1774; *New York Mercury*, February 21, 1774; *Pennsylvania Packet*, February 21, 1774; *Virginia Gazette* (Purdie & Dixon), January 27-March 10, 1774; Eola Willis, *The Charleston Stage in the XVIII Century* (Columbia, 1924), pp. 65-66; *South Carolina and American General Gazette*, April 22-May 27, 1774.

9. *South Carolina and American General Gazette*, May 27-July 1, 1774; *Virginia Gazette* (Purdie & Dixon), supplement, June 16, 1774; *South Carolina Gazette and Country-Journal*, June 14-21, 1774; *South Carolina Gazette*, July 15, 1774. During the American Revolution the *Sea-Nymph* was captured by the British who converted it into a war vessel and renamed it the *Hope* (Samuel Graves to Philip Stephens, December 4, 1775, PRO Ad. 1/485).

10. *New York Gazetteer*, June 30, 1774, December 29-February 2, 1775; *New York Mercury*, July 4, 1774; William Dunlap, *History of the American Theatre* (New York, 1832), p. 35; Worthington C. Ford and others, eds., *Journals of the Continental Congress, 1774-1789* (Washington, 1904-34), I, 78; Joseph Jackson Manuscripts, University of Pennsylvania; Richardson Wright, *Revels in Jamaica, 1682-1838* (New York, 1937), p. 63.

CHAPTER XIII

1. Albert Croll Baugh, ed., *A Literary History of England* (New York, 1948), III, 777; *Virginia Gazette* (Purdie & Dixon), August 29, 1766.

2. Thomas Davies, *Dramatic Miscellanies*... (London, 1785), II, 401; I, 34-35; *Virginia Gazette* (Purdie & Dixon), April 1, 1773; George C. D. Odell, *Annals of the New York Stage* (New York, 1927), I, 66.

3. John Doran, *Annals of the English Stage*... (London, 1899), II, 25; Joseph N. Ireland, *Records of the New York Stage, from 1750 to 1860* (New York, 1866), I, 35.

4. Charles Dibdin, *A Complete History of the Stage* (London, 1800), IV, 32.

5. *Ibid*, IV, 32; Doran, *Annals of the English Stage*, II, 389; Dane Farnsworth Smith, *The Critic in the Audience of the London Theaters from Buckingham to Sheridan: A Study of Neoclassicism in the Playhouse, 1761-1779* (Albuquerque, 1953), p. 173; John Hampden, ed., *Eighteenth Century Plays* (London, 1928), p. xi.

6. Dibdin, *Complete History of the Stage*, IV, 22-23; *Virginia Gazette* (Purdie & Dixon), December 3, 1772; Hampden, *Eighteenth Century Plays*, p. vii.

7. Colley Cibber, *An Apology for the Life of Mr. Colley Cibber, Comedian, and Late Patentee of the Theatre-Royal, with an Historical View of the Stage During His Own Time* (London, 1740), p. 426; Thomas Davies, *Memoirs of the Life of David Garrick* (London, 1808), I, 130.

8. "A Note on Certain of Hamilton's Pseudonyms," *William and Mary Quarterly*, 3rd series, XII (April, 1955), 297n. The lines referred to are probably II, vi, 79-80 and IV, iv, 81-82.

9. *Virginia Gazette* (Purdie & Dixon), November 12, 1772; *New York Royal Gazette*, March 20, June 10, 1779; Alfred Spencer, ed., *Memoirs of William Hickey* (London, 1918), II, 24; Richardson Wright, *Revels in Jamaica, 1682-1838* (New York, 1937), pp. 21, 27-29, 342.

10. Obituary of L. D. Hallam quoted in Wright, *Revels in Jamaica*, pp. 113-14; *New York Daily Advertiser*, May 2, 1787; Bayle Bernard, "Early Days of the American Stage...," *Tallis's Dramatic Magazine* (March, 1951), p. 138; Peter Early to John Gibson, January 17, 1793, Society Miscellaneous Collections, Pennsylvania Historical Society; John Hodgkinson, *A Narrative of His Connections with the Old American Company*... (New York, 1797), pp. 5-7; Paul Leicester Ford, ed., *Journals of Hugh Gaine, Printer* (New York, 1902), II, 164; Galt manuscript Medical Account Books, 1788-93, Research Department, Colonial Williamsburg, Inc.; William Dunlap, *Diary of William Dunlap 1766-1839*..., edited by Dorothy C. Barck (New York, 1930), I, 162.

11. Playbill in Kingston *Royal Gazette*, August 25, 1781, quoted in Lewis P. Waldo, "The French Drama in the Eighteenth Century and Its Influences on the American Drama of that Period" (Unpublished doctoral dissertation, University of Michigan, 1940), p. 65; Wright, *Revels in Jamaica*, pp. 48, 54, 103, 156.

12. Wright, *Revels in Jamaica*, p. 49; Charles Durang, *The Philadelphia Stage: From 1749 to 1821*, First Series, Chapter XII (Philadelphia *Sunday Dispatch*, 1854-56).

13. Wright, *Revels in Jamaica*, p. 50.

14. *Ibid*, p. 48; Joseph N. Ireland, *Records of the New York Stage, from 1750 to 1860* (New York, 1866), I, 34.

15. Ireland, *Records of the New York Stage*, I, 34; Mrs. Mary Durang's manuscript account of the second Mrs. Morris, Harvard Theatre Collection.

16. Robert Hamilton Ball, "Samuel Greville, First Player," *Princeton Alumni Weekly*, XXX (1929), 124.

17. Theatre Royal Account Book, New-York Historical Society; Theatre Royal Book of Poetry Kept by Henrietta Hobart, New-York Historical Society.

18. Hunter D. Farish, ed., *Journal & Letters of Philip Vickers Fithian, 1773-1774: A Plantation Tutor of the Old Dominion* (Williamsburg, 1957), p. 97; *Virginia Gazette* (Pinkney), January 5, 1775; playbills of the Baltimore Theatre, 1782-83, New-York Historical Society.

19. Abstract of a dispatch to the Lords of Trade from Lieutenant-Governor Carleton, dated October 25, 1766, "Abstracts of Letters from American Governors, &c.," LI, Shelburne Papers, William L. Clements Library, University of Michigan.

20. Anne Arundel County Judgments, EB No. 2, 99-100; Hall of Records, Annapolis, Maryland; *Virginia Gazette* (Dixon & Hunter), August 19, 1775; (Purdie), August 18, 1775; (Pinkney), August 17, 1775; "A List of Taxable Articles in the City of Williamsburg Taken by Robert Nicholson for the Year 1783 under the Revenue Acts," *William and Mary Quarterly*, XXIII (October, 1914), 136; Coleman-Tucker Manuscripts, Miscellaneous Accounts and Receipts, Colonial Williamsburg, Inc.

21. Vestry Proceedings, St. Anne's Parish, 1775, p. 150, Hall of Records, Annapolis; Eola Willis, *The Charleston Stage in the XVIII Century* (Columbia, 1924), pp. 75-76; *Virginia Gazette* (Purdie & Dixon), July 1, 1775; York County Records, Deeds, VI, 94; Ledger of Humphrey Harwood, B, p. 88, Colonial Williamsburg, Inc.; [Lucinda Lee Dalrymple], *Journal of a Young Lady of Virginia, 1782* (Baltimore, 1871), pp. 27-28.

INDEX

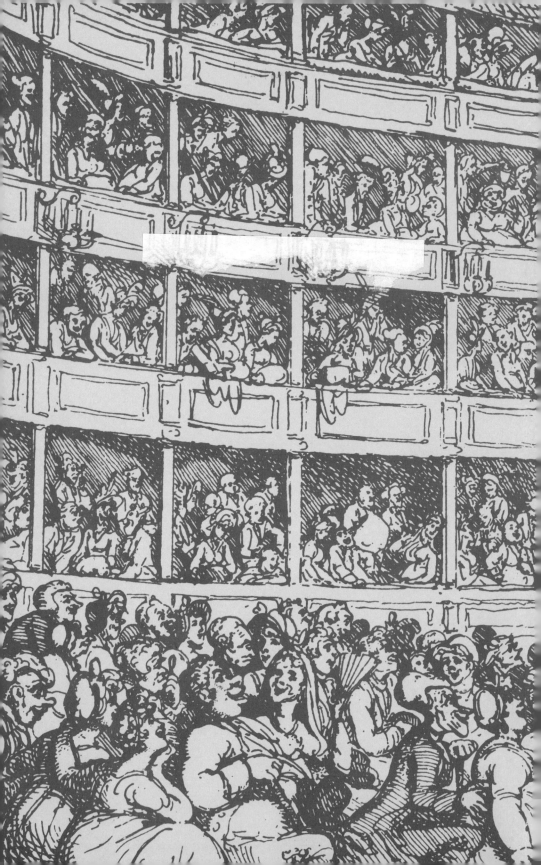